Reaching and Teaching *All* Instrumental Music Students

Kevin Mixon

Published in partnership with
MENC: The National Association for Music Education
Frances S. Ponick, Executive Editor

Rowman & Littlefield Education
Lanham • New York • Toronto • Plymouth, UK

Published in partnership with
MENC: The National Association for Music Education

Published in the United States of America
by Rowman & Littlefield Education
A Division of Rowman & Littlefield Publishers, Inc.
A wholly owned subsidary of The Rowman & Littlefield Publishing Group, Inc.
4501 Forbes Boulevard, Suite 200, Lanham, Maryland 20706
www.rowmaneducation.com

Estover Road
Plymouth PL6 7PY
United Kingdom

British Library Cataloguing in Publication Information Available

Library of Congress Cataloging-in-Publication Data

Mixon, Kevin.
　Reaching and teaching all instrumental music students / Kevin Mixon.
　　　p. cm.
　"Published in partnership with MENC"—T.p. verso.
　Includes bibliographical references (p.　).
　ISBN-13: 978-1-57886-558-1 (pbk. : alk. paper)
　ISBN-10: 1-57886-558-1 (pbk. : alk. paper)
　1. Music—Instruction and study. 2. Musical instruments—Instruction and study. I. Title.
　MT1.M68 2007
　784.071—dc22　　　　　　　　　　　　　　　　　　　　　　　　　2006029604

Printed in the United States of America

♾TM The paper used in this publication meets the minimum requirements of
American National Standard for Information Sciences—Permanence of
Paper for Printed Library Materials, ANSI/NISO Z39.48-1992.
Manufactured in the United States of America.

This book is dedicated with love to my mother, Barbara Anne McCoy, whose lifelong teaching and learning serve as continual inspiration.

Contents

Foreword

Each year thousands of new educators, many of them music teachers, graduate from universities across the country and begin their careers, brimming with enthusiasm and burning with a desire to enlighten students and make the world a better place. Thank goodness for these young professionals! Many will discover, however, that the teaching situation in which they find themselves placed is vastly different from what they expected. So many inspiring events will have shaped their own vision of the aesthetic experience of music, but a "real-world" teaching position in quite a different environment may cause inexperienced educators to feel isolated, ill-prepared and unable to deal with the tidal wave of issues and problems that are suddenly thrust upon them. Even experienced teachers who transfer to other schools may develop similar feelings, questioning their teaching skills and their own resolve to continue in the profession.

As *Teaching and Reaching* All *Instrumental Music Students* illustrates, those of us who have taught in situations where the students and community were of a cultural or socioeconomic background with which we were not accustomed often realized that our own education was really just beginning! Seasoned and successful teachers have managed to both persevere and adapt through these challenging early years, continually honing their skills. Along the way these effective educators have also learned how to enlist the support of parents, colleagues, and administrators while making a meaningful difference in the lives of their students through music.

After twenty-seven years teaching instrumental music to students at levels ranging from kindergarten to doctoral, I have had my share of experiences

in a wide variety of educational settings. Something I found was that regardless of the age group, the quality of the ensemble, or the difficulty of the literature, many things remained the same. A teacher's approach, attitude, enthusiasm, people skills, and philosophy will dictate success or failure in any circumstance—just as much as their musical expertise! Anything we can learn to aid us in reaching and teaching students only improves our ability to communicate to our students, their parents, and our communities that the arts and their expressive elements are important.

Reaching and Teaching All *Instrumental Music Students* provides a practical and sensitive approach to teaching music in a variety of situations. While we may initially perceive the conditions described by the author as "something less than ideal," the way he manages his students and the value he places on every one of them will make the reader soon realize that the power to change a "less than ideal" situation into a rewarding one is within the reach of any creative and committed teacher. This book provides excellent tools, insightful suggestions, ideas, and methods for dealing with many of the challenges faced in any school or population of students. Not only is this a valuable resource for pre-service teachers, but it is a terrific read for experienced teachers as well. I hope that this book will encourage all teachers to renew their commitment to share the joy of music with ALL students—NOT just the ones that are the easiest or most convenient to teach. If we don't do it—who will? We are so fortunate to be a part of such a magical and magnificent art form!

—Robert Sheldon,
Alfred Concert Band Editor
Alfred Publishing Company

Acknowledgments

$\mathcal{I}$ would like to thank the following teachers for their helpful advice while writing this book: Bob and Pam Phillips, Alfred Publishing; Jill DiBattista, String Teacher, West Genesee School District, Camillus, New York; Jeanne Porcino Dolamore, Poughkeepsie City School District, New York; and Rebecca Pena, General Music Teacher, Syracuse City School District. My thanks also to Steve Frank, instrumental music teacher, West Genesee School District and Onondaga Community College, Syracuse, New York, for allowing me include his instructional game. I am also indebted to these outstanding colleagues for reviewing final drafts of the book: Robert Sheldon, Carol Frierson-Campbell, Sandra Dackow, Bob Phillips, Edward S. Lisk, Larry Clark, and Edward O'Rourke.

I very much appreciate Fran Ponick and Ashley Opp at MENC and Erin McGarvey at Rowman & Littlefield for their guidance throughout the project. Thanks also to The National Association of Music Merchants, the Music Achievement Council, for permission to reproduce materials, and the Conn-Selmer Company for assistance in researching aptitude tests.

Finally, I am grateful for the patience of my two children, Chelsea and Kevin Jr., who often put their immediate needs aside and gave me time to complete this book. I am blessed and proud beyond words to have such great kids.

Introduction: New Perspectives

NEW EXEMPLARS: MOVING AWAY FROM THE SUBURBS

*W*ell-funded and supported instrumental music programs have had the spotlight for so long that many directors have come to believe that quality instruction and high student achievement can only take place in ideal circumstances. Much of the current educational literature applies theories and techniques to model instrumental ensembles, but directors cannot always emulate circumstances.

Model ensembles often represent well-funded suburban school districts (though not all suburban schools are affluent, of course). Though excellent teaching and learning takes place in these programs, using them as instructional examples has obvious limits. Many schools do not have the same economic advantages, schedules, or types of student needs, particularly in urban or rural areas.

Rather than pit teaching in the field against the educational decrees of the ivory tower, this book aims to take small doses of the valuable research conducted in the hallowed halls of academia and integrate it with the less than ideal circumstances in real classrooms.

"Less than ideal" doesn't mean "urban." It means not enough instruments. It means cuts in rehearsal time. It means having to teach to a broad range of learning styles at once.

I have written this book to address issues that many instrumental music texts might overlook. Many academics hypothesize, postulate, and theorize without any experience in challenging classrooms. Such academic

work is important, and throughout this book I cite scholars, researchers, and master teachers from whom I have "borrowed," and I hope you will consult these sources directly as well as consider how I have adapted these methods to suit my personal education philosophy and unique teaching environment. I have distilled their ideas, philosophies, and theories down to one thing: How could this work in *my* classroom? I hope you will do the same with this book.

I have adapted well-known approaches to work within the constraints surrounding my instrumental music programs. Because the following strategies are often borne of my own experience and tempered with personal philosophy and values, they do not have universal application without modifications.

NEW STRATEGIES: BUILDING A STRONG FOUNDATION

The first two chapters, "Getting Students Started" and "Maintaining Interest," discuss effective ways to recruit and retain students with strategies that have relevance in most educational environments.

General strategies may need to adapt to certain environments, such as in urban schools. For example, in chapter 3, "Gaining Support," I show how, regardless of socioeconomic circumstances, parental support is vital to instrumental music programs, but I give additional ways directors might get support to serve diverse students and their families. Many people wrongly assume that parents in less affluent communities have less concern for their children's education. This assumption is categorically false, based on both my own experiences and academic research. Researchers repeatedly report the strength of familial bonds and the importance of garnering support from parents for academic achievement in urban schools (Hale, 2001; Kuykendall, 1992; Wilson & Corbett, 2001).

NEW WAYS OF TEACHING

In an educational era where cutbacks have become commonplace, directors must make the most of what they have. In chapter 4, I address a key

issue facing most music programs: lack of instructional time. Instead of lamenting increasing time constraints, I offer practical ways in which directors can maximize their rehearsal time.

Making every minute of rehearsal productive for all students means you must teach all students according to the ways in which they learn. Embracing diverse students, situations, and music requires an acceptance of diverse learning styles, a topic I explore in chapter 5, "Teaching for Diverse Learning Styles." I show specific ways in which teachers can teach fundamental musical concepts to all students.

NEW STUDENTS: EXCEPTIONAL LEARNERS

Regardless of economics or diversity, all directors need to make ensembles accessible—and rewarding—to exceptional learners. Aside from the fact that legislation mandates inclusion, a mission that promotes music for all children dictates that it is simply the right thing to do. In many programs, exceptional learners gain membership only when parents and other advocates seek access.

But you can welcome exceptional learners without compromising the quality of performing ensembles, which many directors fear. Because special education is usually not an area of expertise for directors, a collegial approach that involves special education staff and parental input is the key to success. In time, directors become comfortable with working with exceptional learners and realize their value as ensemble members.

NEW ACTIVITIES: IMPROVISATION AND COMPOSITION

The National Standards set forth by MENC: The National Association for Music Education considers improvisation and composition as vital components of a complete, comprehensive music education in general, choral, and instrumental music settings (MENC, 1994). Directors often sacrifice opportunities for improvisation and composition in order to focus on performance, an equally creative endeavor (Reimer, 1989, p. 71), though different in many respects. Lack of experience, texts, other (and often costly)

resources, and instruction time requires easily implemented improvisational and compositional activities that actually support and enhance performance goals. I devote chapter 8 entirely to improvisation and composition, and present efficient activity ideas that tap students' creativity.

My musical mission is that you will take what you can from this book and adapt it to your unique classroom, to teach and reach *all* instrumental music students.

Getting Students Started

$\mathcal{T}$hough recruiting practices vary, successful program building depends upon carefully matching students to instruments by considering their aptitude and preferences. Many administrators and other policymakers measure instrumental program value by the size of enrollment in ensembles, and many directors believe that as many students as possible deserve the opportunity to play an instrument. Pragmatically, instrumental music programs depend on large recruitment numbers because the number of student participants tends to decrease in higher grade levels. Recruiting many students is crucial, but take care in how you introduce these students to instrumental music.

Many directors successfully recruit large numbers of students with very little enticement. Many younger students are already excited about learning to play an instrument without much of a sales pitch from the ensemble director. Holding recruiting sessions to generate interest are still important nonetheless. They are useful also for matching interested students with instruments that complement their abilities—thereby increasing the likelihood of students' success and decreasing the rate of attrition.

Successful recruiting depends upon knowing how to deal with people. A fine arts administrator recently said that the two most important qualities he looked for when hiring new music teachers was musical competence and people skills. Every aspect of instrumental music teaching, program building, and maintenance depends upon interacting with people in such a way that fosters long-term musical study.

Many directors hold an evening meeting for parents and students that provides an opportunity for them to meet with instrument dealers and to fill out necessary forms. Prior to this parental meeting, consider planning smaller, more informal meetings for students during the school day, with only one or two classrooms at a time (no more than fifty students). These sessions allow prospective students to see instruments "up close," hear those instruments demonstrated by the director or current students, and ask more questions. Smaller sessions also generate fewer behavior management issues.

Directors might consider scheduling these recruiting sessions judiciously at the beginning or end of the school year, when classroom teachers can more conveniently send both prospective students and current students. Directors can "sweeten the deal" by supervising these sessions themselves so that classroom teachers get an extra, well-deserved break. (I have found this to be quite a motivator, particularly at the end of the school year!) Directors might schedule sessions during general music classes, particularly if they integrate them with a unit on instrument families. Though you can demonstrate instruments in many ways, recruitment sessions simply must include demonstrations to help students decide what instruments they prefer.

Individual students have unique skills and preferences, which obviously affect their choices. Unfortunately, some directors let students and their parents select instruments entirely on their own. Although student preference is paramount, selecting an instrument without advice from a knowledgeable director may lead to students quitting. Despite their best efforts, students mismatched with an instrument may trail behind their peers because the instrument is too hard to play. This lack of progress may lead to an unnecessary instrument switch later in the year or, even worse, a loss of interest in instrumental music altogether.

Instrument selection without director guidance also leads to unbalanced ensemble instrumentation and reduced sonority and repertoire selection, restricting enriching musical experiences for all students. Once initiated, this imbalance may stay with the same group for several years as students advance together.

You can avoid losing prospective players by considering four components important to the recruiting process: instrument demonstration, skills assessment, dissemination of the information letter, and tone production assessment.

INSTRUMENT DEMONSTRATION

Typical recruiting sessions include demonstrations by the director or by current students. Even if you use a commercial demonstration video, display real instruments and show students how they are played. Presuming your playing proficiency will give a favorable impression of the instrument, introducing prospective students to unfamiliar instruments and reminding them about familiar ones are crucial factors in matching students to instruments.

Instrument timbres are particularly important to beginners. Edwin Gordon (1997) suggests, "Although elementary school students may be attracted initially to an instrument because of its appearance or other irrelevant reasons, ultimately they find the most success when they play an instrument that has a tone quality that appeals to them" (p. 274). Though experience has shown me that other factors need consideration as well when selecting instruments, demonstrating instruments for prospective students helps them decide which instrument timbres they prefer.

Using current instrumental music students to demonstrate instruments is even more effective than demonstrating them yourself. Prospective students are interested in how "real kids" perform. Current students enjoy introducing prospective students to an activity in which they themselves are proud to participate.

Reasonably proficient demonstrators close in age to your prospective students show students that early success on an instrument is certainly possible (such as fifth graders demonstrating for fourth graders). Ending the playing demonstration with a favorite piece from the most recent concert emphasizes the progress that can be made in a short time, often within a single school year.

Because student demonstrators are still new players, I use several students (rather than a soloist) on each instrument because it generates a more satisfactory sound from most beginner groups. Except for the final piece that I conduct, I play along with students on all of the different instruments in addition to my role as presenter. I find that using proficient second-year students for recruiting sessions works quite well. You may want to consider using advanced students as demonstrators, but students from middle or junior high and high schools may pose transportation, scheduling, and other logistical problems arising with multiple recruiting sessions.

SKILLS ASSESSMENT

A portion of the recruiting session should include assessing the skills of prospective students, and I use short tests such as those provided by instrument purveyors.

While most of these tests do not rigorously measure aptitude with the precision of more rigorously researched aptitude tests, they can assist directors with instrument selection, particularly with wind and percussion instruments. In some cases, good scores on these tests can be effective in persuading hesitant students—particularly those with low self-esteem—to participate because the test may indicate unrecognized musical skill. Of course, a poor score certainly should not exclude a student from participation. Use assessments only to report strengths to parents and students, in order to encourage instrumental music study. Their purpose for directors is to aid instrument selection in conjunction with other factors, not to dictate it.

Because of time, attention, and cost constraints, this assessment should take only about 20 minutes for the entire group to complete using paper and pencil. Refer to the test as a "game" to alleviate anxiety, and include practice items so that students as young as eight or nine years old or those with limited English language proficiency easily understand how to "play" it. Rigorous, more precise aptitude tests take more time and materials to administer, but an assessment "game" to aid in instrument selection should be short and simple enough to maintain student interest. The Selmer Music Guidance Survey (Conn-Selmer, n.d.) is an inexpensive assessment that fits these guidelines, though I eliminate a few test questions to save time. Examples of test items (questions) are either recorded on CD or written out so that you can play them on the piano. You can also ask music dealers or colleagues for similar tests.

Test materials are often inexpensive videos or CDs, but student answer cards can be costly. If on a tight budget, you can use these tests as models to create your own. The Music Achievement Council's (n.d.) "Musical Instrument Game" is no longer available, but has been reprinted with their permission:

Each section of the Musical Instrument Game consists of six items, which you can quickly score by using an answer key. The first section re-

quires students to indicate if the second of two pitches played on a typical wind instrument is higher, lower, or the same as the first. The second section also requires students to indicate if two groups of four quarter note melodies are the same or different (quarter note = ca 120 beats per minute, 4/4 meter). The third section, which is easiest, requires students to determine if two four-beat rhythm patterns performed on a single pitch using quarter, eighth, and sixteenth note durations are the same or different (quarter note = ca 120 beats per minute, 4/4 meter).

Some scholars encourage directors to select appropriate tests in general based on the degree of reliability, validity, usability, and usefulness (Boyle and Radocy, 1987, p. 154). I have found that tests such as the one mentioned are certainly "usable" in that they are easily administered and "useful" because they suggest which students might progress at about the same rate as other students on instruments requiring certain skills, particularly with wind and percussion instruments.

Table 1.1 Musical Instrument Game

Name _____

School _____

Classroom Teacher _____

Follow Instructions and Listen Carefully

A. Pitch Recognition

A-1	A-2	A-3	A-4	A-5	A-6
High	High	High	High	High	High
Same	Same	Same	Same	Same	Same
Low	Low	Low	Low	Low	Low

B. Melody Memory

B-1	B-2	B-3	B-4	B-5	B-6
Same	Same	Same	Same	Same	Same
Different	Different	Different	Different	Different	Different

C. Rhythm Memory

C-1	C-2	C-3	C-4	C-5	C-6
Same	Same	Same	Same	Same	Same
Different	Different	Different	Different	Different	Different

For example, a score of four to six correct answers on the first section of the Musical Instrument Game and five to six on the second section indicates a student who usually has enough tonal discrimination to discern the close "higher" and "lower" partials on the horn, or to adjust the embouchure naturally in reaction to pitch discrepancies on an oboe. Students who answer only two or three items on the first section but answer the majority of items correctly on the second section are still probably able to discern the high and low pitches needed to negotiate partials on other brass instruments and intonation adjustments on all winds.

Five or six correct answers in the third section requiring rhythm discrimination indicate potential satisfactory progress on some percussion instruments (though versatile percussionists playing timpani and keyboard instruments will need to demonstrate the same skills as other instrumentalists).

All string instruments require the same pitch and rhythm abilities, so pitch and rhythm assessments have limited use in predicting instrument success. However, as mentioned earlier, you can use favorable test results to encourage reticent parents and students to participate (Lamb, 1990, p. 142; Hamann & Gillespie, 2004, p. 203).

Though certainly not as precise but necessary due to time constraints, I often must test individual students quickly "on the fly" if they missed the recruiting sessions. We "play" the game quickly; I play examples at the piano, the students answer verbally, and I mark their responses. If really pressed for time, I may modify this further and have them simply match three or four different pitches that I sing. In addition to testing pitch discrimination, I have students echo-clap rhythms while I simultaneously clap a different rhythm to assess students' rhythm memory as well as the independence required to play individual percussion parts.

THE INFORMATION LETTER

Sign-up letters for students to take home should be distributed at the conclusion of the instrument demonstration and skills assessment session.

These promotional letters should tell parents briefly about the program and specifically describe any commitments, such as after-school rehearsals. Include a section on the form that allows students to indicate instruments that interest them. Students who return a signed information letter are scheduled for a tone production assessment. Figure 1.1 is an example of an information letter I find useful.

Of course, not every child or parent is interested in instrumental music study, and "hard sell" tactics are not necessary or beneficial. But directors can consider contacting parents of students who did not return the sign-up sheet but obtained a high score to let parents know that their child demonstrates musical ability and might succeed playing an instrument. I usually call or send home a letter because I believe that students and parents should know about student's potential success even if the student chooses not to participate. Parents and students are usually pleased to hear such news and these calls and letters usually add a couple more new students to the roster.

TONE PRODUCTION ASSESSMENT

The fourth component of recruiting allows students to try producing sounds on the instruments. After the deadline for students to return completed forms included in the parental information letter has passed, I schedule students for a tone production assessment. Similar to the initial meeting, I schedule this by classroom. Because of the time involved, only students who have returned the form are assessed. By this time I have the skills assessment sheets scored and I am ready to use them as guides for discussing instrument suitability.

It is widely purported that some physical characteristics such as lip and teeth structure prohibit satisfactory progress on some instruments. Though true for some pronounced physical barriers (which may be a concern with some exceptional learners), many of these biases have no support (Gordon, 1997, p. 274; Schleuter, 1997, p. 14; Westphal, 1990). However, you can gauge potential success by having students produce sounds on wind instrument mouthpieces or by fingering and bowing

Anytown Beginning Orchestra or Band
Anytown School
Street Address
City, State 12345
(555) 555-5555
John or Jane Q. Smith, Director

Dear Parent:

Classes are currently being organized for this year's orchestra or band! [A few brief comments about the benefits of instrumental music in general and specific events planned for the year that might generate enthusiasm.] Participation in instrumental music has been linked to academic achievement, as well as many other benefits. But students report that the participation in band or orchestra, though challenging, is also fun!

[Include planned performances or activities here.] We are very excited about the year ahead and are looking forward to winter and spring concerts, as well as our district-wide band or orchestra performance.

All instruction is free and all that is necessary for you to do is rent an instrument from a district-approved music dealer. The school owns a few of the larger band or orchestra instruments students may borrow for the year at no cost.

[Insert any specific program requirements.] If your child begins band or orchestra instruction, he or she must stay for rehearsal one day a week until 3:15. Buses are available to bring students home. Once a week, students have a lesson during the regular school day.

For now, simply complete this form and return it to school by September 3. Information about renting an instrument and other details will be discussed during an information meeting for parents on Thursday, September 25 at 7:00 p.m. in the Anytown Elementary auditorium. Parents should also feel free to call me at Anytown Elementary School (555-5555) on Monday or Tuesday, Anytown Middle School (555-5555) on Wednesday through Friday, or at my home after school hours before 9:00 p.m. at 555-5555.

Yours in music,
John or Jane Q. Smith

Please detach and return to Mr. or Ms. Smith by Sept. 3
Name of Student _____
Instrument:
    1st Choice   _____
    2nd Choice _____
    3rd Choice   _____
Classroom Teacher This Year:_____
Classroom Teacher Last Year (and school, if different): _____
[Last year's information is helpful if recruiting at the beginning of the school year]
Parent Name: _____
Street Address: _____
City, State Zip: _____
Telephone Day: _____ Evening: _____
Best Time to Call: _____
Parent Signature: _____

Figure 1.1   Sample Recruiting Letter

string instruments. Tone production assessment helps students see firsthand how difficult popular instruments like the flute may be for them or how holding the cello feels more comfortable than violin, thus promoting balanced instrumentation.

For wind instruments, after an initial demonstration by the director, students should try to produce sounds on a flute head joint, and an oboe, clarinet, trumpet, baritone or trombone, and tuba mouthpieces. (Directors should have plenty of sanitizer to use between each student.) Potential flute players can often immediately produce a strong "whistle" on the head joint. It takes a long time to test all students on every type of mouthpiece available in the band, and because of its popularity, controlling the number of saxophonists can be a concern. I have only students who can play the most characteristic and controlled tones on the clarinet mouthpiece also try the saxophone mouthpiece. Though I realize that the two embouchures required are different, I have found that initial success with the clarinet mouthpieces can indicate success on the saxophone mouthpieces.

Students should demonstrate the ability to "buzz" naturally. They usually have "low end" or "high end chops," which is the natural inclination of more (high buzzes or "high end") or less (low buzzes or "low end") lip pressure on the trumpet and trombone, baritone, and euphonium mouthpieces. Students who can buzz in the high range may do well on the trumpet, and those buzzing in the medium to high range can succeed on the horn. "Low end" buzzes indicate future success on the lower brasses. Directors should demonstrate the loose "lip-flapping" required for tuba away from the mouthpiece. Once students can imitate it, they should try to produce a low buzz on the mouthpiece.

Strings require a different tone production assessment. Unlike winds, individual string instruments do not require specific musculature for embouchure formation that varies widely between students. It is still very helpful to have students "test drive" instruments as part of the selection process to promote the underrepresented viola, cello, and bass to undecided students.

After students have experienced their initial success with instruments firsthand, directors will find less interest in overrepresented instruments. Based on the skills assessment, instrument preferences indicated on the sign-up forms, and the tone production assessment, I

usually recommend two or three instruments that students may consider. Because students have listed three instrument choices on their sign-up forms, we easily come to an agreement, though students must be happy with this decision. If students (and, in some cases, parents) still insist on a particular instrument, directors can suggest a trial period. Students sometimes surprise the directors with initial success. In other cases, the student realizes—usually within the first two or three weeks—that they should consider another instrument.

After students have tried the instruments, I call every parent with the results. It is important to have two or three choices in mind. Parents, like students, may have gender biases ("The tuba is too big for Sally; how about a more ladylike instrument like the flute?"), preferences based on personal history ("I played the drums, and I think Juan wants to, also"), and instrument partiality due to availability ("Rashonda's older brother used to play the saxophone and we still own one"). Most of the time, however, parents accept the recommendations of the director.

Directors can also extol to parents the financial benefits of playing the underrepresented but often school-owned lower strings and winds. Most importantly, share why you recommend certain instruments with parents, based on the information you collected through the skills and tone production assessments. Even if parents do not follow director recommendations, they see the director as competent and sincerely concerned about both the ensemble and individual students.

The final recruiting session may be a general meeting at night for students, parents, and local music dealers. (Dealers are usually present if purchasing instruments is a requirement.) To avoid damage to instruments, you should instruct dealers to deliver instruments directly to you so that students can demonstrate proper assembly (usually shown at the first lessons) before taking them home.

At the meeting, I give a motivational talk tempered a bit with details about the effort required to meet practice expectations and the commitment necessary to attend rehearsals and performances. If parents cannot make this very brief but important general meeting, calling parents can inform them of important dates, program expectations, and the phone numbers of music dealers so that they can independently make rental arrangements.

ECONOMICALLY DISADVANTAGED
SCHOOLS AND STUDENTS

This section has particular relevance for those teaching in schools with significant levels of poverty, especially generational poverty. Prevalent in many communities, Payne (2001) defines it as "having been in poverty for at least two generations; however, the characteristics begin to surface much sooner than two generations if the family lives with others who are from generational poverty. . . . [It] has its own culture, hidden rules, and belief systems" (p. 64). When recruiting urban students, directors may need to consider the importance of entertainment and humor, relationships, matriarchal family structures, and oral language traditions. If such things shape your students' lives, you must be prepared to work within these structures rather than struggle to make students conform to conventional standards.

Less positive characteristics of generational poverty include a belief in fate rather than destiny mitigated by choice, the desire to live in the moment rather than considering future consequences, and lack of organization (Payne, 2001). For underprivileged students, school-owned instruments have tremendous potential to foster responsible behavior while relationships help recruitment.

School-Owned Instruments

Because of widespread poverty, schools in some districts provide most or all instruments for students to borrow, usually with a small rental fee. Philosophically, instrumental music should be offered to every child who wishes to participate. From a pragmatic perspective, there are usually more interested students than available school-owned instruments, so choices often need to be made about who participates, at least at first. Because of instrument shortages, I keep an active waiting list and begin teaching students throughout the school year.

When assigning school-owned instruments, directors need to consider that not all students should transport instruments to and from school because of dangerous neighborhoods and unstable home environments. Directors can allow students to practice at school as a solution, but home practice is a typical expectation and directors must consider

the demonstrated responsibility of students and their families when deciding who borrows an instrument. As a new teacher in an urban school several years ago, I did not account for student responsibility, and I promptly lost three instruments within the first month. To make matters worse, budget constraints prevented replacing them, so fewer students could participate.

The recruiting letter example asks parents or guardians to provide the names of both the current and previous teacher so that directors can confer with classroom teachers about students' demonstrated responsibility. If a teacher gives compelling reasons why a student may not properly care for an instrument, I either make arrangements for students to practice at school or privately share these concerns with the student if I think they can change the behavior. I then put the student on the waiting list to begin later in the year. This way, the student has an opportunity to show the responsible behavior necessary to properly care for an expensive instrument while he or she waits for an available one.

Relationships

Relationships are central for people living in generational poverty because they often provide a way to survive socially and economically. Getting to know students before you recruit them helps to establish a congenial relationship. If students know and like a teacher, that relationship might motivate a student to begin music study more than the activity itself. Students like enthusiastic, personable, and sincere teachers. When communicating with students, teachers should make eye contact and strive to be good listeners. Names mean a lot to students, and teachers should learn them quickly and pronounce them correctly. Directors who show they care about students usually impress them—and their colleagues too.

To meet and recruit students, directors should make themselves visible by participating in activities outside instrumental music. Directing vocal groups or teaching general music classes makes the director more familiar. For example, as an instrumental music teacher with general music teaching duties for several years, I consistently have several general music students in my instrumental music ensembles. Students get to know and like me in my general music class, and they become interested in joining my instrumental ensembles.

Building relationships with parents is as important as developing them with students, especially for those families living in generational poverty. These parents have many strengths, love their children, and want them to succeed in school as much as more affluent parents. Though gaining parental support is universally important across settings, directors can adopt strategies designed specifically for particular socioeconomic demographics.

Parents living in poverty want their children to do well in school, but they often don't know how to negotiate school organizational structures or may have a fear of schools based on their own negative experiences. Though parents may view school unfavorably, they, like their children, support teachers they like. If directors want parental support, they must strive to make contact with parents or guardians of prospective students during the recruiting process using the same interpersonal skills they use to recruit students.

Parent contact may take more effort in some cases. Sometimes families do not have phones, and directors must visit homes to discuss recruiting information. In other cases, parents may not speak English. Fortunately, students can often translate, and school personnel and community members may know the language. Software programs can translate recruiting letters into common languages such as Spanish (though someone fluent must proofread them, since these translations are often imprecise).

True, cases exist where the lack of parental concern is heartbreaking—and this neglect is not exclusive to underserved students in disadvantaged schools. But with some tenacity, the director can get strong support early in the recruiting stage from most parents, greatly aiding student success by encouraging home practice, attending performances, and meeting other program expectations.

A well-planned, diligent approach to recruiting students establishes a strong foundation for your instrumental music program. Carefully matching students with appropriate instruments and encouraging the participation of parents and family members sets up your music students for long-term success.

· 2 ·

Maintaining Interest

$\mathscr{R}$etention practices across all teaching environments generally have far more similarities than differences. Instruction that motivates students has similar power in suburban, rural, and urban schools, but directors may need to modify some techniques because of local economic conditions or cultures. Committed directors can foster success and motivate students to continue instrumental music study, regardless of teaching and learning environments.

Successful recruiting is of little significance if directors do not make an effort to retain students once they have begun study. Current trends in scheduling, mandatory testing, and other issues have led to widespread instrumental program attrition in general, and many of these weighty issues require a degree of advocacy beyond the scope of this book. The current discussion centers on retaining students from a structural and instructional perspective, from within the instrumental music program itself.

After the excitement of learning a new instrument wears off, the reality of home practice takes its place. Dropout rates of up to one-third of the original recruiting number are not unusual between the first and second year of beginner programs. In a study of orchestra programs, Hamann, Gillespie, and Bergonzi (2002, as cited in Hamann & Gillespie, 2004, p. 208) report a national average retention rate (students staying in the program) of 73 percent between the first and second year, another 73 percent between elementary and middle or junior high school, and yet another 73 percent retention rate between middle or junior high school and high school with a

15

total retention rate of 53 percent of students from beginner program to high school. The total attrition rate equals 47 percent of students.

This rate reflects the approximate retention average in my beginning ensembles, though I structure my program so I can replace these students with new ones throughout most of the school year. Nonetheless, this percentage rate presents an alarming amount of attrition for some directors, particularly if their programs do not have revolving enrollment and recruitment numbers are low to begin with. Administrators, parents, and other district instrumental music teachers closely scrutinize numbers to assess program justification in the elementary schools, projected strength in the higher grades, and director competence.

A certain amount of attrition is unavoidable, but large attrition numbers can be kept to a minimum when as many students as possible have the opportunity to participate and when directors pay proper attention to providing every student with motivating and meaningful experiences.

The large numbers desired when recruiting are necessary, in part, to account for the inevitable dropout of some students. A study by Boyle, De-Carbo, and Jordan (1995) describe causes of attrition:

> Loss of interest by students is the most cited factor that affects participation. Other major factors that have been reported include lack of communication, interest in participation in other activities and sports, and class scheduling conflicts. Financial concerns, although cited, generally was not a factor in determining participation in instrumental music programs. (p. 2)

The research suggests that some factors exist beyond directors' immediate control, but it also shows what they can address. When multiple activities vie for students' time, not all students share the necessary commitment to learn an instrument. Directors can keep students in the program by discussing the reasons for waning interest to find solutions. They can consult other teachers or administrators about scheduling conflicts. Parents can illuminate problems that students may be too timid to discuss with the director.

Strategies that motivate students and improve retention may require an examination of program structure as well as instruction. As a teacher, you must have clear expectations and strive to be firm but fair—and even likable! Work to keep students engaged by monitoring rehearsal pace, and include games and game-like activities to add interest. Perform often, praise often, and

communicate often with parents. You have to keep a lot of balls in the air at once, but your students—and their continued interest—will reward you.

TWO PROGRAM STRUCTURE SOLUTIONS

Directors may need to consider program policy structure and instruction in their efforts to reduce attrition. Some directors mistakenly believe that they must retain all students, regardless of demonstrated commitment, because program merit is assessed solely on ensemble numbers. Others directors feel that some students' interest and commitment "blossoms" with maturity and they encourage them to continue, even without ample home practice, lesson attendance, or other typical expectations. It takes only one or two uncommitted students to make even a large ensemble sound poor, though, and many uncommitted students only make it worse.

Ensemble quality is important even to young students, particularly those who believe that high performance quality is a goal of study. All students must bear the burden of having unprepared students in the ensemble. It is often not the few unprepared students who are most frustrated, but the more motivated students in the ensemble. These motivated students may quit and join other ensembles, pursue musical experiences as soloists, or much worse, discontinue instrumental music study altogether.

Many programs have the benefit of both small-group instruction or "lessons" (typically using the "pull-out" system where students miss portions of other classes, usually on a rotation schedule) and large-group instruction or rehearsals. To avoid a large disparity in skill level, directors might require students to demonstrate prerequisite skills to participate in the full ensemble. Benchmarks for participation keep the pace of success rewarding for students. Clearly explain requirements, assess them objectively, and report progress to parents and students.

Students who do not demonstrate the necessary prerequisite skills may not participate in the full ensemble until they are proficient. Encourage them to continue their music study, but they may need individual lessons because those in group lessons are further ahead. The present discussion involves typical students who struggle because of a lack of practice, attendance, or motivation to fulfill other program requirements; a detailed discussion of modifications for exceptional students will take place in chapter 6.

In many cases, individual instruction without ensemble participation does not retain students because they sense they are atypical, and ensemble participation usually works as a powerful motivator for continued study. Some struggling students become more motivated and responsible enough to practice and fulfill other expectations when they get a bit older. Rather than allowing them to quit permanently because of a temporary maturity, encourage them to start later.

My first-year groups are open to fourth and fifth graders, and I have a second-year, more advanced group that consists primarily of fifth graders (though the actual grade levels vary depending on program structure in other schools). Because fourth graders typically move at a slower pace, the older fifth-grade beginners can both begin an instrument and acquire most of the skills of the second-year fifth graders by year's end. This accelerated pace is an expectation at the outset, and the older beginners are usually motivated to catch up to their peers.

The multi-grade beginner option allows students who were not successful in one grade to try again a year later, often with noteworthy success. It may be useful in programs that do not have schedules that allow students to catch up in small-group or individual instruction. Multi-grade structure also permits new students moving from schools where programs began at different ages (for example, all beginners started in fifth grade instead of fourth grade) to join.

I have had some struggling students "repeat" a year in the first-year groups, particularly when their friends or relatives either began as fifth graders or repeated the year with them (so they had a buddy). Rather than having some students complete and then repeat a second year, it might be better to have them discontinue study and resume the next school year. Starting beginners in more than one grade may not be possible in all programs, but can be an option when trying to decrease attrition while maintaining adequate ensemble progress.

TEACHER DEMEANOR AND EXPECTATIONS

Teacher demeanor is as important for retaining students as it is for recruiting them. Some directors misinterpret positive demeanor and adopt the saccharin persona of a children's television show host. Directors do not

need be excessively sweet to be effective, even with young students. If they are enthusiastic—indeed, passionate—about teaching music and are "hip" to the given age group, they usually inspire and engage students.

Instrumental music study requires effort, and students tolerate and even expect a consistent and objective director who insists that students meet high expectations. In my experience, students often describe these teachers as "strict," but not "mean." "Mean" teachers demonstrate sarcasm, spite, inequity, and other indications of animosity toward some or all children. "Strict" teachers have expectations for students and ensemble quality, and are consistent in reaching those goals.

AVOIDING BOREDOM

Fortunately, playing an instrument is inherently engaging, but overly long periods of teacher-talk, working with individual sections, or managing behavior restricts playing time and invites boredom. Directors should plan thoroughly to keep things moving, but plans must be abandoned if they are not working. Whenever I do not complete objectives for the sake of optimal pacing, I note unfulfilled objectives in my lesson plan so they can be included in future classes.

Understanding or mastering the "stuff"—content, concepts, and skills—of instrumental music study is often just plain work. But work in the form of play constitutes the single most powerful approach I can recommend for meaningfully engaging students. To be considered instruction rather than recreation, these games must have very clear objectives and assessments to monitor attainment of objectives.

Given limited instruction time, games should not take too long, have complex rules, or require several materials. Games can be the same as those familiar to students, or be game-like activities, meaning tasks structured in the manner in which children play (see below for example). They effectively introduce, reinforce, review, or assess.

Learning activities, modeled after familiar children's games, provide engaging contexts. Instrumental music educator Steve Frank of West Genesee Central School District in Camillus, New York, contributed the following "Video Baseball." It has student appeal, and achieves and assesses a specific goal: accuracy in reading music notation.

In order to play "Video Baseball," identify performance material, such as short passages groups can use that also contain "tricky" situations that truly test reading ability.

I use a baseball format for this "video game," but the game can be easily adapted. In this version, the students receive a certain number of "at bats," based on the difficulty of material or available time. Each student takes a turn playing one line of music at a time. For example, the first student attempts a perfect performance of line 1 and if he or she plays it correctly the first time, the student earns an extra "at bat." Students earn an extra "at bat" only if they play the line correctly during the first attempt. A correct performance on the second or third attempt allows them only to proceed to the next line of material.

If a mistake is made, the student is "honked" immediately upon making the mistake. (I make a sound resembling the buzzer used at athletic events.) "Honking" the mistake immediately allows students to know where they made a mistake and they can immediately check to see what they did wrong. When a student "strikes out," I "honk" to signal the mistake while signaling "out" by thrusting my thumb upwards (imitating a baseball umpire). Imitating a mechanical computer-generated voice, I say, "game over." The kids love this part. . . .

Students can't advance through the material until they play the line correctly or "strike out" trying. Play continues, alternating from student to student, through the designated material until everyone has played everything or has "struck out" trying. Everyone can be a winner—anyone who stays "at bat" up to the end of the material wins.

Students of all ages find games like this one motivating, provided that the games are modified for specific age levels. Due to the proliferation of mature video games with violent themes, consider benign contexts such as sports-oriented video games.

It is quite possible that the same students will consistently win the music reading game because they are naturally more skilled notation decoders. And no one enjoys the game when the same people win (except the winners, of course). Students have different strengths; using games for other skills such as intonation, breathing, or expression will likely produce multiple winners. If competitive elements in games cause concern, structuring games that require teamwork can reduce competition and encourage students—particularly those who are struggling.

Game-like activities draw from children's play experiences, but lack the structure required for games. For example, after students learn proper breathing technique and have had opportunities to practice it, di-

rectors can engage students with this challenge: "Let's see if we can all 'sizzle' (or 'hiss,' which is similar to breathing required for wind instruments) for ten seconds." After correcting any breathing errors, directors can challenge all students to "sizzle" for 15 seconds, then 20 seconds, and so on, correcting breathing errors after each challenge. The goal is demonstrating proper breathing technique away from the instrument; assessment comes from teacher and student observation. The activity, presented as a contest, de-emphasizes competition as all students breathe together; no student gets singled out for scrutiny and there are no individual winners.

For game ideas, resources such as *Teaching Techniques and Insights for Instrumental Music Educators* (Casey, 1993) and *Band Rehearsal Techniques: A Handbook for New Directors* (Dalby, 1993) devote entire sections to games. Directors can adapt age-appropriate and relevant board games and video games. The possibilities are limitless, and playful activities that have clear goals and assessment have great instructional and motivational power.

PERFORMING

I still remember terse advice prominently posted in a university computer cluster that read "Save Early. Save Often." Conspicuously posted because of the many incidences of losing crucial data, this advice has equal import with respect to students if it reads "Perform Early. Perform Often." Like games, performing motivates and prevents students from losing the important material they have mastered. Because the motivational benefit of performance wanes within a couple of weeks, schedule more than just the perfunctory winter and spring concerts. Performances need not be formal like those in winter and spring; they may only involve playing a segment or entire piece in front of the principal, teacher, or group of students. Soloists, a few students in a lesson group, or the entire ensemble can perform. These informal "concerts" help minimize performance anxiety, and I include as many of these impromptu performances as I can when preparing students for solo and ensemble festivals.

PRAISE AND PUBLIC RECOGNITION

"What constitutes reward?—That which the student will work toward" (Madsen & Madsen, 1983, p. 54). Madsen and Madsen further identify words (spoken and written), expressions (facial and bodily), closeness (nearness and touching, though touching obviously is not recommended in today's schools), activities and privilege (social and individual), and things (tokens, food, playthings, money) as the types of rewards children work toward (1983, p. 59).

Students respond much better to "positive techniques" of reinforcement rather than negative ones of disapproval or punishment, as Madsen and Madsen crucially observe (1983, p. 59). The computer advice could read "Reward early. Reward often" to prevent the loss of students. The following are for using praise and public recognition effectively because of their shared power in retaining and instructing all students through motivation.

Teacher approval communicated through verbal praise is rewarding to most students. Praise can bolster students' feelings of competence of self-efficacy, which some research suggests plays a role in prolonged music study (O'Neill & McPherson, 2002, chap. 3).

Verbal praise must be clear and specific in order to reward and instruct the student. Other students present work toward receiving the same reward. Vague, nonspecific praise, even if genuine, is ineffective because students do not know what to work toward. Thus, "Nice work, cellos!" rewards cello students, but "Nice work, cellos. I like the way you kept your bows parallel to the bridge throughout the entire passage" is specific enough to be instructive. It rewards cello students and instructs the whole class by providing an incentive to work toward proper bow angle. Skillful use of this type of praise saves rehearsal time because the director gives instruction and reinforcement at the same time.

Public recognition that rewards achievement powerfully motivates students. Some students earn special recognition for activities, such as regional honor groups, but these exemplary students do not make up the entire ensemble, and every member needs an opportunity for recognition. Announcing "Band or Orchestra Student(s) of the Week" during morning or afternoon announcements is effective for elementary students, and is instructive if

students know the criteria for selection. Though exemplary students may earn this distinction during the first few weeks, other students should receive the award for achievements, such as an outstanding lesson or display of citizenship, so that as many students are rewarded as possible by the end of the year.

You can display achievement posters in prominent locations in the school that motivate students of all ages (though you might need to adjust the "coolness" factor for middle and high school students). Students sign their names on the posters as they earn predetermined goals for each level, such as a specific number of parent-signed practice records or successful performance of a passage or entire piece.

Individualize goals to increase success rates. For example, one student might earn their signature on the Achievement Level 1 poster for successful completion of an étude, while another student reaches the same level for two consecutive weeks of prompt and prepared lesson attendance. Students sign the posters themselves after fulfilling predetermined requirements, and each level can bring a reward of some sort, like a ribbon, a note home, and so on. In schools with bilingual students, achievement level posters can be written in all represented languages.

Students aim to arrive at all achievement levels by the end of the school year, and I find that ten levels work well for this length of time. Although older students often act ambivalent about the reward system, I see that the achievement level display is a necessary stop for students of all ages when visiting the school with their parents. Again, clearly communicated criteria for the various levels can simultaneously reward and instruct students.

PARENTS

Positive communication that builds bridges to parents is vital for keeping students in ensembles. Despite the best efforts of directors to motivate students, their interest has peaks and valleys. Parents can encourage students through those valleys of low interest, and a strong partnership between director and parents are often the key to helping students through them. Sharing students' success either by phone, note, or in person helps to build necessary parent partnerships that retains students.

CONSIDERING STUDENTS LIVING IN
POVERTY AND DIVERSE CULTURES

Revolving enrollment, practicing, and competition have particular import when trying to decrease dropout rates of students living in poverty. Consider learning styles, competition, and culturally relevant music to retain students from diverse cultures.

Revolving Enrollment

In order to keep numbers up in schools with high levels of student poverty, particularly if you have more interested students than school-owned instruments available, directors may need to start students throughout most of the school year as instruments become available. During the last third of the year, students may simply take lessons in preparation for the following year.

Remember that ensemble participation with peers is important to students and a key factor in retaining them, so they need to participate in rehearsals as soon as possible. Directors can reward student effort by phasing in participation. For example, a goal to learn all or merely a part of the easiest piece the ensemble is currently preparing can serve as a condition of participation for the new student. The part can even be simplified at first. Expect that the new student will continue to work to catch up to the ensemble as the year progresses.

Programs that don't have "lessons" can phase students in gradually, but students simply cannot play during pieces or passages they do not know. Although they want to learn pieces quickly so they can play more during rehearsal, directors should realize that students new to the ensemble can feel overwhelmed by the advanced skill level of peers. Clearly defined, individualized, incremental goals help encourage new students.

Peer tutors can help students catch up. This strategy helps the tutee, but also challenges the tutors as they draw on more advanced thinking skills by teaching the material (Kaplan & Stauffer, 1994). Directors can assign new students to a competent peer to help during rehearsals, lessons, and even practice at home. With students who are learning English, consider tutors who can also serve as translators.

Practicing

Some students may live in dangerous neighborhoods, have neighbors or family members who complain about noise, or are not allowed to transport large instruments on crowded buses. Practicing at school may be an option for students who cannot practice regularly or at all at home, or who cannot transport instruments to and from school. I converted a storage area within view of the music room for this purpose. Students can practice during, before, or after school hours. Students who must practice at school have the benefit of added guidance from the director, so the practice sessions are usually very effective. Practicing at school for as little as twenty minutes every other day can be the deciding factor in keeping a student progressing at a pace necessary to stay in the instrumental music program.

Cultural Learning Styles

The learning styles increasingly represented in economically disadvantaged schools suggest that planning instruction that motivates students helps to decrease dropout rates. Scholars describe ideal African American learning experiences as relevant, purposeful, social, and offering high degrees of stimulation (Hale, 2001; Kunjufu, 1986, 1990, 2002). Through my experiences in urban and rural schools, I have found that teaching practices to account for cultural learning style characteristics posited by these scholars work well with students in general. Though playing an instrument addresses many of these learning needs inherently, teachers need to plan instruction that ensures ample playing time as well as similarly engaging experiences, like singing, during those brief periods when students do not play.

Competition

Warily approach the dynamics of competition and cooperation. "Some cultures highly value group success and therefore encourage cooperative behavior over competitive behavior" (Colarusso & O'Rourke, 2004, p. 19). In other instances, children from generational poverty often lack skills necessary to mediate behavior, especially in competitive environments. They may have experienced little success in school and give up easily with the perception of failure. To respect certain cultural perspectives, avoid

peer conflicts, build a sense of esprit de corps, and keep perceived failure at a minimum, directors should consider activities that reward students for group achievements. Structuring activities for group success accounts for the social learning styles ascribed to some cultures, and it helps all students positively perceive success.

Cultural Relevancy

A rich diversity of cultures exists in some schools. Students like to play musical styles that reflect their own cultures, though culturally relevant music should not be the only music they learn. Much of the band and orchestra music available is Eurocentric and may not motivate students because of its unfamiliarity. Older students in particular tend to have trouble staying motivated when they play only Western-styled music. Danny Lopez, an urban instrumental music teacher in Texas, offers a compelling rationale for culturally relevant ensembles by describing his own experiences:

> All my kids have probably seen mariachi from the time they were small. In San Antonio, it's traditional at every wedding to have a mariachi. You really don't see bands that often unless you go to a high school football game or a college football game—and my kids ordinarily don't go to college football games or concerts. . . . My kids don't know a lot of the folk songs in the beginning band books. They're inner-city people and they don't know "Go Tell Aunt Rhody". . . . [Y]ou've got to start with "their" music. You've got to find out what kids are listening to, and then use that music in class. (Taylor, Barry, & Walls, 1997, pp. 69–70)

The type of culturally relevant music differs, based on geographic area or student ethnicity and may be unfamiliar to directors. In the case of mariachi, band and orchestra instruments are used (with the addition of guitars or voice), but other culturally relevant ensembles may require nontraditional instruments. A growing number of printed and recorded resources for teaching these ensembles have become available. Directors can immerse themselves more fully in a musical style by attending workshops and clinics.

Such instrumental ensembles sometimes exist in schools as extracurricular activities. Volunteers often teach them, and ensembles tend to focus on entertainment value rather than the serious study of authentic performance. This should not be the case if a certified music teacher is avail-

able. Directors must remember that these ensembles, like traditional bands and orchestras, have a standard of performance quality, and can conform to national, state, and district standards. *Strategies for Teaching Specialized Ensembles*, edited by Robert A. Cutietta (1999), provides an excellent resource to help directors align alternative ensembles with music standards. These ensembles are as legitimate as traditional ones, and directors should strive to provide motivating, substantive music experiences that also reflect students' cultures.

Traditional bands and orchestras should play culturally relevant music as well. Much of the so-called multicultural music in the past merely constituted arrangements of folk material from different parts of Europe. Fortunately, a growing number of pieces at all skill levels have become available that more authentically reflect world music styles. You can introduce students to instrumental music study by using the cultural music with which they identify, but they should perform varied music from all over the world. Substantive music originates from all cultures.

If directors cannot find or afford world music literature, they can arrange pieces in a given music style themselves. Given the limited budgets of economically disadvantaged schools, this may be a necessity. These arrangements do not need to be complex; writing a simple unison melody often suffices for beginners. As dictated by the style of music, arrangements for older students may need the addition of harmony, bass line, and percussion parts. Whether performing published pieces or arrangements written by the director, students find "their" music motivating to play and audiences usually respond enthusiastically.

Student retention depends on many factors, some of which you can control, and others you can't. Put your energy into inspiring students to achieve high standards by implementing classroom policies that motivate, reward, and, ultimately, retain.

· *3* ·

Gaining Support

*B*ecause funding for instrumental music programs often gets called into question, directors need to search continually for ideas that publicize their program's achievements and elevate their prominence. You can do many things to inform parents, administrators, and other stakeholders about the viability of instrumental music programs. Directors who establish good public relations celebrate student achievement and successfully build support for programs.

PARENTS

As an inexperienced teacher several years ago, I was uneasy with parents in general, and nearly terrified of a few of them in particular. I was not prepared for the power that parents could wield. Through the advice of mentors and doing a good bit of reading and reflection on my own, I learned that parents are powerful allies, but I would have to enlist their support proactively. I have since improved my rapport with parents a good deal. In fact, I have built programs in some otherwise adverse conditions through parental support, and subsequent administrative support.

    Early and frequent communication with parents provides a sense of legitimacy. Large numbers of students are typically involved in the instrumental music program, so their parents create a powerful force that can preserve program vitality in the face of scheduling and funding crises.

Though often quite strong in elementary schools, frequent communication with parents wanes with the increasing age of the student. Maturing students press for autonomy and independence, especially in the middle and high school years. Though they do not object to peripheral involvements such as fund-raising, students expect less overt involvement from parents, particularly at school. However, older children still seek the approval of parents, who continue to affect their children's success no matter what their age.

Assessment reporting provides a simple yet crucial way to keep parents informed of their child's progress and program expectations. Grades or other assessments provide effective communication if they accurately and objectively identify students' strengths as well as areas for improvement. A program with clear, identifiable, and measurable goals communicates the "academic" legitimacy of instrumental music study. Brophy (2000) argues, "When music teachers are armed with assessment data that demonstrate learning and student progress toward attaining educational standards, their programs are much more supportable when districts face budget cuts" (p. 2). Students, in turn, find favorable assessments rewarding. Assessment has vital importance for both instruction and advocacy.

As the director, you need to initiate relationships with parents—a difficult task. Written announcements that detail upcoming events are necessary forms of communication, but these are impersonal. The director talks to parents during functions at school, but there are usually too many parents to greet in a short amount of time.

Phone calls present opportunities to discuss student progress while building personal rapport. It is best to call parents when they are free to talk, so ask what time of day is most convenient to receive calls when collecting phone numbers. Even if parents are not home, you can leave brief messages such as a congratulatory note about a good lesson or other praise. In my experience, some parents have trouble contacting me at school. In all correspondence, I have chosen to provide my home number. You may want to consider giving out an e-mail address, but most of my students' parents don't have computers (and I don't have one at school).

I have never had problems with giving out my home phone number in any school in which I have taught, even in newsletters. The advent of "caller ID" has virtually ended prank phone calling, though I tell students clearly that my phone number is for parent use (as friendly students merely wanting to chat have called in the past!). Of course, not everyone should give out e-mail

and home phone numbers. In many cases, directors manage large programs and might become inundated with work-related issues if dealing with calls and e-mails when they—and their families—need the time away from work.

I try to speak personally to parents at least three times a year. Sometimes these conferences are congratulatory phone calls, and merely let parents know that their child is doing well. These phone calls reward students powerfully. They excitedly tell me how happy their parents were to receive good news. Even if I call with a problem, I find one or two student strengths to share with parents to temper the tone of the call.

In all direct communication with parents, directors must communicate problems concerning student progress precisely and objectively. For example, instead of vague language and details such as, "C. J. is doing poorly," directors should use objective language supported by evidence: "The last two lessons, C. J. could not keep up with the rest of the group and seemed unfamiliar with pieces on page ten. I spoke to him privately after both lessons and he told me he was having a hard time practicing at home. I don't want him to fall behind. How can we work together to solve this?"

Directors should also listen carefully to parents and acknowledge their feelings, validate their concerns, and check for understanding by asking questions such as, "It is clear to me that you are frustrated. If I understand you correctly, you are upset that Shahadah is being treated unfairly, right? Well, I am glad that we have this opportunity to talk about it." Please note that directors should never have to endure verbal abuse or insults, and they should end conversations that take this course. But directors should try to understand feelings and arrive at solutions, even during those unpleasant phone calls where parents become upset. Experience has shown that such frustration usually results from lack of communication, and I have fewer of these types of calls as my efforts to communicate with parents improve each year. I have come a long way since my first couple of years of teaching!

Even when students drop from the program, I make sure I call parents to thank them for their support and to ensure that no one has any hard feelings. Even before I get around to calling, some parents call or write on their own to explain that their children's discontinuation of study was not my fault, and to thank me for my efforts. Even though their child is no longer in the program, these parents remain ardent supporters and encourage participation with younger family members or friends.

To effectively communicate and build support, directors need to understand local cultures and values. Directors often do not come from the communities in which they teach and may have different values and perspectives, encountering "oppositional frames of reference" (Ogbu, 1992, p. 9), particularly if the director is white or another ethnicity not largely represented in the community. These different frames of reference may exist because of history, socioeconomics, ethnicity, and geographic location. Directors can talk to veteran teachers in the district, read articles and books written by experts on certain cultures and communities, and be sensitive to different perspectives by carefully observing students, parents, and community members.

Numerous resources discuss successful parent-teacher conferencing, active listening, and other effective communication techniques that help you get along well with parents as well as colleagues, administrators, and students. Though frequent, individual communication with parents is time consuming in large ensembles, the relationships that you develop generate great support for the ensemble—something well worth the effort. Some of the most powerful feedback administrators receive about your program comes from parents; the more parents who provide feedback, the more powerful the message.

Parental support has as much importance in economically disadvantaged schools as it does in affluent schools. Many teachers, particularly if they view family structure through a white, middle class perspective, criticize and underestimate the parental support of their students. Realize, however, that students of diverse ethnicity or students living in poorer communities may have extremely strong familial bonds. Kuykendall (1992) points out that "some [teachers] would be surprised to learn of the tremendous strength that exists in non-nuclear, but 'extended' Black and Hispanic families" (p. 98).

Other researchers promote extended family support, but they also underscore the impact parents themselves can have on students' efforts at school. A study by Wilson and Corbett (2001) sought to ascertain what type of teachers urban middle school students prefer, and their statements are illuminating:

> [Interviewer]: Why are you getting an A in reading when you did so poorly last year?

[Student 1]: I work hard. She's [the teacher] hard on us. I like that. It's helping me.

[Researcher]: What does she do?

[Student 1]: She called my house and talked to my mom.

[Student 2]: A teacher who stays on you is one who tells you to do your work, calls your house over and over and over, says "You're missing this and that" and "You need to turn this in."

[Researcher]: What do your best teachers do to help you the most?

[Student 3]: She knows my mom real good. She stays on my back. She says she'll call my mom. (p. 72)

In their own words, these students show how much power parents and teachers have, especially when combined, in molding student behavior.

Some parents distrust teachers and act generally hostile toward school representatives because of bad experiences they or their children had, or cultural differences that language barriers possibly heightened. They may not place the same value on education as teachers do. But directors must realize that these parents will develop positive relationships with teachers they like and trust; building bridges to ambivalent parents is possible.

Contacting parents can be more challenging in areas with high levels of poverty. Because many of these parents can find only low-paying jobs, they often need to work several hours beyond the average work week, often with varied schedules. In these cases, students often stay with extended family or friends during evening hours. Many families living in poverty are grappling with day-to-day survival. They might fear phone calls from school only bring more bad news, so perhaps they screen them.

Thus, I make some of my parent contact by leaving messages with family members or on answering machines. As with speaking to parents directly, these messages always include positive comments about the student. Although I share positive comments freely, I save any areas of concern for discussion directly with the parent. In some cases, if I understand the particular family dynamics well enough, I'll discuss these concerns with extended family members as well.

When families do not have access to phones, I ask students for phone numbers of other family members. I also frequently mail home congratulatory notes. I try to visit homes as often as possible because these visits are usually very positive and successful in garnering family support, but directors need to judge whether or not it is safe to visit homes alone in some environments. Some teachers make home visits with other teachers, while others

bring spouses. Though some families resist getting to know me no matter what, working to secure family support regardless of economic conditions is central to building and maintaining a healthy instrumental music program.

ADMINISTRATORS AND COLLEAGUES

Parental support is a powerful ally in maintaining an instrumental music program, but building administrators often make the decisions that determine your program's fate. Principals must manage near the bottom of the power structure in a top-down bureaucracy. Regardless of district size or structure, government mandates frequently determine the decisions administrators must make. However, recent widespread adoption of site-based management models often allows building principals autonomy in scheduling, building use, and funding allocations. In many instances, administrators—including building principals—can either crush or cultivate instrumental music programs. It's best to have them on your side.

Keeping administrators aware of instrumental program events and achievements reminds them that your program is vibrant and vital. Administrators can reward and encourage students by sharing program achievements through building announcements and conversations with the students themselves. Praise and recognition from people in positions of authority are quite motivating for students.

Similar to administrators, developing relationships with fellow teachers can enhance both your job and your program. Teaching with other colleagues increases visibility and builds collegial bonds that often lead to support of the instrumental music ensemble. Collegial partnering can be as simple as having science students come to the music room for a demonstration of sympathetic vibrations for a few minutes, or as involved as an entire unit on Shakespeare's *Romeo and Juliet* and its contemporary adaptation: *West Side Story.* Even non-academic support, like volunteering the music room for certain students who need time out, or covering another teacher's classroom for a bathroom break helps garner their support.

Publicize your program's events as much as possible. Distribute announcements about upcoming performances to administrators, as well as news about success meeting standards and other curricular developments typically sent home to parents. Principals usually require that you submit

these notices to them for approval before distribution to parents. Even if your school does not have this policy, you should submit any correspondence for distribution outside school to principals first to keep them in the loop. Besides program achievements, keep them informed regarding program needs, and issues concerning scheduling, instructional space, and budget.

One-on-one conversations provide an obvious opportunity to promote your program. When directors must pose problems to the administrator, they can posit two or more viable solutions, if possible. Because problems presented by new teachers may be viewed as insignificant or a result of inexperience, new teachers can consider having an experienced colleague participate in the discussion. The presence of supportive colleagues shows that you have productive relationships with other staff members—a critical assessment component in many teacher evaluations.

Skillful and competent administrators judiciously weigh instrumental program needs along with other numerous considerations. Unfortunately, the weight assigned often correlates to the value administrators place on music and the arts in general. Savvy administrators who do not personally value instrumental music still work to cultivate and maintain healthy programs if parents and other community members strongly support the program.

Build support by including administrators in performances. Most principals enjoy being on stage as much as students do! Have them serve as narrators or even as performers. "First Performance: A Demonstration Concert" for band (Feldstein, 2000) and orchestra (Feldstein, 1994), a chart distributed by the Music Achievement Council, constitutes a performance that requires a narrator. My building principal enthusiastically accepts my invitation every year. I recently wrote a beginning band piece integrated with English or Language Arts classes that included vignettes performed by building administrators and other teachers. Students feel important when they perform with administrators, and the performance itself provides an opportunity for administrators to display their support for instrumental music programs.

COMMUNITY AWARENESS

Though sharing program achievements with parents and administrators constitutes a form of publicity, directors must make the greater community aware of program vitality. Announcements of community interest include

Press Release
For release: [date]
Contact:

LOCAL ORCHESTRA PERFORMS CONCERT

The [name] School Orchestra will give a free concert of [day of the week], [date], at [time] in the school auditorium.

[Name of director], a music educator at [school], will conduct the orchestra in the performance, which will feature both popular and traditional selections.

For more information about the concert, call [name and phone].

Figure 3.1   Sample Press Release

Press Release
For more information, contact: [Your name] at [your phone number]
For Immediate Release

[Your Name] Returns from Attending
Prestigious Music Education Conference in Bellevue, Washington

[Date of Release] [Your city, state]—[Your name] recently returned to class at [your school] after attending the 2005 Northwest Division Conference of MENC: The National Association for Music Education.

[Your name], who [describe your teaching experience or level or include other pertinent information], attended the meeting to [describe your goals and reasons].

[Your last name] was one of thousands of music educators who convened in Bellevue, Washington, February 18–20, 2005, to experience workshops, exhibits, and performances by school ensembles and by the All-Northwest Honor Groups, consisting of more than 900 of the most musically accomplished high school students in the Northwest region of the United States. Other highlights included an Evening of Jazz, music education exhibits, and a Get America Singing . . . Again! program by Kirby Shaw.

"[A quote describing your experience at the conference, how it will help you in your teaching, and the importance of music in school is appropriate to add here]," says [your name].

Figure 3.2   Sample Press Release

performances, honors and awards, and professional accomplishments of the director. Greater publicity motivates students because it recognizes their achievements to others outside school. Parents and administrators appreciate the community notices the program, in turn strengthening their support. Figure 3.1 is a press release template appropriate for announcing instrumental music concerts.

In addition to program achievements and events, directors should consider announcing their own professional development and accomplishments. Publicity of such announcements depends on the size of community and targeted readership or audience of the media outlet. If published or broadcast, these announcements strengthen the instrumental music program by showing that it has a skilled director committed to further training and service to the profession. From a motivational perspective, students take pride in a director who has acknowledged achievements, and they need not be extraordinary. Figure 3.2 is a press release template provided by MENC: The National Association for Music Education, which should be printed on school letterhead.

Becoming a public relations expert gives your students the chance to shine—and get recognized for it. Everyone who comes into contact with your program is a potential instrumental music supporter, and the more of them, the better. Show them what you do and how well you do it, and just watch the ruckus they make if your program is endangered!

· 4 ·

Maximizing Rehearsal Time

$\mathcal{C}$urrent school policies place ever-increasing time constraints on most ensemble directors, meaning that efficiency in rehearsal, though certainly a priority in the past, is even more critical now. To combat limited rehearsal time, I have modified some time-tested practices that flow from basic teaching and learning principles. I review some general rehearsal planning and procedures tenets, and provide some specific techniques that you can adapt to fit any rehearsal environment. They have a successful track record in rural, suburban, and urban schools.

The key elements to success with limited rehearsal time are action and adaptation. Action through involvement with advocacy efforts in local, state, and national campaigns facilitates public awareness of diminished rehearsal time and other cuts to instrumental music programs. Adapting rehearsal preparation and practices helps to battle time constraints after cuts have occurred. Effective rehearsal planning and procedures are imperative for the many directors who, like me, consistently race the clock while trying to cultivate excellent programs.

In spite of concentrated advocacy and publicity efforts, like many directors, I have faced near-crippling cuts in rehearsal time in some of my previous programs, though in retrospect the cuts would have probably been much worse without my publicity efforts. Faced with these inevitable reductions, I continued my advocacy and publicity efforts, but decided to also combat the problem internally by evaluating my occasionally inefficient teaching practice and program infrastructure. I began instituting some

new procedures that helped me run rehearsals more efficiently. Malleable enough to fit any teaching and learning environment, these practices stem from sound principles first introduced in undergraduate education classes, and apply to practical, real–world situations.

LESSON PLANNING

Planning rehearsals that account for every minute available maximizes teaching time and curbs behavior problems. Though seemingly obvious, knowledge of the score and other musical material planned for the rehearsal saves time. There are no quick routes to score study and lesson planning; they simply take time outside rehearsal.

Battisti and Garofalo (1990) warn that "[t]o communicate the expressive potential of a musical composition to an ensemble in an effective and efficient manner, a conductor must first acquire an understanding of the score" (p. 1). Thorough score analysis that encompasses both musical and technical elements allows directors to understand the music and develop ways to meaningfully and efficiently share it with students.

Even after several years of teaching certain pieces, I still study scores for both musical and technical details that might pose performance problems and then carefully write lesson plans. "An outstanding rehearsal is well organized and planned in advance" (Blocher & Miles, 1999, p. 37). Like most experienced teachers, my lesson plans appear meaningless to others because I use an abbreviation system that I have developed to save time. One crucial item in the lesson plan that I still diligently include is the "reflection" or "evaluation" portion at the end of the plan. After rehearsal, I note what worked, what did not, problem areas in the score, and any other details needed to plan the next lesson. The few minutes it takes to reflect in writing saves me time in the next rehearsal because I know exactly what we need to accomplish.

PHYSICAL SET–UP AND ROUTINE

Another fundamental element that contributes to efficiency in any classroom involves the set–up of the physical environment before instruction—

also known as "controlling the environment before it controls you." Make sure you set up the room so you can move about as freely as possible during rehearsal. Doing so allows you to move closer to students who might misbehave. Directors who "mix it up" and move about the room are simply more interesting to students. Mobility free of obstruction enables directors to have access to students who may need individual assistance, or to monitor and coach peer tutors or teacher's aides assisting new students or exceptional learners.

Directors also hear and see ensembles differently from different areas of the room. Critically looking and listening nearer to instrument sections located farther away from the podium assists in identifying problems with technique as well as help with aural error detection.

Students can help prepare for rehearsal by distributing music and putting equipment in place. Be sure to put the daily repertory order on the board, and place lesson plans, written reminders, announcements, blank paper, and a pencil on the conductor's stand for "Notes to Self" during rehearsal.

I also make sure I have baton, tuner, metronome, and other instructional aids in place near the podium. Any trips out of the room not only wastes instruction time, but it also compromises orderliness as students begin off-task behaviors. To further alleviate misbehavior when students enter the room, I always try to stand at the podium or near the front door to greet them. I discourage any horseplay and help students mentally prepare for the rehearsal by playing music recordings that relate to the repertory planned for the day.

Students should know rehearsal routines such as instrument storage and tuning procedure. For example, once students are seated and setting up instruments, I do not allow any playing because we warm up together after class begins. Some directors—particularly those of older students—train students to warm up and even tune independently, but I find that silent preparation creates a more orderly environment for younger students. Such order prevents unnecessary distraction and helps keep students focused on the work ahead.

AVOIDING EXCESS TALKING

You can easily observe restless body language in rehearsals run by directors who talk too much. For new concepts, I use the learning style sequence discussed in the next chapter, which requires auditory, visual, and tactile or

kinesthetic representations of material. For verbal corrections, directors save time and maximize student attentiveness by making very brief, specific comments that include both a succinct statement of the problem and a means to rectify it. Directors maintain rehearsal focus if they remember to "teach more; talk less" (Moore, 2002, p. 31).

To further expedite my direction with less talk, I have devised hand signs for common problems such as intonation, hand position, and embouchure that I use while conducting that, together with eye contact, quickly make individual players aware of a problem without the embarrassment of public scrutiny. Of course, the success of these nonverbal cues depends on the ability of students to watch my conducting. The time I spend training students to respond to conducting gestures and other cues alleviates the need for excess verbiage.

REPAIRS

Save time by avoiding instrument repairs during rehearsal. Of course, students should maintain their own instruments, but the extent to which this is possible depends upon the age of the student. Directors should teach and reinforce proper care of instruments and monitor student efforts in lessons so that stuck valves and other maintenance-related mishaps occur less often in rehearsal.

Most directors keep extra reeds and oils on hand for emergency use, but I also have at least one loaner instrument available for every instrument type—two for clarinets and flutes. If the school does not own them, instrument dealers may lend them for the school year. A necessary accessory to loaner instruments is plenty of disinfectant to sterilize mouthpieces. When budgets are tight, inexpensive, mint-flavored rubbing alcohol (available at most pharmacies) transferred to a spray bottle is a quick sterilizer, but to avoid possible mouthpiece discoloration, you can use antibacterial dish or hand soap and water.

Note that students play better on their own instruments, to which they are accustomed. Any more than a couple of forgotten instrument episodes requires some attention by the director, which often includes a phone call home. As directors work with students and parents to remember instruments, and when instruments are out for repair, loaners help keep students progressing.

CLASSROOM MANAGEMENT

Classroom management is vital to effective rehearsals and a particularly challenging issue for directors. Participation in instrumental music is almost always voluntary and a director who is too permissive loses effectiveness and time in rehearsals, while a director who is too stern loses students. Remember, a carefully planned rehearsal keeps students focused and alleviates most behavior problems.

Directors can keep behavior problems from slowing down rehearsal with a policy that consists of fair, consistently enforced, and clearly defined rules with consequences—basic principles covered in most classroom management classes. Because I am fair and consistent, my students often describe me in their vernacular as "strict" (enforcing appropriate behavior), but not "mean" (uncaring, hostile). Students actually prefer "strict" directors, but few will participate in the programs of "mean" ones. Though designed for elementary and middle school students, the following classroom management techniques also work for high school students, if rewards and consequences are modified.

INDIVIDUAL BEHAVIOR

A plan that accounts for individual and group behavior is effective as it adequately accounts for the varied types of behavior issues. To quickly rectify incidents of individual students' misbehavior, I use a two-card system that everyone understands, but that minimizes public humiliation.

At the onset of behavior problems, I use a couple of techniques usually covered in classroom management classes: eye contact and temporarily moving within closer proximity to the off-task student(s). If necessary, I place an index card with the word "Reminder" written in blue ink on the music stand behind the music folder of the student. Although other students are aware of the reprimand, it is less severe than a verbal admonishment, and requires no discussion. It merely warns students that they need to monitor their behavior. If the student fails to follow rehearsal rules after receiving the warning card, I place a "Report to Parent" card, written in red ink, behind the folder. This "report" can constitute either a phone

call or a note mailed home that identifies some positive attributes of the students, a description of the incident, and a way to address it.

I usually do not have to issue more than two red cards at the beginning of the year, as word gets out about my parental phone call or letter. Students learn that I commit to keeping order in rehearsal. Whether blue or red, after rehearsal students must return the cards to me, at which point we privately discuss behavior and expectations. I include positive comments along with a clear statement of the problem and solution, just as I do when I talk to their parents.

GROUP BEHAVIOR

Because misbehavior often involves more than two or three students, I have instituted a group goal that students do not "lose their marbles" during rehearsal. Serving as a team-building technique, each rehearsal begins with three marbles in a plastic cup. Every group infraction of rehearsal rules (usually talking or other off-task behavior) means a lost marble. If students can go the entire rehearsal without losing all three marbles, they receive a predetermined reward, such as ending the rehearsal by playing a popular piece, points toward a band party, and so on. I have had great success in quickly managing even very large groups. Most of the time, I merely have to shake the cup to immediately silence the room!

Some directors claim that they expect and receive complete silence during the entire rehearsal. This is unreasonable to expect with younger students during rehearsals that last more than 30 minutes. Attention problems occur after extended periods of the same activity, even a naturally engaging one like playing an instrument. If activities are prolonged, students become increasingly less attentive toward the end of rehearsal, and I lose time trying to engage them. Varying activities throughout the rehearsal keeps them focused. During particularly intense rehearsals, I provide a break by leading the group in a quick movement activity involving concepts covered in rehearsal (rhythm patterns, dynamics, and so on). These movements help relax tense playing muscles and release the excess energy that might lead to behavior issues that interrupt rehearsal.

Though not recommended by some directors, I tell students they have 30 seconds to a minute between rehearsal segments to get out the next piece.

I usually allow controlled individual conversations pertinent to the activities at hand during this time to provide a brief period of respite between the intense periods of concentration needed to play. Students often use this time to help each other solve performance problems. I encourage and reward this whenever possible, particularly because I have revolving enrollment and often assign tutors to students who have begun later in the year.

Even during brief periods of transition you must maintain an orderly climate or you waste time trying to regain rehearsal focus. When groups of people are called to order, immediate cessation of talking rarely occurs, and the leader usually repeats the call a few times as students conclude their thoughts before ending conversations. Rather than asking for silence several times, I make the request for quiet once and then count down by five from about 15 seconds (15, 10, 5, 0), which controls the flow of rehearsal while allowing students a chance to prepare percussion instruments and otherwise transition to the next piece. If the room is not quiet when I reach zero, I take a marble. Students do not like "losing their marbles" and, after losing all three during a rehearsal at the beginning of the year, calling the room to silence usually does not pose a problem thereafter, particularly if they truly desire the reward.

STUDENTS AS HELPERS AND LEADERS

I expect students to help me with rehearsal efficiency. With my beginners, I notice that they have varying levels of independence. Consequently, I used to waste rehearsal time by providing solutions that students themselves can easily remedy. Now, at the beginning of the year, I demonstrate how students can avoid excessive teacher direction particularly when preparing for rehearsal.

For example, if students come to me about not having a music stand, I indicate the extras in the corner of the room and explain that they are expected to quietly get one. If a student raises his or her hand to report that another student won't move over to provide enough room for a large instrument, I clearly articulate my expectation that all students work together to provide ample space, and that I am available to help with irresolvable conflicts, but I expect ensemble members to work as a team in rehearsal. Of course, I must intervene at times, but a consistent expectation that students

rely on their own resourcefulness—both as individuals and as team players—frees rehearsals from unnecessary, time-consuming mediation.

To further aid student independence, I designate one to three leaders in each instrument group. Though often the strongest players, I also choose responsible students with leadership qualities. You can use these leaders for the entire school year or institute a rotating policy where all students have opportunity to lead. Section leaders answer questions from less experienced students, pass out notices, check sections at the end of rehearsals to ensure that all equipment and music is put away correctly, or deal with frequent problems, such as lost music or missing percussion equipment. Clearly define their power from the beginning, and deal with any abuses immediately. I seldom have problems with student leaders and they greatly expedite time-consuming tasks.

While lack of rehearsal time is irritating if not downright overwhelming, don't let it get the best of you. Plan your time well and let your students become your allies in generating productive rehearsals. You might not be able to control the amount of time you have, but you can control what you do.

Teaching for Diverse Learning Styles

*L*ike their students, directors respond to certain learning styles better than others, and it can be challenging to collect and incorporate teaching techniques for all ways of learning. The following teaching sequence accommodates all learning styles and becomes second nature with a little initial planning and practice. The benefits outweigh the effort, as directors who account for both individual and cultural learning styles reach and teach more students.

Teachers often use the lecture-style method of instruction, and its ineffectiveness for nonauditory learners is well-known. I vividly remember observing students who seemed to not listen to my explanations. Actually, they were quite attentive; they were simply looking at pictures or diagrams in the book that showed the concept that I was verbally describing. The "light went on" for some students because the visual representations in the method book taught them more effectively than my lecture.

Like many teachers, I made largely verbal presentations, and further study convinced me that I could have taught more effectively and saved time if I had accounted for different learning styles. I now use a teaching sequence in rehearsal and lessons that maximizes my teaching effectiveness by accommodating the different types of learners in my ensembles. Recently, I have also considered strategies that account for learning styles that have a cultural foundation.

First, we must understand these learning styles. Several models explain individual styles, but I have found that planning instruction by adding

Fleming's (1995) read/write learning style to Celli-Sarasin's (1999) auditory, visual, and kinesthetic model easily and adequately accommodates diverse learning styles. Understanding the characteristics of four learning styles prepares you to plan effective instruction.

DIFFERENT TYPES OF LEARNERS

Read/write learners "reveal a preference for accessing information from printed words" (Fleming, 1995, p. 2), which is the most common method of information exchange in educational settings. These students learn by seeing and writing printed words, and are prolific note-takers in lecture-style presentations. Though they are usually successful in lecture-style presentations, their preferred learning style needs consideration in instrumental music settings.

Auditory learners, as the term suggests, approach education experiences effectively through listening. These learners process verbal instruction easily. It seems that all students drawn to music would be auditory learners because of its aural nature, but an assessment of learning styles in rehearsal would reveal that this is not the case. As Gardner (1999) posits, a student with high musical intelligence can have a preference for any one of the four modes of processing. Therefore, lecture-style demonstrations, group discussions, and modeling with the voice or instrument may help only some of your music students process information effectively.

Visual learners often have trouble in rehearsal because directors usually use verbal instruction. These students benefit from graphic representations and visual demonstrating of skills and concepts. A teacher's aural example may not be enough for visual learners; actually seeing a diagram or "picture" of the sound may help.

Kinesthetic learners learn by doing. This type of learner has been traditionally the most neglected in education settings (Celli-Sarasin, 1999). Fortunately, instrumental music easily caters to this learning style because of the "hands-on" nature of playing an instrument. But the built-in interaction with the instrument does not always help this type of learner understand new skills, concepts, or content. These learners often benefit from teaching techniques that allow them to "feel" the concept or skill away from the instrument first.

When introducing new information, I use a teaching sequence that accounts for all four types of learners. Although each step addresses a different learning style, all students benefit from each step because it helps learners process information through modes that differ from those that they use naturally. Celli–Sarasin (1999) elaborates:

> [I]t is not necessary to limit tactile learners to the tactile, visual learners to the visual, and auditory learners to the auditory. Students naturally gravitate to parts of the lesson with which they feel most comfortable. However, if lessons are designed holistically . . . all students will experience all parts of the lesson and have the chance to learn through their areas of strength, as well as develop their weaker style areas. (p. 85)

The combination of a holistic teaching model and a practical teaching sequence makes my rehearsals effective.

The first step ("hear it") includes demonstrations of the desired behavior and sound and helps auditory learners. This step may also include verbal review of prior knowledge and group discussions, which activate the interest of all students. In the second step ("see it"), present a graphic representation and accommodate read/write learners by writing words that explain the graphics. The third step ("feel it") appeals to tactile or kinesthetic learners because it provides a way to understand through the body. All students understand and demonstrate the new skill or concept before becoming encumbered with the instrument, which is especially important for beginning students whose executive playing skills are not yet second nature. Once students show they understand a skill by simulating it away from the instrument, they then demonstrate it while playing.

TEACHING SEQUENCE TO ACCOMMODATE DIFFERENT LEARNING STYLES

Concept: Proper Articulation for Winds

Let students:

Step 1: *Hear what it sounds like.* Engage auditory learners through verbal analogies or class discussion. Make sure to demonstrate the skill or concept with your voice or instrument if applicable. For example, explain to beginning students that the proper articulation and note length should sound like the notes are almost touching with the tongue separating each note.

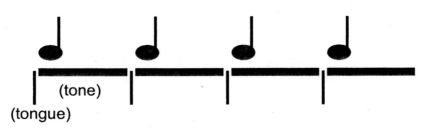

(tone)

(tongue)

"TaaaaaaaaaTaaaaaaaaaaTaaaaaaaaaaTaaaaaaaaaa"

Figure 5.1

Step 2: *See what it sounds like.* Draw a diagram or model. Be sure to include word descriptions for read/write learners. Figure 5.1 shows a visual example of proper articulation and note length for beginners.

Step 3: *Feel what it sounds like* away from the instrument with the body. Students can demonstrate the example by "air playing," where they finger the desired note on the instrument, but tongue quarter notes while forming the embouchure away from the mouthpiece. Brass players can do the same, but buzz on the mouthpiece.

Step 4: *Do it* on the instrument. Monitor progress and repeat steps above if necessary.

Concept: Tuning for Strings and Winds

Let Students:

Step 1: *Hear what it sounds like.* Explain that a pleasing sound on string or wind instruments does not occur by simply pressing strings, keys, or valves. Demonstrate "out-of tune-ness" by playing "in tune" first. Then play sharp and flat. Play a unison pitch with a student and bend the pitch sharp and flat relative to the student's pitch. Guide students' perception of the "wobbles" (beats) that occur when you play sharp or flat. Conclude by playing in tune with the student.

Step 2: *See what it sounds like.* Play a pitch in tune as indicated by an electronic tuner. Then play pitches out of tune while having students note the sharpness and flatness indicated by the electronic tuner. Draw a picture, such as the one in figure 5.2 to further aid the beginner. (I continue to use this graphic as a visual reminder to students even after they have a basic grasp of the basic concept of "in-tune-ness.")

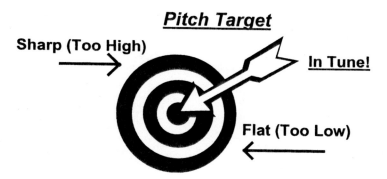

Figure 5.2

Step 3: *Feel what it sounds like* away from the instrument. Have students sing pitches "in the bull's eye" (in tune) as indicated by an electronic tuner. Next, they sing intentionally sharp and flat. They conclude by singing pitches in the bull's eye (in tune).

Step 4: *Do it* on the instrument. Two students play a unison pitch on similar instruments and try to get rid of the "wobbles" (beats) in the air by having one student adjust the embouchure and the length of the instrument. Also have individual students play pitches using the tuner. After they accurately play a pitch in tune, have them try to bend the pitch sharp and flat, according to the tuner. Conclude by playing pitches in tune.

If you observe that students need more help to demonstrate understanding, move through the sequence again, but try a different explanation. Use a graphic representation, followed by a new demonstration away from the instrument. I have found that a review of the visual aid ("see it") and the movement away from the instrument ("feel it") usually suffices.

You can learn new teaching techniques through method books, professional journals, or by attending clinics at professional conferences. In time, a teaching sequence such as this one becomes seamless. My experience has shown that it saves time because my teaching becomes more streamlined and students grasp skills and concepts more quickly. You might even find that they get it right the first time.

Though typical learners have a preferred way of processing (a detailed discussion of exceptional learners follows in the next chapter), they can still process information to some extent in the other three modes.

Many so-called at risk learners, or those with a perceived high likelihood of failure in school, benefit from the sequence because their avoidance behaviors often stem from learning disabilities.

CULTURAL LEARNING STYLES

How cultural values become manifested in specific culture-based learning styles is a current hot topic. Colarusso and O'Rourke (2004) describe the conflicting ways in which teachers approach students: "One culture might encourage spontaneity and creativity in children, and yet another teach the importance of restraint in all behaviors. . . . One teacher might perceive a student's shouting out of answers and ideas as disruptive, while another teacher sees it as a reflection of the student's interest and active participation in the learning process. Individuals from different cultures often view the world from vastly different perspectives" (p. 19). Varying cultural learning styles affect how directors plan and deliver instruction.

Lessons that relate to students' lives and involve social interaction are recommended for many African American (Hale, 2001; Kunjufu, 1986, 1990, 2002; Ladson-Billings, 1994) and Hispanic students (Kuykendall, 1992). As a tenet of constructivist pedagogy, lessons relevant to personal experience benefit all learners (Boardman, 2002; Brooks & Brooks, 1993). The more "people-oriented" (Kunjufu, 1990, p. 13) learning style attributed to some cultures has also been observed generally in adolescent students, when peers replace the significance of adults (Steinberg, 1996). Most instrumental music students in the midst of adolescence are "field-dependent learners" (Kuykendall, 1992, chap. 3), motivated by social and personal relevance.

Directors can structure some activities to involve working with peers. For example, practice buddies involve older students, usually a sibling, extended relative, family friend, or neighbor, who checks on younger instrumental music students at home between lessons. I have had accomplished eighth-grade students choose a fourth- or fifth-grade buddy to help with home practice during the younger student's first year of study. After I prepare them for how best to help, the eighth graders practice with the younger students once a week after school.

This form of interaction proves particularly beneficial, as all students are motivated to some degree by their social context. Older students

deepen their own understanding as tutors (a benefit of cooperative learning), and younger students are encouraged to practice by a significant peer. Younger students also look forward to being practice buddies when they reach eighth grade.

Directors sensitive to the social dynamics of student relationships prove more effective in reaching and teaching their students. Fortunately, the ensembles naturally create a socially relevant context. An ensemble requires the cultivation of esprit de corps, or the "one-for-all-ness" in the ensemble, as opposed to the accomplishments of individuals. I often tell students that audience members are not usually trained musicians that can pinpoint strengths and weaknesses of individual players. Typical listeners generally describe the performance as either good or bad and give praise or criticism to the entire group. Students must support one another so that the entire group is rewarded for collaborative successes. Such teamwork frames a positive social learning environment and provides meaning for field-dependent learners.

Social dynamics can make getting singled out of a group for scrutiny a particularly uncomfortable experience. Like issues associated with social and personal relevance, heightened sensitivity could stem from cultural values or simply from the developmental age of the student. Instead of addressing single players, directors should address the entire section, or simply refer to groups of players: "Do you hear some people not blending? We all must be listening so that our sounds blend together." Directors should describe the problem and recommend solutions to minimize public humiliation and competition amongst players, and to emphasize the importance of every player within the group.

Students learn according to the ways in which they process information within their social and cultural contexts. Adapting instruction to accommodate varied styles of learning engenders thorough and streamlined instruction.

· *6* ·

Including Exceptional Learners

$\mathcal{A}$lthough many directors approach inclusion with apprehension, reservations usually prove unfounded so long as directors adequately prepare themselves to instruct students with exceptional needs. Preparation includes professional study by the director, and collaboration with special education and clinical staff, administrators, parents, and students themselves. A plan that realistically accounts for student strengths and limitations helps directors and students get started. Diligent assessment in light of goals for all students fosters a successful, inclusive classroom.

The Education for All Handicapped Children (1975), now Individuals with Disabilities Education Act (IDEA), has led to mainstreaming exceptional learners in all school program areas, to the extent possible in the "least restrictive environment" (Pub. L. No. 94-142). The term "exceptional learner" has a broad definition in the present discussion and refers to students with learning disabilities, cognitive deficits, and physical limitations that require school services.

Inclusion causes concern for many directors because they feel that accommodating students with special needs will lead to rehearsal disruption and diminished performance quality. The "least restrictive environment" refers to the satisfactory learning progress of typical students as well as that of exceptional students. Therefore, directors need to balance an individual learner's special needs with the needs of the other ensemble members. To do this, directors usually require support from special education staff, administration, and parents. A collaborative effort ensures enriching experiences for all ensemble participants.

55

Despite any disability, it may be quite possible that exceptional learners simply won't dedicate the necessary level of commitment to home practice and other program expectations. Regardless of special need, student commitment should predicate participation and resultant success, and students and parents must understand this from the beginning. In my experience, lack of commitment, as with typical learners, is the most frequent reason exceptional learners do not succeed in instrumental music.

Of course, if dedicated exceptional learners exhibit performance or behavior issues directly attributable to special needs, directors may need to provide further modification. Directors might consider recruiting, consultation with staff and parents, selecting appropriate instruments, preparing and involving student peers, and music modification when including exceptional learners.

RECRUITING

Directors often recruit exceptional learners in the same sessions in which they recruit typical students. If scheduling these sessions during the school day, directors should check with classroom teachers to see if students need added assistance to participate. If this is the case, teachers or teacher's assistants familiar with these special needs should accompany students.

In particular, the skills assessment portion of the session, if included, may require adaptation for some students. Classroom staff can provide extra assistance to individuals while the director administers the assessment for typical students. In some cases, administering assessments at a different time ensures that you can accurately determine the skills of exceptional students. For example, if a student has difficulty understanding responses provided on the answer sheet, he or she will likely provide incorrect answers, but they have nothing to do with music skills. Students may need more detailed instructions and practice questions, or to respond orally rather than with written responses. Special education teachers familiar with particular students can guide modifications.

Some exceptional students may not have the cognitive skills to indicate a preference about whether or not to participate in instrumental music study. Recruiting drives may miss other students who do not participate in general classrooms frequently, but such students usually take part in ei-

ther mainstreamed or specialized music classes. General music teachers can recommend students who show interest in playing classroom instruments, and special education staff can provide further insight as to the appropriateness of instrumental music study for their students.

WORKING WITH COLLEAGUES AND PARENTS

Approach decisions about instrumental study as a team. Special education staff should make recommendations based on expertise as well as experience with particular students. When considering the best way to include an exceptional learner, I confer first with special education teachers and, if warranted, psychologists and physical and occupational therapists. I want to have adequate information when recommending instruments and possible adaptations before I make decisions concerning exceptional students and their parents.

After this consultation, I am better equipped to discuss inclusion options with parents. Some parents have had to fight to have their children included in other school programs and quickly develop an aggressive position if they sense unreceptive directors. Instead, use a proactive approach that respects parental input, and you will garner their support. My experience shows that parents support teachers who genuinely commit to including exceptional learners. A realistic plan that respects the needs of individual learners while accounting for the interests of all other students in the ensemble usually proves possible.

Sometimes parents may resist the recommendations made by special education staff and director. They may not think that their child should have individual lessons instead of group lessons, or ensemble participation with the support of a teacher's aide. The parent might feel that their child "loves music" and won't exhibit the same inappropriate behavior in instrumental music classes that warrants extra support in a general education classroom. I never assume I know students better than parents, but I insist that students receive the same support in the instrumental music class as their other classes until I get to know the student. I always encourage parents to attend the first lesson or two so that we can monitor progress together. They provide helpful input and their presence supports my efforts. Special education staff can observe and provide additional input.

Directors usually need to take the initiative to learn about the nature of specific disabilities. An increasing amount of information has become available regarding several disabilities and how to address them when playing musical instruments, particularly in publications such as MENC's *Music Educators Journal* and *Teaching Music*.

Lack of support from school personnel can lead to unsuccessful inclusion. For example, teacher's aides often support exceptional students, but their breaks are sometimes scheduled during general music classes and other "specials." Lack of support and a music teacher's unfamiliarity with exceptional students can pave the way for failure. The director has the responsibility to provide music instruction and the right to rely on teacher's aides in instructional support roles, since students initially require the same services in both general and music education classrooms. My experience repeatedly shows that once the director becomes familiar with the student's needs and the modifications prove successful, you may no longer require extra support.

Administrators have an obligation to ensure proper support. For example, a building principal should endorse staggered breaks so that special education staff can assist students during music classes. I have also had cases where the principal had to alter teacher's aide's pay for after-school rehearsals. Before asking for help from administrators, directors should confer with special education colleagues to make sure that everyone agrees about the appropriateness and viability of a solution. Administrators can then make informed decisions that facilitate inclusion.

SELECTING APPROPRIATE INSTRUMENTS

Directors must take into account physical or cognitive challenges when selecting appropriate instruments for exceptional learners. Percussion instruments are possible choices for students with physical or cognitive challenges. Directors can easily modify percussion music to meet several student performance levels without reducing ensemble performance quality. You can adapt instruments and beaters so that almost every student with physical limitations can play them. Clark and Chadwick's (1980) *Clinically Adapted Instruments for the Multiply Handicapped* offers several examples of how to adapt percussion instruments and beaters, as well solutions for adapting wind and string instruments.

I have had success with the two-mallet grip used primarily by keyboard percussion players (in which two mallets are held in the same hand), particularly with students with limited use of only one arm or hand (two mallets are held in the more functional hand). Professional marimba players demonstrate the independence possible with both mallets held in the hand, especially with such techniques as single-handed rolls. This grip is not limited to percussion keyboard instruments, as I have had students with limited use of one hand use this grip with almost all percussion sticks and mallets with great success. Mastering these techniques, of course, takes a good bit of practice.

Percussion instruments frequently provide solutions, but you can modify other instruments, though often less easily. Woodwind and string instruments require a good deal of fine motor facility, even at the beginning level. Straps can hold clarinets (some younger players use them anyway), and you can fashion holders to help secure string instruments. String instruments can also be re-strung to be played with opposite hands, but you should consult with an instrument repair technician first.

Brass instruments pose similar problems with embouchure formation, but some can also be played with opposite hands if finger facility is a concern. Trombone is an option if both hands have limited finger use. I had one horn student with limited use of the right hand who played the horn in the customary manner because the hand functioned adequately in the bell of the instrument, and a strap similar to those used for saxophones helped to support the instrument.

Suitable unmodified instruments often suffice for students with physical limitations. For example, students with limited finger movement may have difficulty with a woodwind or string instrument, but not with operating the slide of the trombone. The Moss Rehabilitation Hospital Settlement Music School Therapeutic Music Program produced *Guide to the Selection of Musical Instruments with Respect to Physical Ability and Disability* (1982). It identifies the movement that band and orchestra instruments require. Though the writing is technical and geared toward an occupational therapist, directors and trained school personnel can explore the physical movement needed to play specific instruments before making recommendations to students and parents.

Despite the realistic recommendations of the director, like typical students, exceptional learners may insist on a particular instrument. Students may surprise directors with success in some cases, but most students

quickly realize that they must consider another instrument if they have not made progress after two or three weeks.

PEERS

Respecting and valuing differences is a benefit of inclusion, but directors may need to prepare ensemble members for the arrival of the exceptional learner. Typical students can then help exceptional learners succeed.

If the student is new to the school, new to a more advanced program where students have played together for a while, or new to inclusion in that particular school, directors might consider preparing typical learners in the lesson group or ensemble for the inclusion of the new student. Directors should confer with the exceptional student, if appropriate, parents, and special education staff about the best way to introduce him or her to other students, remaining sensitive to privacy issues. Because of the prevalence of inclusion in general classrooms, most students likely know exceptional needs students prior to participation in band or orchestra.

STUDENT HELPERS

Before using student helpers, remember that in beginner programs, all students are new to instrumental music and must devote their full attention to their own skills. At the beginning, exceptional learners may need to have a special education teacher or aide present, but as typical students progress, a buddy might take his or her place. Typical students often assist exceptional learners they know on their own, especially in inclusive schools.

Helping exceptional peers effectively and greatly contributes to success of typical learners as well, as they reinforce their own learning in the process, but student helpers must first have satisfactory playing skills before they assist special learners. Throughout the process, exceptional learners should not rely too heavily on their helpers to the point where they learn less on their own or restrict the development of their helpers.

LESSON AND REHEARSAL PARTICIPATION

Because I am not usually familiar with students, I schedule individual lessons with exceptional learners so I can better assess the effectiveness of any modifications. If an exceptional learner progresses at a typical rate, I move him or her into group lessons. I have had some students remain in individual lessons permanently because of their needed specialized instruction, though most of them participate in the full ensemble. For programs that have only large-group instruction, directors may want to consider individual instruction for exceptional students, at least at first. If individual instruction is not possible, a special education teacher or paraprofessional can assist the exceptional learner during large-group instruction.

I have clearly specified requirements for ensemble participation. As with typical students, if exceptional learners are capable but do not meet these expectations—most often because of a lack of home practice—they may not participate in the ensemble until they have met the necessary requirements. Obviously, instances occur where the participation requirements for exceptional learners need to be modified or waived, depending on previously identified strengths and weaknesses.

MODIFYING INSTRUCTION OR MATERIALS

Devise a plan for teaching exceptional students based on information you have already gathered. Once instruction begins and you implement your plan, assess and document progress. If exceptional learners show dedication, have an appropriate instrument, but do not progress as predicted, remain open to modifying their instruction. Modifications may involve instruction sequencing or modifying music print or parts.

Task Analysis

Zdzinski (2003) recommends that teachers implement task analysis for special learners with cognitive challenges. Teachers analyze the larger task and break it down into smaller ones, in planning instruction for some instrumental music students. The special education field depends heavily upon

this approach, but it is also essential in teaching and learning in general. Through task analysis, learners sequentially master smaller, more achievable tasks along the way to the larger goal.

For example, task analysis is usually needed to teach small children to tie shoelaces (the larger goal). Many steps (smaller goals) are required to make the double-bow knot. In the next chapter, I apply task analysis to reading notation. And though the steps I describe for introducing notation are temporary for most students, task analysis is required for almost all instruction for some of those who have cognitive challenges.

Modifications

Besides task analysis, consider modifying music. You can simplify parts for exceptional learners, and delete passages that are too difficult. These simplifications or deletions might be permanent or provide a temporary solution until learners can successfully play the part. Ensemble quality doesn't suffer if directors simplify music for some learners.

Consider color coding notation or use other visual cues. Large-print or Braille music helps students with impaired sight. Sight-impaired students as well as several other exceptional students often learn quickly from rote learning or "playing by ear." Hearing-impaired students could require amplification devices. These are only a few examples given to illustrate the many adaptation possibilities.

Necessary modifications usually coincide with those used in students' other classes, though special education staff can help directors with any new challenges that surface specifically with instrumental music study. A growing body of literature available in professional journals and methods texts provides information about specific needs and strategies to meet these challenges in instrumental, general, and choral settings.

BEHAVIORAL CHALLENGES

Aside from physical and cognitive challenges, some students have behavioral difficulties that need attention. Directors should make sure they know behavior plans for a consistent approach.

"ADD" (attention deficit disorder) and "ADHD" (attention deficit hyperactivity disorder) has received a good deal of attention recently. Familiar terms even outside education, ADD and ADHD create controversy because of varying opinions on causes, treatments, or if they even constitute credible disorders (Armstrong, 1999; Kunjufu, 1990). I am not expert and will not speculate on the controversy here, but I do know that some children seem to need a higher degree of stimulation than others to stay attentive, and these students often exhibit a good deal more kinesthetic activity (movement).

Fortunately, the inherent active participation of instrumental music study is ideal for many of these students. Like typical students, they stay more engaged when well-planned lessons allow the entire ensemble to play as much as possible. I often keep these active or easily distracted students engaged by assigning them duties that help expedite rehearsals (such as passing out notices, music, or other managerial tasks). When addressing off-task behavior, I use predetermined visual cues from the podium to help these students stay focused on required tasks. These nonverbal signals help minimize scrutiny by peers. As with other exceptional learners, consult with colleagues and parents to ensure a consistent approach in addressing behavior concerns.

With proper research and preparation, directors can include most exceptional learners in their ensemble in a way that benefits all students.

• 7 •

Introducing Notation

$\mathcal{H}$ow directors teach students to decode music notation (reading music) is controversial because many different strategies stem from several approaches. Regardless of method or technique, reading music notation while performing requires several tasks performed simultaneously.

Aside from the meanings the music symbols represent, executive skills such as bowing, breathing, tonguing, and holding the instrument also need attention at the same time. All of these many simultaneous tasks can be quite challenging for beginners.

Many directors teach reading notation and executive skills separately. Directors usually introduce executive skills necessary to play the instrument prior to notation, but revisit them only after students have formed bad habits, and experienced directors know the difficulties associated with remedying undesirable habits after they occur. Students need a sequence of instruction that helps them decode music notation, but still enables a way to monitor the executive skills that playing the instrument requires.

The following sequence presents a task analysis of simultaneously playing and reading notation. Drawing on the principles of the influential Swiss educator Johann Heinrich Pestolozzi (1746–1827), this sequence allows directors "[t]o teach but one thing at a time—rhythm [and] melody . . . to be taught and practiced separately, before the child is called to the difficult task of attending to all at once" (Monroe, 1907, p. 145, as cited in Schleuter, 1997, p. 27). I analyze the larger task of reading notation while playing, divide it into five subtasks, and arrange

the sequence in the following order: reading rhythm symbols, reading tonal symbols, fingering passages on the instrument, attending to playing techniques, and putting all steps together by slowly playing on the instrument.

While designing the sequence, I drew from pedagogues such as Campbell and Scott-Kassner (1995), Hamann and Gillespie (2004), Gordon (1997), Grunow and Gordon (1989), Robinson and Middleton (Kohut, 1996; Middleton, Haines, & Garner, 1998), and Schleuter (1997). It should be noted that I modify these methods and techniques and use them differently than originally intended, so I encourage you to consult the cited references as well.

LEARNING SEQUENCE FOR BEGINNING INSTRUMENTAL MUSIC READING AND PLAYING

Strings

1. *Tap* basic beat (with heels of both feet with toes anchored to floor), *Pat* beat divisions (with one hand on thigh while other hand holds or supports instrument), and *Rap* melodic rhythm (using rhythm syllables or other counting system).

2. *Tap* basic beat (with heels), *Pat* beat divisions (with one hand on thigh while the other hand holds or supports instrument), and *Sing* passage (using tonal syllables or letter names).

3. *Sing* (using tonal syllables or letter names) and *Finger* on instrument.

4. *Finger* on instrument and *Air Play* without bow (optional: grasp pencil or straw).

5. *Play* (on instrument). Repeat passage several times and gradually increase speed until secure at desired tempo.

Winds

1. *Tap* basic beat (with heels of both feet with toes anchored to floor), *Pat* beat divisions (with one hand on thigh while other hand holds or supports instrument), and *Rap* melodic rhythm (using rhythm syllables or other counting system).

2. *Tap* basic beat (with heels), *Pat* beat divisions (with one hand on thigh), and *Sing* passage (using tonal syllables or letter names).

3. *Sing* (using tonal syllables or letter names) and *Finger* (trombones slide) on instrument.

4. *Finger* (trombones slide) on instrument and *Air Play*. (Form embouchure, tongue, and control breathing as if playing on instrument. Brass players may, at the discretion of the teacher, buzz with or without the mouthpiece instead of "Air Playing." For all wind instruments, check for proper tonguing and articulation and breathing.)

5. *Play* (on instrument). Repeat passage several times and gradually increase speed until secure at desired tempo.

Keyboard Percussion

1. *Tap* basic beat (with heels of both feet with toes anchored to floor), *Pat* beat divisions (with hands on thighs), and *Rap* melodic rhythm (using rhythm syllables or other counting system).

2. *Tap* basic beat (with heels), *Pat* beat divisions (with hands on thighs), and *Sing* passage (using tonal syllables or letter names).

3. *Sing* melody (using tonal syllables or letter names) and *Finger* bars on instrument with forefingers. (Sticking may be monitored here.)

4. *Air Play* (play part in the air, approximating proper intervals between bars). Check for proper stroke, grip, and sticking.

5. *Play* (on instrument). Repeat passage several times and gradually increase speed until secure at desired tempo.

Drums and Accessories

1. Simultaneously *Tap* basic beat (with heels of both feet with toes anchored to floor), *Pat* beat divisions (with hands on thighs), and *Rap* rhythm (chant using rhythm syllables or other counting system).

2. *Tap* basic beat (with heels), *Clap* rhythm, and *Rap* rhythm (using rhythm syllables or other counting system).

3. *Clap* rhythm.

4. *Air Play* (play part in the air). Check for proper stroke, grip, and sticking.

5. *Play* (on instrument). Repeat passage several times and gradually increase speed until secure at desired tempo.

Table 7.1   Comprehensive Sequence at a Glance

	Step 1	*Step 2*	*Step 3*	*Step 4*	*Step 5*
Strings	*tap, pat, rap*	*tap, pat, sing*	*sing, finger*	*air play*	*play*
Winds	*tap, pat, rap*	*tap, pat, sing*	*sing, finger*	*air play*	*play*
Keyboard Percussion	*tap, pat, rap*	*tap, pat, sing*	*sing, finger*	*air play*	*play*
Drums and Accessories	*tap, pat, rap*	*tap, clap, rap*	*clap*	*air play*	*play*

Reinforce the italicized words in the sequence to help students remember them for home practice.

RHYTHMIC FEELING

Gordon (1997), Lisk (2001), and Schleuter (1997) warn that toe-tapping is ineffective as a means of developing rhythmic accuracy. I think that some musicians at all skill levels naturally tap their feet while playing, but I concur that training all young instrumentalists to tap their feet does not help them maintain a steady pulse. Rhythm is felt kinesthetically, as Gordon (1997) points out, and Schleuter (1997) recommends large-muscle movement to facilitate rhythmic sensation in preparatory phases of study.

Because instrumentalists are usually seated, Schleuter (1997) recommends that children respond to "tempo-beat" feeling while sitting "by keeping the toe anchored and raising the heel off the floor" (p. 83), which is large-muscle movement. I adopted this movement during the first two steps of the sequence for both sitting and standing (percussion and string bass) players, but you might notice that I do not include this "heel-tapping" in the steps involving the instrument. Large-muscle movement aims to help students sense rhythm, not train them to move their feet while playing.

Having students pat the beat divisions (such as eighth notes) on the thighs further helps students to feel a steady basic beat. It also prepares beginners to accurately perform beat divisions and subdivisions (such as sixteenth notes).

I have used rhythm syllables such as those associated with Music Learning Theory (developed by Edwin Gordon) and with Kodaly approaches with success, and endorse their use. However, these and other well-known systems are most effective if used consistently over a long period of time. In my school district and many others, student transience is

quite common, and often no uniform rhythm syllable system is used so that students have instructional consistency when changing schools. Further, I start older beginners in higher grades throughout the school year and must get them caught up to their peers quickly. Consequently, I now use the counting system adopted as standard ("1, and, 2, e, ah") from the beginning of instruction. In any case, the present sequence accommodates the use of either rhythm syllables or counting system.

SINGING AND PITCH

Singing is integral to the sequence because instrumental music students often learn most efficiently when they first attempt skills through the most natural instrument: the voice. Among other things, incorporating singing activities helps students develop a sense of tonality, musical phrasing, and style of articulation. Further, virtually all music teachers agree that the ability to sing pitches facilitates proper tuning and intonation. You can monitor pitch accuracy when students sing in steps 2 and 3 for strings, winds, and keyboard percussion.

Acquiring musical understanding is facilitated by audiation, defined as hearing and comprehending musical sound in the mind that is not merely memorized or imitated. Gordon (1997) extols the importance of singing in realizing audiation: "To audiate a melody, students must be able to sing, because when they engage in tonal audiation they unconsciously sing silently" (p. 37). He advocates singing solfège syllables because they help students understand the syntax of typical tonal patterns (in Western music, that is) such as the dominant function of "so" and "ti" typically resolving to "do" at cadences.

I endorse the moveable do/la–based minor solfège system (Gordon, 1997; see also Grunow & Gordon, 1989; Schleuter, 1997) to foster an understanding of Western musical syntax. You can use it consistently across various grade levels and music classes (general music, choir, orchestra, and band). But because of specific issues that affect my program, I have had to adapt a different solfège system for pitches. Although I hesitated to tinker with established methods at first, I am now certain it is necessary to adapt methods and techniques to work effectively in the varying conditions of instrumental music programs.

Established methods that assume a consistent approach over several years are not realistic in some situations. For example, many directors face multiple feeder schools and student transience, particularly in large urban districts, and the consistency of instruction suffers. Additionally, the amount of time I have and the instructional goals I desire for my program usually mean that I must distil, adapt, or meld existing methods and techniques. I also created my own methods, as I did with pitch names.

Band instruments present transposing issues, and students need consistent "concert pitch" syllables for singing when using the notation reading sequence. As an example of adapting established techniques, I teach solfège syllables with a fixed "do" on concert Bb and a do-based minor for singing (which requires the use of different solfège syllables such as the flatted third and sixth). Dalcroze and other European pedagogues advocate this system, but they use C as "do" (the most familiar key for pianists), aiming to acquire perfect pitch (Landis & Carder, 1990, p. 20). However, Bb is the most familiar key for wind instruments in band programs, particularly for those using most current method books. I use a fixed "Bb-do" system simply as a matter of practicality within ever-increasing time constraints.

I attach the letter name to pitches as Grunow and Gordon (1989) endorse. For example, with instruments in concert pitch, the pitches of the Bb major scale would be referred to as Bb-do, C-re, D-mi, Eb-fa, and so on; for instruments that transpose, such as clarinets and trumpets, the same pitches are referred to as C-do, D-re, E-mi, F-fa, and so on. In this system, all students sing the same tonal syllable regardless of instrument transposition by omitting the letter name while singing, but they still learn the universal letter names specific to instrument transposition.

Given a unison passage, students can thus sing the same solfège syllables and pitches and alleviate confusion with transposition in heterogeneous group lessons and rehearsals. When students leave for other programs, they know the universal letter names already and easily adapt to new solfège systems, if necessary.

Again, I use the stationary "do" system for practical reasons. If using Bb concert as stationary "do," "Bb" is always "do" regardless of key. Further, this method means that all pitches, solfège syllables, and letter names remain the same regardless of key. Students consistently refer to

the same solfège syllables and pitches with the same fingerings or slide positions.

Using the stationary "do" system helps reduce performance errors. For example, beginning band students often confuse the pitch A with the pitch Ab concert (especially when learning the key of Eb major after Bb major). With stationary "do," "A–ti" in Bb major becomes "Ab–te" in Eb major. The combined pitch, letter, and fingering/slide change ("A–ti" to "Ab–te") helps students remember the new pitch in Eb major.

In the previous sequence, students sing a different solfège syllable as they change fingering or slide positions, thus pairing the aural change ("ti" to "te") with the kinesthetic change of fingering or slide position (concert A to Ab). This aural-kinesthetic clarity is important when students change keys, and when accidentals appear in familiar keys.

Though critics may argue that ample audiation training makes aural-kinesthetic association unnecessary, the audiation techniques they offer often assume dated instrumental music program designs that are increasingly rare in the present day, such as the assumption that students begin together at the beginning of the school year and remain together for subsequent years. Solfège syllables with stationary "do" work well with many exceptional needs students, those with limited musical ability, in situations where limited time is available for instruction, and when students enter programs at various times.

In my opinion, solfège syllables provide the best but not the only option. You can use letter names, particularly with strings. They are in concert pitch and students sing the same letter names regardless of instrument grouping. However, when working on unison passages in heterogeneous settings with transposing instruments, such as full orchestra or band ensembles, students sing different letter names. Students grow accustomed to this, and it should not pose a significant distraction if you use the sequence regularly.

EXECUTIVE SKILLS

Playing techniques such as posture and hand and finger placement can be monitored in the sequence. I designed the fourth step primarily for the reinforcement of technique. For example, this step for winds ("Finger and Air

Play") very effectively prevents wind students from breathing after every note, which beginners commonly do. "Air Playing," or forming the embouchure, tonguing, and controlling breathing as if playing while fingering the instrument allows teachers to monitor when students take breaths.

You can effectively observe tonguing, or the proper absence of such, as in the case of slurring. I usually have brass players buzz into mouthpieces while fingering during this step. In large groups, this buzzing may overpower the sound of woodwind "air players," so brass players must air play with lips slightly parted. Trombone players slide instead of fingering, of course, but they must "air play" by buzzing the lips away from the mouthpiece while sliding, or buzz into the mouthpiece while approximating slide positions in the air without the instrument due to the way it must be held while playing. Even with these necessary modifications, the step is still effective for young trombonists.

"Air playing" effectively improves precise entrances ("attacks") and releases. In my experience, uniform releases pose more of a problem than uniform entrances, and "air playing" effectively monitors them. With more problematic releases, modifying the Breath Rhythmic Impulse Method (BRIM) first developed by Robinson and Middleton (Kohut, 1996; Middleton, Haines, & Garner, 1998) can help. I have wind students pulse beat subdivisions using the diaphragm, much like the common technique used for teaching diaphragm vibrato. For example, when a half note receives two beats at a moderate tempo, students would subdivide into four eighth notes and say "ta ha ha ha" while "air playing" (See figure 7.1). Students and I call breath impulses "pushes." "Air Playing" with "pushes" helps students feel exactly how long to sustain the tone and release it without being encumbered by the instrument.

The BRIM technique is an excellent way to coordinate where to take breaths. Most wind players have difficulty coordinating the release of the tone and intake of air at the ends of phrases properly while maintaining a steady pulse, and they "breathe with the beat" instead. For example, they play a half note at the end of a phrase for only one beat and breathe on the second beat instead of sustaining the tone. Subdividing durations with breath impulses ("pushes") coordinates phrasing and breathing for wind students at all skill levels.

Wind players should use breath impulses frequently at first so that students become accustomed to the technique. They can do "pushes"

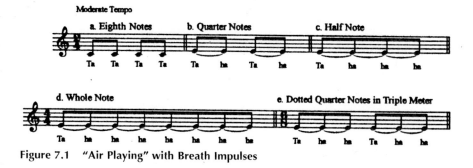

Figure 7.1   "Air Playing" with Breath Impulses

while playing the instrument, but I usually have students do them only while "air playing." Again, as with the Gordon method, I strayed from Middleton's original BRIM technique to serve my own goal to hone uniform durations and releases. Middleton's method has benefits beyond my purposes, if used consistently and in the manner he intended. If unfamiliar with them, I encourage you to read further about Gordon's and Middleton's methods and techniques, as well as those developed by other pedagogues cited, and see if you can incorporate them more fully in your practice.

At the beginning stages of instruction or when you introduce new bowing techniques, strings should "air play" and demonstrate proper grip, hand, and arm motion by simulating bow gestures (without the bow) while still fingering the strings with the left hand. To assist proper bow grip formation, students may hold pencils, and to encourage a relaxed grip, students can hold straws, which bend if they apply too much pressure (Hamann & Gillespie, 2004, p. 50). "Air playing" for strings helps to check executive bowing skills without the encumbrance of the bow's weight.

For keyboard percussion, "sing and finger" encourages students to keep their eyes on the music while using peripheral vision to find the bars of the instrument, an often-neglected skill necessary for successfully reading notation for the keyboard percussion instruments. Other common problems include proper sticking, grip, and stroke. Through "air play," you can monitor the mallet and drums or accessories. The relaxed stroke and rebound used while playing in the air is similar to the desired technique for striking percussion instruments, and particularly benefits stroke development.

At the beginning stages of instruction or when you introduce new bowing techniques, strings should "air play" and demonstrate proper grip, hand, and arm motion by simulating bow gestures (without the bow) while still fingering the strings with the left hand. To assist with proper bow grip formation, students may hold pencils. To encourage a relaxed grip, students hold straws, which bend if they apply too much pressure (Hamann & Gillespie, 2004, p. 50). "Air Playing" for strings helps to check executive bowing skills without the encumbrance of the bow's weight.

WHEN TO USE THE SEQUENCE

Use this sequence when you first introduce music notation or when encountering problematic passages. The learning sequence is effective for short (four to eight measure) songs or passages. Providing a means to remedy problems during home practice is a crucial component of properly training students; so teach this sequence for school use as well as home practice.

Even though this method is for introducing notation, "rote before note" or "sound before symbol" methods still apply when considering best practice for beginners. The first pitches, meters, and rhythms included as part of many method books are best introduced through movement activities, rote learning (imitating the teacher), and playing by ear, all of which should precede reading notation and this sequence. All my students play by rote and by ear exclusively the first couple of weeks, and continue later in the form of improvisation. Contrary to some established methods, I cannot use these activities for extensive periods because of time constraints.

Notice that the learning sequence consists of five steps for all instruments and that I modify and correlate them to instruments found in typical beginner ensembles. You can use the sequence for both mixed group and homogeneous lessons or rehearsals.

OMITTING AND ISOLATING STEPS

Although you should use the sequence when students first learn to read, remember that students join band and orchestra to play instruments, not to sing and chant. Furthermore, they cannot rely on this sequence indefi-

nitely. As teachers note progress, they should monitor students to see if they read and perform proficiently enough to omit all or part of the sequence. After the first couple of weeks of reading (or even sooner with older beginners), see if students can read songs or passages without the sequence. It serves little purpose (and students find the process boring) if they must use it with familiar music that they already play well or with music they can read easily.

You need not use the sequence in its entirety. For example, you can obviously omit step 3 ("sing and finger") for string instruments during the open strings stages and add when introducing fingering. "Air bowing" in step 4 is useful for teaching basic bow techniques needed before introducing notation.

As students become more proficient at playing and reading, you can gradually omit steps, depending on the problems observed by the teacher. For example, with a few weeks of experience, wind players can probably articulate properly with the tongue without breathing after every note, so you can omit "air play" until an articulation, breathing, or release problem occurs again. As students gain more experience reading but later encounter an unfamiliar or problematic passage, abbreviate the sequence to only include the "tap, pat, and rap" and "sing and finger" steps for strings, winds, and keyboard percussion, and the "tap, pat, and rap" and "clap" steps for drums.

You can isolate steps to remedy problems with more advanced students. Quite possibly, only one aspect of student performance is weak when performing a given passage. Directors can isolate a step to address the problem and see if the passage improves when played again. For example, if the pitches were played correctly with the proper articulation but the rhythm was inaccurate, students can "tap, pat, and rap" (step 1) the rhythm of the passage and see if rhythmic accuracy improves. After students have read notation for a few weeks, this process of diagnosing and remedying problems with isolated steps in the sequence saves precious time and maintains student interest in the rehearsal or lesson.

SOME TIPS FOR SUCCESSFUL IMPLEMENTATION

To help younger students understand the sequence, change terminology to better describe basic beats and beat subdivisions, such as "big beats"

(with the heels) and "little beats" (with the hands on the lap). Some students have trouble coordinating these two movements at first, but tapping basic beats with the heels while patting beat divisions on the thigh aids accurate performance of rhythm patterns and steady pulse maintenance, a common problem with young players. If coordination is a problem, have students get the "big beats" first and then add the "little beats" after the "big beats" are secure. Then students may proceed with the rest of the given step ("rapping" rhythms or singing). Most students gradually improve their coordination with simultaneous heel movement (basic beats) and lap patting (beat divisions) by using this process consistently over time.

I use heel-tapping for all instruments because it is a large-muscle movement appropriate for students seated in close proximity, and even for percussionists and string bassists who typically stand. Other movements are also effective, such as swaying the upper body back and forth in response to the basic beats while still patting the beat divisions on the thighs. You can vary movements to feel both basic beats and beat divisions to add variety and maintain interest, particularly with younger students.

Despite all the positive results attributed to singing, some teachers prefer that students not sing passages before playing them. I believe that this hesitancy may sometimes stem from the directors' unease with singing themselves, but they often argue that if a student sings passages incorrectly, confusion results when played pitches differ from sung ones. The possibility of a real detriment seems remote when this occurs, and the benefits of singing outweigh any temporary confusion caused by a possible discrepancy between passages. Providing many opportunities to sing during instruction at school improves pitch accuracy at home.

Most band method publishers also offer accompaniments and playing exemplars on compact disc that students may use at home to help them sing and play accurately. Some publishers even offer free CDs and access to websites where students can download accompaniments and other aids. When using the recordings, students hear correct pitches and a consistent beat that helps them as they use the sequence at home. They can play along with the recording after they have performed all the steps in the sequence to check their performance accuracy.

EXCEPTIONAL LEARNERS

Many exceptional learners find the sequence helpful, and may only require slight modification. For students with more pronounced cognitive challenges, you may need to break these steps down further, and some exceptional learners need to use the sequence longer than typical students.

The sequence also helps students who may not have intervention services, but may trail behind peers when decoding notation symbols. Students who fear failure and give up easily have particular success with this sequence, and the better readers remain engaged when repeating the sequence a few extra times for those struggling. If some students continue struggling to read notation after the first few weeks, other techniques (as well as a possible lesson group change) may need to be considered. Typical students grow tired of the sequence when they don't need it.

Reinforcing good musical habits early improves performance, skills, and overall enjoyment in both the long and short run. Break the rules a little bit and try modifying established methods that are practical to use in *your* classrooms.

• 8 •

Improvisation and Composition

$\mathcal{M}$ost music educators agree that the creative activities of improvisation and composition are components of a complete music education. According to the MENC National Standards, "The curriculum for every student should include improvisation and composition. Many students gain considerable information about music and acquire rudimentary performing skills, but too few have ample opportunities to improvise and compose music" (MENC, 1994, p. 4). You can, however, include improvisation and composition even in rehearsals with very limited time. Using an efficient method is the key.

Like performance, improvising and composing has varied skill levels, but every student can engage in these activities to a certain extent. Some music educators argue that limited opportunities to try such skills contribute to why we have so few improvisers and composers. Increased exposure dispels the sense of mystery and apprehension often associated with improvisation and composition. Unfortunately, directors' inexperience and the demand to prepare for performances limit students' opportunities to pursue these creative endeavors.

A great deal of the improvisational resources available centers on jazz. Composition teaching techniques come from the general music realm and may have limited application in instrumental music classes. Yet by adapting some of these existing techniques, as well as designing others specifically for instrumental ensembles, you can introduce creative, expressive activities that expose students at all levels to improvisation and composition while

actually reinforcing performance goals. Thus, the time spent to learn how to improvise and compose does not detract from building performance skills. Indeed, if designed and implemented correctly, the two creative endeavors actually strengthen students' performance ability.

IMPROVISATION

Jazz (and even Western European or so-called classical music) has always relied on improvisation. Because of this prevalence in music throughout the world, a comprehensive instrumental music education simply should include improvisation activities. Elliot (1995), in his philosophical treatise, *Music Matters*, feels strongly enough about the importance of improvising to assert that "performing and improvising (when improvising is germane to a practice) ought to be the foundational and primary forms of music making taught and learned in music education programs" (p. 172). Unfortunately, while students learn to perform in instrumental music classes, they are rarely taught to improvise.

Some directors feel that instrumental music classes have too little time to teach improvisation because of performance demands. However, a research study by Azzara (1993) found a correlation between beginning students who engage in improvisation and an increased ability to perform while reading notation.

Good improvisers play by ear proficiently. Some musicians, particularly in non-Western and jazz styles, prize "ear playing" and have little or no need for notation. Interestingly, McPherson and Gabrielsson (2002) conclude that ear playing as a pre-notation activity actually helps students better understand notation.

Most directors realize the depth of study required to improvise in the jazz style, and naturally conclude that only jazz students should learn improvisation. True, traditional methods of teaching jazz improvisation are not often easily adapted for several music genres at various skill levels. For this reason, while drawing on eminent pedagogues' works such as Azzara, Grunow, and Gordon (1997), Azzara and Grunow (2006), Gordon (1997), Grunow and Gordon (1989), and Schleuter (1997), I developed a method to teach students in large ensemble groups how to improvise quickly with

limited instruction time. In a few minutes during rehearsal or lessons, this sequence taps into students' creative abilities, helps them play by ear, improves reading skill, and serves as warm-up exercises at the beginning of rehearsals or lessons.

IMPROVISATION SEQUENCE

Rhythm Sequence:

1. Start with rote activity: You chant a neutral syllable ("lu") and students echo. After students echo your four-beat rhythm without pausing, insert a four-beat rest before you chant the next rhythm (see figure 8.1). Keeping this four-beat rest consistent throughout the sequence helps students improvise in step 5.

2. Add rhythm syllables or other counting system. You chant using rhythm syllables ("du" or "ta" for quarter notes) or counting system and students echo. Note: I have students softly say "mmm" for the duration of all rests, as rests move, but quietly.

3. You chant on neutral syllable ("lu") and students chant back using rhythm syllables or counting system. You can monitor students to see if they audiate the rhythm patterns rather than merely echo back the rhythm in rote fashion. To correct errors, chant the rhythm back with students after they have tried to chant it on their own. If errors still occur after several corrections, begin the sequence again, as students may not be ready for this step.

4. You sing on a comfortable playing note using pitch name, and students sing rhythm back on the same pitch. I begin with concert D-mi with band students (as notated in figure 8.1), one of the first and easiest unison pitches my students learn. This step allows students to sing the rhythm accurately before adding the skills necessary to play it on the instrument.

(Rest four beats before beginning next pattern.)

Figure 8.1   Beginning Rhythm Pattern Example

5. You sing a neutral syllable or play rhythm pattern, and students play back (such as on D–mi).

6. Individual students improvise rhythm patterns, and the rest of class plays back. Students take turns improvising in a call-and-response manner. You should demonstrate a few patterns and take volunteers at first, and then point to any student during the four-beat rest between each call and response. Students have the option to "pass," but they all should become willing participants with experience.

Note: For steps 1 through 4 above, students should tap basic beats with the heels and pat beat divisions with one hand on thigh as described in the previous chapter.

Melody Sequence:

1. You sing on a neutral syllable ("lu") and students echo. Start with only two pitches and very simple rhythms at a slow to moderate tempo. Be sure to include the rest after each pattern (see figures 8.2 and 8.3).

2. You sing syllables (do, re, mi or letter names), and students echo.

3. You sing pattern on a neutral syllable, and students sing back the pattern using pitch names. At first, give the starting pitch name to students during the rest at the end of the melody to get them started. They will make a few mistakes at first, every time you add a new pitch; students must audiate before responding. To correct these errors, sing the melody back with students after they have tried to sing it on their own. This method of correcting errors as they occur becomes a game, as students become increasingly motivated to sing the pattern correctly and check their accuracy in the "sing back" with the teacher. Omit the "sing back" with the teacher if students respond with the correct pitch names. If errors still occur after several "sing backs," begin the sequence again, as students may not be ready for this step.

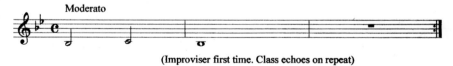

(Improviser first time. Class echoes on repeat)

Figure 8.2   Beginning Melodic Pattern Example

Demonstrates common do-so/tonic-dominant tendency

(Improviser first time. Class echoes on repeat)

Figure 8.3   More Advanced Melodic Pattern Example

4. You sing on neutral syllable or—better yet—play a melodic pattern, and students play back. Similar to the error correction in step 3, if you hear errors, sing the melody with pitch names after students have attempted to play the pattern by themselves.

5. An individual student plays, and the rest of the group plays back in call-and-response fashion. You should demonstrate a few patterns and ask for volunteers at first, and then later simply point to students during the rest between patterns.

USING THE SEQUENCE

Not only does this sequence help students start improvising, but the first steps of this sequence constitute rote or ear-playing activities that you use before beginning students are ready to play together. In my first couple of years of teaching, I would not begin rehearsals for a month or two after lessons began to allow students time to gain the necessary skills to play together in unison. Now I can begin rehearsals concurrently with lessons. In programs without lesson or small-group instruction, this improvisation sequence can be used during the very first rehearsals.

Steps 1 through 4 of the rhythm sequence and steps 1 through 3 of the melodic sequence are appropriate even before students can play instruments together because they do not involve playing. I find that the reading accuracy of both rhythms and pitches improves when students are introduced to them through improvisation first.

To help the success of younger players, this improvisation sequence also initially isolates rhythm and pitch. I begin with four-beat quarter note/quarter rest rhythms (see figure 8.1), and add more complex rhythms as the year progresses. New pitches also adhere to this idea of gradual complexity. To save time, introduce new pitches in individual or group lessons, if possible, because of the extra time needed to learn new fingerings and other executive skills.

Students need not use the entire sequence every time they improvise. Instead, progress through each step in the sequence only when learning new rhythms (eighth notes, dotted quarter/eighth, for example) or when learning new pitches. Considering limited time, I find that approximately six typical melodies or rhythms are sufficient for the easier steps. For example, with "do" and "re" melodies, directors may begin with do-re-do, re-do-re, do-do-re, re-re-do, do-re-re, and re-re-do, using the rhythms in figure 8.2. Students will require more patterns at steps requiring audiation (step 3 in the rhythm sequence and steps 3 through 5 in the melodic sequence). Be sure student performance is accurate at each step before moving on to the next one.

Steps 1, 2, 4, and 5 with rhythms should only take a couple of minutes each, and steps 3 and 6 should take five to ten minutes. I have found that students have more difficulty with melodies than rhythms, so steps 3 through 5 may each take a rehearsal or lesson session of five or ten minutes at first. All steps do not need to occur in a single session. For example, one rehearsal may involve only steps 1 and 2. The next rehearsal might begin with a quick review of the first two steps using the same melodies and the addition of step 3.

As students get used to improvising, these steps take even less time and become seamless. After a month with rehearsals meeting two to three times weekly, I can introduce a new rhythm or pitch using the entire sequence in only one five- to ten-minute rehearsal session. Rehearsal time can be maximized even further if you structure the rhythms and melodies to replace warm-ups. For example, rapid rhythm improvisations can serve to get tongues, fingers, and bows moving, while melodies with longer durations can serve as long tones and intonation exercises.

Limiting choices ensures success with rhythms and beginning improvisation. Gradually add more pitches and more complex rhythms as students gain proficiency. I start with two pitches, preferably before students have seen them in notation, and use the same half note/half note/whole note/whole rest rhythm (see figure 8.2) for several weeks, even though I may add three or four additional notes. As mentioned earlier, I find that students struggle with melodies more than rhythms, so I keep the melodic rhythms simple and consistent.

The whole rest at the end of melodies is important because it gives students the extra time needed to audiate them. In other words, students

have time to process what they have heard into pitches or syllables and, later in the sequence, into pitches that they can play. As students gain experience with improvisation using this sequence, they develop skills to "play by ear."

It helps if students know solfège syllables, particularly in band, because the many letter names for transposing instruments are a little confusing (though certainly not impossible). For ease in improvisation activities, I teach the combination of letter and solfège names advocated by Grunow and Gordon (1989). For example, Bb-do, C-re, D-mi are used for concert pitched instruments; C-do, D-re, E-mi for Bb instruments; G-do, A-re, B-mi for Eb instruments, and so on. In mixed-group settings, we easily refer to pitch names simply as do, re, mi, omitting the pitch letter name at the beginning.

As previously discussed, Gordon advocates the use of "movable do" (where solfège syllables change with tonality) and directors should consider this technique first. Because of my program structure and the time allowed for beginning instruction, I have had more success with "immovable" or "stationary do," where the solfège syllables remain the same regardless of tonality.

BEYOND THE BEGINNING STAGE

Separating rhythm and melody for improvisation becomes much less crucial as students gain experience with melodies. When directors introduce new or complex rhythms, melodies should remain simple, and new pitches and complex melodies should have simple rhythms.

Though a few new pitches and rhythms provide the context for improvisation experiences at first, improvisation can expand to include entire major and minor scales as students progress. Soon after the beginning stages, you should help students understand the commonly accepted syntax of pitch intervals within melodies. For example, you can discuss the leading tone's tendency to move to the tonic, the static quality of the tonic, the tonic-dominant relationship, and so on (see figure 8.3).

Gordon (1997) uses the clarification of interval relationships as a rationale for using movable "do," because regardless of key, "ti" or "so" typically resolves to "do," "re" resolves to "do" or "mi," and so on. However, in the stationary "do" system, I illustrate these tonal tendencies in the key

of Bb, the initial key that my band students learn. Thus, the first scale degree is "do," the dominant is "so," and so on. Because "do" is concert Bb regardless of key, I ensure that students understand scale degrees and can refer to "mi" as the third, "so" as the fifth, and so on.

I later apply these interval relationships to other keys and refer to intervals by number, as traditionally done when discussing music theory. For example, I tell students that, in the key of Eb, "te" (concert Ab) is the fourth, and "do" (concert Bb) is the fifth. Regardless of whether you use stationary or movable "do" systems, point out common interval tendencies to help student improvisations develop from mere random pitch or rhythm selection into communicative, expressive improvisation.

Understanding harmonic structure is fundamental to generating meaningful improvisation. Soon after learning the first scales, introduce harmony using the sequence for melodies. Students can improvise and echo using root, third (major or minor), and fifth, or the ensemble can sustain first and fifth scale degrees (sometimes referred to as drones) or triads (first, third, and fifth scale degrees) while a soloist improvises scale patterns. Certain scale degrees sound better than others, and with your guidance students quickly discover what pitches they think fit best. After harmonic structure, introduce the concept of harmonic progression by having individual students improvise over chord roots of simple harmonic progressions played by the ensemble (see Azzara & Grunow, 2006; Azzara, Grunow, & Gordon, 1997).

After triads and harmonic progressions, introduce sevenths, and students are on the way to jazz improvisation. With respect to the traditional jazz style, I find that the rhythm sequence helps to teach students to swing eighth notes. Directors may also use the melody sequence with the blues scale and scale modes, beginning with the first two or three scale degrees and adding pitches as students demonstrate proficiency.

In designing this sequence, I accounted for the development of beginning improvisers as well as advanced students while also allowing for the limited time usually devoted to rehearsals. Consequently, I can improvise with my beginning groups using only about five minutes each rehearsal. Not only do I provide students with a more complete instrumental music education, but also my students feel that improvisation is one of the most enjoyable parts of their instrumental music experience.

Composition

Reimer (1989) feels that "while some degree of progress has been made in recent years toward effective methods of involving students in musical composition, this aspect of music education . . . remains a major piece of unfinished business for the profession" (p. 71). Part of the problem is that so many resources on how to teach composition, how students compose, and appropriate composition activities are geared only to the general or classroom setting. Further, preparing music for perfomance becomes the top priority. Directors can, however, design composition activities that still reinforce performance goals.

The "degree of progress" in student compositions to which Reimer refers is partly due to the advent of computer technology and software devoted to music notation and playback. Directors save valuable time designing composition activities using the computer. Once designed, you can save these activities for years to come. Using the computer for student composition is probably most appropriate for general music instruction or in instrumental music programs where students have sufficient time and ample access to computers and necessary software. Regardless of access to computer technology, composing by hand first has advantages similar to writing letters and words before learning to type.

Although a computer can render a performance simulation in classroom music settings, using live musicians is more instructive and satisfying. Elliott (1995) feels that "[m]usic is a performing art. The intended outcome or work in the performing arts is not a self-sufficient object (like painting, novel, or sculpture) but rather a performance" (p. 172). Instrumental music ensembles provide this opportunity to both create and perform.

Playback features available with notation software render sterile and inaccurate virtual performances. Students need to learn instrument ranges, abilities of live players, transpositions, and so on. Virtually every book on composing, arranging, and orchestration recommends performance of compositions by live musicians as a critical component in gaining necessary skills and experience as a composer. Even if they use software to notate compositions, students benefit most from hearing compositions played by their peers who can accurately evaluate composition strengths and areas for improvement.

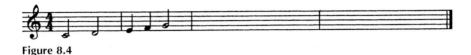

Figure 8.4

Motivation

Student motivation provides another reason for student composers and their peers to perform their compositions. These compositions have social significance as well as real-world relevance, and students have greater concern for composition if other ensemble members perform and evaluate it. In accounting for social learning styles, I sometimes let students work together on assignments, if I feel it motivates particular students.

I further motivate students (and get support from families) by encouraging students to perform their compositions for family members in preparation for the lesson in which they will perform their piece. I highly recommend that beginners perform for their parents weekly, and even have students indicate on their weekly practice records if they have done so. These performances have even more meaning if a student plays his or her own composition. For example, Giana proudly titled one of her compositions "Farming Circle" (a method of farming in which tasks are divided amongst a group) because of feedback her mother gave her.

The opportunity for expression also motivates some students. For example, in one lesson group Saquan titled his composition "Kirk Park" in reference to his football team, which served as the inspiration for the spirited and bombastic style of the piece. In the same lesson group, Malaysia titled her composition "Semaj" (figure 8.7) in honor of her younger sister. The settings students choose for pieces serve as sources of compositional ideas as well as relevant expressions of students' lives.

SOME HELPFUL TIPS

To avoid transposition and time issues, I give short composition assignments for younger musicians to play and evaluate during homogeneous les-

Figure 8.5

son groups. In programs where there is no small-group instruction, directors can transpose student compositions so the whole group can play, or small groups of students with homogeneous instruments can perform while others evaluate.

In order to ensure success, tasks begin with a high degree of structure and gradually require more student knowledge of notation and music theory, and compositional freedom increases with subsequent assignments. Because time is always critical, I expect carefully and legibly written compositions so that we may use them as études as well as composition activities during lessons.

Figure 8.4 shows a beginning activity where the student finishes the melody using C, D, E, F, and G pitches, and quarter note and half note durations. Students might complete the composition and prepare for its performance together. Figure 8.5 is an example of student work.

Of course, improvisation and composition assignments can be modified depending on the needs of the students. For example, a student percussionist with severe cognitive challenges may only improvise rhythms. The director should choose other students in the section to improvise melodies on keyboard percussion instruments while the exceptional learner echoes and improvises on drums. Figure 8.6 is a beginning composition activity (see figure 8.4) modified for an exceptional learner who has difficulty reading notation. The duration of notes may be shown graphically by drawing dashes under the notes (as shown). You can also color code notes to help students identify them.

For "advanced beginners," use a less structured composition assignment. Provide a blank staff and have students compose a short piece for their particular instrument, using the rhythms and pitches they have learned. I encourage students to keep it simple and to write neatly so that they and the other members of their section can easily read and perform the song. Figure 8.7 is an example of student work.

Directors should design composition assignments that focus on specific skills to reinforce performance and reading as students and peers play

Figure 8.6

Figure 8.7

through pieces. For example, students may be given an assignment to compose a four-bar étude that uses slurs.

It often takes one or two weeks of revising before performing a composition in the lesson group. Directors might need to reassign a composition for individual students if it is illegible, has wide intervallic leaps, or has notation mistakes so that they don't waste precious time when "reading it down." Students will soon realize that revision is a necessary component to composing. If individual students require significant revisions, directors should try to conference with those students privately to avoid peer scrutiny. As long as sensitive directors create an encouraging environment and respect and value students' efforts, students do not feel humiliated when they must revise compositions.

To save time, compositions by every student need not be performed every week, though all should receive feedback. This feedback should both acknowledge accomplishment (praise) as well as offer constructive critique. Evaluate compositions by using rubrics or other effective evaluation criteria clearly communicated to students when first giving the assignment.

Though I evaluate every composition assignment, to save time, I note which student pieces have been played in the lesson to ensure that all students have pieces played by peers (usually twice a quarter). The compositions that students play depend on the progress of individual students in the lesson group. For example, Sonimar's piece titled "The Goal" (figure 8.5) served as an exemplar for other students in her lesson group when they needed another week to revise their compositions. The following week, two revised compositions were performed. Sometimes I choose certain compositions because of their effectiveness in reinforcing other learning goals. Malaysia's composition was similar to a bass line in a piece that students were learning at the time, so they played "Semaj" (figure 8.7) to reinforce it.

There is usually enough time for students to perform two short, legible, and otherwise error-free compositions during the typical group lesson. I do not plan composition activities at certain times of the year, particularly around festival season and toward the beginning and end of the

school year. Directors can plan composition assignments based on projected performance demands prior to the start of the school year, and adjust plans as needed.

One advantage of composition is that it affords students more time to prepare complex pieces rather than spontaneous improvised creations. After beginners compose simple melodies, you can adapt improvisational ideas and use them as composition assignments. For example, instead of having the ensemble play bass lines while individuals improvise, students can compose both bass lines and appropriate melodies and perform them in lesson groups. As student learn more harmonies, dynamics, and other musical elements, composition assignments can incorporate them.

The following resources have helpful ideas on improvising and composing:

Azzara, C. D., & Grunow, R. F. (2006). *Developing musicianship through improvisation.*

Froseth, J. O., & Froseth, D. (1995). *Do it! Improvise I* and *Do it: Improvise II: In all the modes.*

Hamann, D. L., & Gillespie, R. (2004). Practical approaches to teaching improvisation in the school orchestra. In *Strategies for teaching strings: Building a successful string and orchestra program.*

Lieberman, J. L. (2002). *The creative band and orchestra.*

Improvisational and compositional activities reward your students when they realize their creative and expressive potential. Learning how to improvise and compose reinforces what players are learning, preparing them even better for performance.

Afterword

Some directors look for easy, quick fixes, but like most solutions to challenging issues in music education, many of the solutions I offer require diligence and patience. Directors may say they simply do not have the time to improve existing conditions in which they teach. These directors often mean that they are not willing to devote the time outside school hours to put new ideas into practice. Though directors who devote too much time to their jobs burn out, they need to diligently devote time outside class to plan, administrate, provide extra student instruction, foster parent and community relations, and tend to their own professional development, practice, and reflection. Directors also need patience because many improvements are gradual.

To meet challenges, I draw from sound teaching and learning principles that apply to all instrumental music settings. Nonetheless, I cannot help but recommend some context-specific practices from my own teaching experience that align with my personal teaching philosophy. Even if individual circumstances preclude adoption of some of my strategies, I hope that I demonstrate that either adapting established methods and techniques or creating new ones can provide solutions in any teaching environment. I encourage you to do the same.

I also hope that this book fosters or replenishes the tenacity in directors who work in less-than-ideal circumstances or deal with difficult challenges, as most directors do. I have certainly worked in unfavorable conditions and faced seemingly insurmountable challenges. I made those

conditions better and solved tough problems through committed, sustained effort—because my students were worth it. Maintaining excellent, inclusive instrumental music programs in all school environments that serve all children regardless of privilege requires hard work. Sharing the personal and musical rewards with students makes it all worthwhile.

Fight on! Your students need you.

References

Armstrong, T. A. (1999). *ADD/ADHD alternatives in the classroom*. Alexandria, VA: Association for Supervision and Curriculum Development.

Azzara, C. D. (1993). Audiation-based improvisation techniques and elementary instrumental students' music achievement. *Journal of Research in Music Education, 41* (4), 328–42.

Azzara, C. D., & Grunow, R. F. (2006). *Developing musicianship through improvisation*. Chicago: GIA Publications.

Azzara, C. D., Grunow, R. F., & Gordon, E. E. (1997). *Creativity in improvisation* (Book 1). Chicago: GIA Publications.

Battisti, F., & Garofalo, R. (1990). *Guide to score study for the wind band conductor*. Ft. Lauderdale, FL: Meredith Music Publications.

Blocher, L. R., & Miles, R. B. (1999). *Scheduling and teaching music*. Springfield, IL: Focus on Excellence.

Boardman, E. (Ed.). (2002). *Dimensions of musical learning and teaching: A different kind of classroom*. Reston, VA: MENC: The National Association for Music Education.

Boyle, J. D., DeCarbo, N. J., & Jordan, D. M. (1995). Middle or junior high school band directors' views regarding reasons for student dropouts in instrumental music. Retrieved May 22, 2006, from http://music.arts.usf.edu/rpme/boyledec.htm.

Boyle, J. D., & Radocy, R. E. (1987). *Measurement and evaluation of musical experiences*. New York: Schirmer Books.

Brooks, J. G., & Brooks, M. G. (1993). *In search of understanding: The case for constructivist classrooms*. Alexandria, VA: The Association for Supervision and Curriculum Development.

Brophy, T. S. (2000). *Assessing the developing child musician: A guide for general music teachers*. Chicago: GIA Publications.

Campbell, P. S., & Scott-Kassner, C. (1995). *Music in childhood: From preschool through the elementary grades*. New York: Schirmer.

Casey, J. L. (1993). *Teaching techniques and insights for instrumental music educators* (Rev. ed.). Chicago: GIA Publications.

Celli-Sarasin, L. (1999). *Learning style perspectives: Impact in the classroom*. Madison, WI: Atwood Publishing.

Clark, C. A., & Chadwick, D. M. (1980). *Clinically adapted instruments for the multiply handicapped*. Saint Louis, MO: MMB Music.

Colarusso, R., & O'Rourke, C. (2004). *Special education for all teachers* (3rd ed.). Dubuque, IA: Kendall/Hunt Publishing.

Conn-Selmer (n.d.). Selmer Music Guidance Survey (available from Conn-Selmer, Inc., A Steinway Musical Instruments Company, P. O. Box 310, Elkhart, IN 46515. Telephone: 800-348-7426 or 574-522-1675. Website: www.selmer.com/content/educators.php).

Cutietta, R. A. (Ed.). (1999). *Strategies for teaching specialized ensembles*. Reston, VA: MENC: The National Association for Music Education.

Dalby, M. F. (1993). *Band rehearsal techniques: A handbook for new directors*. Northfield, IL: The Instrumentalist Publishing Company.

Elliott, D. J. (1995). *Music matters: A new philosophy of music education*. New York: Oxford University Press.

Feldstein, S. (1994). First performance: A demonstration concert: Beginning orchestra (distributed by The Music Achievement Council, 5790 Armada Drive, Carlsbad, CA 92008. Telephone: 800-767-6266 or 760-438-8001. Website: www.music achievementcouncil.org).

———. (2000). First performance: A demonstration concert: Beginning instrumental music [band] (distributed by The Music Achievement Council, 5790 Armada Drive, Carlsbad, CA 92008. Telephone: 800-767-6266 or 760-438-8001. Website: www.musicachievementcouncil.org).

Fleming, N. D. (1995). I'm different, not dumb. Modes of presentation (VARK) in the tertiary classroom. In A. Zelmer (Ed.), *Research and development in higher education, proceedings of the 1995 annual conference of the Higher Education and Research Development Society of Australia (HERDSA): Vol. 18* (pp. 308–13).

Froseth, J. O., & Froseth, D. (1995a). *Do it! Improvise I*. Chicago: GIA Publications.

———. (1995b). *Do it! Improvise II: In all the modes*. Chicago: GIA Publications.

Gardner, H. (1999). *Intelligence reframed: Multiple intelligences for the 21st century*. New York: Basic Books.

Gordon, E. E. (1984). *Instrument timbre preference test*. Chicago: GIA Publications.

———. (1997). *Learning sequences in music: Skill, content, and patterns: A music learning theory*. Chicago: GIA Publications.

Grunow, R. F., & Gordon, E. E. (1989). *Jump right in: The instrumental series, teacher's guide, book one*. Chicago: GIA Publications.

Hale, J. E. (2001). *Learning while black: Creating educational excellence for African American children*. Baltimore: Johns Hopkins University Press.

Hamann, D. L., & Gillespie, R. (2004). *Strategies for teaching strings: Building a successful string and orchestra program*. Oxford: Oxford University Press.

IDEA. Pub. L. No. 94-142 (1975).

Kaplan, P. R., & Stauffer, S. L. (1994). *Cooperative learning in music*. Reston, VA: MENC: The National Association for Music Education.

Kohut, D. L. (1996). *Instrument music pedagogy: Teaching techniques for school band and orchestra directors*. Champaign, IL: Stipes Publishing.

Kunjufu, J. (1986). *Motivating and preparing Black youth to work*. Chicago: African American Images.

———. (1990). *Countering the conspiracy to destroy Black boys* (vol. III). Chicago: African American Images.

———. (2002). *Black Students. Middle class teachers*. Chicago: African American Images.

Kuykendall, C. (1992). *From rage to hope: Strategies for reclaiming Black and Hispanic students*. Bloomington, IN: National Education Service.

Ladson-Billings, G. (1994). *The dreamkeepers: Successful teachers of African American children*. San Francisco: Jossey-Bass Publishers.

Lamb, N. (1990). Guide to teaching strings (5th ed.). Dubuque, IA: Wm. C. Brown.

Landis, B., & Carder, P. (1990). The Dalcroze approach. In P. Carder (Ed.), *The eclectic curriculum in American music education* (pp. 7–29). Reston, VA: MENC: The National Association for Music Education.

Lieberman, J. L. (2002). *The creative band and orchestra*. New York: Huiksi Music.

Lisk, E. S. (2001). *The creative director: Beginning and intermediate levels*. Galesville, MD: Meredith Music Publications.

Madsen, C. H., Jr., & Madsen, C. K. (1983). *Teaching/discipline*. Raleigh, NC: Contemporary Publishing Company.

McPherson, G. E., and Gabrielsson, A. (2002). From sound to sign. In R. Parncutt & G. E. McPherson (Eds.), *The science and psychology of music performance: Creative strategies for teaching and learning* (pp. 99–115). Oxford: Oxford University Press.

MENC: The National Association for Music Education (1989). *Music booster manual*. Reston, VA: MENC: The National Association for Music Education.

——— (1994). *The school music program: A new vision*. Reston, VA: MENC: The National Association for Music Education.

Middleton, J., Haines, H., & Garner, G. (1998). *The band director's companion*. San Antonio, TX: Southern Music Company.

Moore, M. C., with Batey, A. L., & Royse, D. M. (2002). *Classroom management in general, choral, and instrumental music programs*. Reston, VA: MENC: The National Association for Music Education.

Moss Rehabilitation Hospital Settlement Music School Therapeutic Music Program (1982). *Guide to the selection of musical instruments with respect to physical ability and disability*. Saint Louis, MO: MMB Music, Inc.

Music Achievement Council (n.d.). Musical Instrument Game (Music Achievement Council, 5790 Armada Drive, Carlbad, CA 92008. Telephone: 800-767-6266 or 760-438-8001. Website: www.musicachievementcouncil.org).

Ogbu, J. U. (1992). Understanding cultural diversity and learning. *Educational Researcher, 21* (8), 5–14.

O'Neill, S. A., & McPherson, G. E. (2002). Motivation. In R. Parncutt & G. E. McPherson (Eds.), *The science and psychology of music performance: Creative strategies for teaching and learning* (pp. 31–46). Oxford: Oxford University Press.

Payne, R. K. (2001). *A framework for understanding poverty* (new revised edition). Highlands, TX: aha! Process.

Reimer, B. (1989). *A philosophy of music education* (2nd ed.). Englewood Cliffs, NJ: Prentice-Hall.

Schleuter, S. L. (1997). *A sound approach to teaching instrumentalists* (2nd ed.). New York: Schirmer Books.

Steinberg, L. (1996). *Adolescence* (4th ed.). New York: McGraw-Hill.

Taylor, J. A., Barry, N. H., & Walls, K. S. (1997). *Music and students at risk: Creative solutions for a national dilemma.* Reston, VA: MENC: The National Association for Music Education.

Westphal, F. W. (1990). *Guide to teaching woodwinds* (5th ed.). Dubuque, IA: Wm. C. Brown Publishers.

Wilson, B. L., & Corbett, H. D. (2001). *Listening to urban kids: School reform and the teachers they want.* Albany: State University of New York Press.

Zdzinski, S. F. (2003). Instrumental music for special learners. In MENC: The National Association for Music Education, *Readings on diversity, inclusion, and music for all* (pp. 120–23). Reston, VA: MENC: The National Association for Music Education.

About the Author

Kevin Mixon began his career in rural and suburban schools in Illinois and currently teaches instrumental music at Blodgett K–8 School, an urban school in Syracuse, New York. His instrumental groups consistently receive the highest ratings at regional festivals and are widely recognized for achievement. Mixon earned degrees summa cum laude at Onondaga Community College, Syracuse University, and University of Illinois (Urbana-Champaign), and he presents sessions internationally at conventions including the International Society for Music Education World Conference, the Midwest Clinic, and MENC regional and national conferences. Several of his articles have appeared in *Music Educators Journal, Teaching Music, The Instrumentalist, The National Band Association Journal*, and he is a contributing author to *Teaching Music in the Urban Classroom: A Guide to Survival, Success, and Reform* (Rowman & Littlefield Education). His highly acclaimed compositions for band and orchestra are available through Alfred Publishing.

Other Hay House Classics Titles by Dr. Joseph Murphy

Believe in Yourself
Miracles of Your Mind
Techniques in Prayer Therapy

Other Books in the MAXIMIZE YOUR POTENTIAL Series:

Book 2: *Maximize Your Potential Through the
Power of Your Subconscious Mind to Create Wealth and Success*

———

Book 3: *Maximize Your Potential Through the Power of Your
Subconscious Mind to Develop Self-Confidence and Self-Esteem*

———

Book 4: *Maximize Your Potential Through the
Power of Your Subconscious Mind for Health and Vitality*

———

Book 5: *Maximize Your Potential Through the
Power of Your Subconscious Mind for a More Spiritual Life*

———

Book 6: *Maximize Your Potential Through the
Power of Your Subconscious Mind for an Enriched Life*

• • •

All of the above are available at your local bookstore,
or may be ordered by visiting:

Hay House USA: **www.hayhouse.com**®
Hay House Australia: **www.hayhouse.com.au**
Hay House UK: **www.hayhouse.co.uk**
Hay House South Africa: **orders@psdprom.co.za**
Hay House India: **www.hayhouseindia.co.in**

Book 1

MAXIMIZE YOUR POTENTIAL
THROUGH THE POWER OF
YOUR SUBCONSCIOUS MIND
TO OVERCOME

Fear and Worry

One of a Series of Six Books
by
Dr. Joseph Murphy

Edited and Updated for the 21st Century
by Arthur R. Pell, Ph.D.

HAY HOUSE, INC.
Carlsbad, California
London • Sydney • Johannesburg
Vancouver • Hong Kong • New Delhi

DR. JOSPEH MURPHY

Maximize Your Potential Through the Power of Your Subconscious Mind to Overcome Fear and Worry is one of a series of six books by Joseph Murphy, D.D., Ph.D., edited and updated for the 21st century by Arthur R. Pell, Ph.D. Copyright © 2005 The James A. Boyer Revocable Trust. Exclusive worldwide rights in all languages available only through JMW Group Inc.

Published and distributed in the United States by: Hay House, Inc.: www.hayhouse. com • **Published and distributed in Australia by:** Hay House Australia Pty. Ltd.: www.hayhouse.com.au • **Published and distributed in the United Kingdom by:** Hay House UK, Ltd.: www.hayhouse.co.uk • **Published and distributed in the Republic of South Africa by:** Hay House SA (Pty), Ltd.: orders@psdprom.co.za • **Distributed in Canada by:** Raincoast: www.raincoast.com • **Published in India by:** Hay House Publishers India: www.hayhouseindia.co.in

Design: Nick C. Welch

Library of Congress Cataloging-in-Publication Data

Murphy, Joseph, 1898-1981
  Maximize your potential through the power of your subconscious mind to overcome fear and worry / by Joseph Murphy ; edited and updated for the 21st century by Arthur R. Pell.
    p. cm. -- (Maximize your potential series ; bk. 1)
  ISBN-13: 978-1-4019-1214-7 (tradepaper) 1. New Thought. I. Pell, Arthur R. II. Title. III. Series: Murphy, Joseph, 1898- Maximize your potential series ; bk. 1.
  BF639.M832 2006
  154.2--dc22

2006016222

ISBN: 978-1-4019-1214-7

10   09   08   07   4   3   2   1
1st Hay House printing, June 2007

Printed in [the United States of America] or [Canada]

CONTENTS

Introduction to the Series

*W*ake up and live! No one is destined to be unhappy or consumed with fear and worry, live in poverty, suffer ill health, and feel rejected and inferior. God created all humans in His image and has given us the power to overcome adversity and attain happiness, harmony, health, and prosperity.

You have within you the power to enrich your life! How to do this is no secret. It has been preached, written about, and practiced for millennia. You will find it in the works of the ancient philosophers, and all of the great religions have preached it. It is in the Hebrew scriptures, the Christian Gospels, Greek philosophy, the Muslim Koran, the Buddhist sutras, the Hindu Bhagavad Gita, and the writings of Confucius and Lao-tzu. You will find it in the works of modern psychologists and theologians.

This is the basis of the philosophy of Dr. Joseph Murphy, one of the great inspirational writers and lecturers of the 20th century. He was not just a clergyman, but also a major figure in the modern interpretation of scriptures and other religious writings. As minister-director of the Church of Divine Science in Los Angeles, his lectures and sermons were attended by 1,300 to 1,500 people every Sunday, and millions tuned in to his daily radio program. He wrote more than 30 books, and his most well-known one, *The Power of Your Subconscious Mind,* was first published in 1963 and became an immediate bestseller. It was acclaimed as one of the greatest self-help guides ever written. Millions of copies have, and continue to be, sold all over the world.

Following the success of this book, Dr. Murphy lectured to audiences of thousands in several countries. In his lectures he pointed out how real people have radically improved their lives by applying specific aspects of his concepts, and he provided practical guidelines on how all people can enrich themselves.

Dr. Murphy was a proponent of the New Thought movement, which was developed in the late 19th and early 20th century by many philosophers and deep thinkers who studied it and preached, wrote, and practiced a new way of looking at life. By combining metaphysical, spiritual, and pragmatic approaches to the way we think and live, they uncovered the secret for attaining what we truly desire.

This philosophy wasn't a religion in the traditional sense, but it was based on an unconditional belief in a higher being, an eternal presence: God. It was called by various names, such as "New Thought" and "New Civilization."

The proponents of New Thought or New Civilization preached a fresh idea of life that makes use of methods that lead to perfected results. They based their thinking on the concept that the human soul is connected with the atomic mind of universal substance, which links our lives with the universal law of supply, and we have the power to use it to enrich our lives. To achieve our goals, we must work, and through this working, we may suffer the thorns and heartaches of humankind. We can do all these things only as we have found the law and worked out an understanding of the principles that God seemed to have written in riddles in the past.

The New Thought concept can be summed up in these words:

You can become what you want to be.

All that we achieve and all that we fail to achieve is the direct result of our own thoughts. In a just and ordered universe, where loss of balance would mean total destruction, individual responsibility must be absolute. Our weaknesses, strengths, purity, and impurity are ours alone. They are brought about by ourselves and not by another. They can only be altered by ourselves, and

never by anyone else. All of our happiness and suffering evolve from within. As we think, so we are; as we continue to think, so we remain. The only way we can rise, conquer, and achieve is by lifting up our thoughts. The only reason we may remain weak, abject, and miserable is to *refuse* to elevate our minds.

All achievements—whether in the business, intellectual, or spiritual world—are the result of definitely directed thought; and are governed by the same law and are reached by the same method. The only difference lies in the object of attainment. Those who would accomplish little must sacrifice little; those who would achieve much must sacrifice much; those who would attain a great deal must sacrifice a great deal.

New Thought means a new life: a way of living that is healthier, happier, and more fulfilling in every possible manner and expression.

Actually, there is nothing new in this, for it is as old and time-honored as humankind. It is novel to us when we discover the truths of life that set us free from lack, limitation, and unhappiness. At that moment, New Thought becomes a recurring, expanding awareness of the creative power within; of mind-principle; and of our Divine potential to be, to do, and to express more of our individual and natural abilities, aptitudes, and talents. The central mind-principle is that new thoughts, ideas, attitudes, and beliefs create new conditions. According to our beliefs, is it done unto us—good, bad, or indifferent. The essence of New Thought consists of the continual renewing of our mind, that we may manifest what is good, acceptable, and the perfect will of God.

To prove is to know surely, and to have trustworthy knowledge and experience. The truths of New Thought are practical, easy to demonstrate, and within the realm of accomplishment of everyone—if and when he or she chooses. All that is required is an open mind and a willing heart: open to hearing old truths presented in a different way; willing to change and to relinquish outmoded beliefs and to accept unfamiliar ideas and concepts—to have a higher vision of life, or a healing presence within.

The rebirth of our mind constitutes the entire purpose and practice of New Thought. Without this ongoing daily renewal, there can be no change. New Thought establishes and realizes an entirely new attitude and consciousness that inspires and enables us to enter into "life more abundant."

We have within us limitless powers to choose and to decide, and complete freedom to be conformed or to be transformed. To be conformed is to live according to that which already has taken or been given form—that which is visible and apparent to our own senses, including the ideas, opinions, beliefs, and edicts of others. It is to live and to be governed "by the fleeting and unstable fashions and conditions of the moment." The very word *conformed* suggests that our present environment has shape, and that we do not and should not deny its existence. All around us there are injustices, improprieties, and inequalities. We may and do find ourselves involved in them at times, and we should face them with courage and honesty and do our best to resolve them with the integrity and intelligence that we now possess.

Generally, the world accepts and believes that our environment is the cause of our present condition and circumstance—and the usual reaction and tendency is to drift into a state of acquiescence and quiet acceptance of the present. This is conformity of the worst kind: the consciousness of defeatism. It's worse because it is self-imposed. It is giving all power and attention to the outer, manifested state. New Thought insists on the renewal of the mind, and the recognition and acknowledgment of our responsibility in life—our ability to respond to the truths we now know.

One of the most active and effective of New Thought teachers, Charles Fillmore, co-founder of the Unity School of Christianity, was a firm believer in personal responsibility. In his book *The Revealing Word,* he wrote (simply, and without equivocation): "Our consciousness is our real environment. The outer environment is always in correspondence to our consciousness."

Anyone who is open and willing to accept the responsibility has begun the transformation—the renewal of the mind that

enables us to participate in our transformed life. "To transform" is "to change from one condition or state to another" (which is qualitatively better and more fulfilling) "from lack to abundance; loneliness to companionship; limitation to fullness; illness to vibrant health"—through this indwelling wisdom and power, the healing presence will remain within.

True and granted, there are some things we cannot change: the movement of the planets, the turn of the seasons, the pull of the oceans and tides, and the apparent rising and setting of the sun. Neither can we alter the minds and thoughts of another person—but we can change ourselves.

Who can prevent or inhibit the movement of your imagination and will? Only you can give that power to another. You can be transformed by the renewing of your mind. This is the key to a new life. You're a recording machine; and all the beliefs, impressions, opinions, and ideas accepted by you are impressed in your deeper subconscious. But you can change. You can begin now to fill your mind with noble and Godlike patterns of thoughts, and align yourself with the Infinite Spirit within. Claim beauty, love, peace, wisdom, creative ideas . . . and the Infinite will respond accordingly, transforming your mind, body, and circumstances. Your thought is the medium between your spirit, your body, and the material world.

The transformation begins as we meditate, think upon, and absorb into our mentality those qualities that we desire to experience and express. Theoretical knowledge is good and necessary. We should understand what we're doing and why. However, actual change depends entirely on stirring up the gifts within—the invisible and intangible spiritual power given fully to every one of us.

This, and only this, ultimately breaks up and dissolves the very real claims and bondage of past unhappiness and distress. In addition, it heals the wounds of heartbreak and emotional pain. We all desire and require peace of mind—the greatest gift—in order to bring it into our environment. Mentally and emotionally, contemplate Divine peace, filling our mind and heart, our entire being. First say, "Peace be unto this house."

To contemplate lack of peace, disharmony, unhappiness, and discord, and expect peace to manifest is to expect the apple seed to grow into a pear. It makes little or no sense, and it violates all sense of reason, but it is the way of the world. We must seek ways to change our minds—to repent where necessary. As a result, renewal will occur, following naturally. It is desirable and necessary to transform our lives by ceasing to conform to the world's way of choosing or deciding, according to the events already formed and manifested.

The word *metaphysical* has become a synonym for the modern, organized movement. It was first used by Aristotle. Considered by some to have been his greatest writing, his 13th volume was simply entitled *Metaphysics*. The dictionary definition is: "Beyond natural science; the science of pure being." *Meta-* means "above, or beyond." *Metaphysics,* then, means "above or beyond physics"—"above or beyond the physical," the world of form. "Meta" is above that; it is the spirit of the mind, which is behind all things.

Biblically, the spirit of God is good. "They that worship God worship the spirit, or truth." When we have the spirit of goodness, truth, beauty, love, and goodwill, it is actually the Divine in us, moving through us. God, truth, life, energy, spirit—can it not be defined? How can it be? "To define it is to limit it."

This is expressed in a beautiful old meditation:

> *Ever the same in my innermost being: eternal, absolutely one,*
> *whole, complete, perfect; I AM indivisible, timeless, shapeless,*
> *ageless—without face, form, or figure. I AM the silent brooding*
> *presence, fixed in the hearts of all men (and women).*

We must believe and accept that whatever we imagine and feel to be true will come to pass; whatever we desire for another, we are wishing for ourselves.

Emerson wrote: "We become what we think about all day long." In other words and most simply stated: Spirit, thought, mind, and meta is the expression of creative presence and power—and

as in nature (physical laws), any force can be used two ways. For example, water can clean us or drown us; electricity can make life easier or more deadly. The Bible says: "I form the light, and create darkness; I make peace, and evil; I, the Lord, do all these things—I wound, I heal; I bless, I curse."

No angry deity is punishing us; we punish ourselves by misuse of the mind. We also are blessed (benefited) when we comprehend this fundamental principle and presence, and learn and accept a new thought or an entire concept.

Metaphysics, then, is the study of causation—concerned not with the effect that is now manifest, but rather with that which is causing the result. This discipline approaches spiritual ideas as scientists approach the world of form, just as they investigate the mind or causation from which the visible is formed, or derived. If a mind is changed, or a cause is changed, the effect is changed.

The strength and beauty of metaphysics, in my opinion, is that it is not confined to any one particular creed, but is universal. One can be a Jew, Christian, Muslim, or Buddhist and yet still be a metaphysician.

There are poets, scientists, and philosophers who claim no creed; their belief is metaphysical.

Jesus was a master metaphysician—he understood the mind and employed it to lift up, inspire, and heal others.

When Mahatma Gandhi (the "great-souled" one) was asked what his religion was, he replied, "I am a Christian . . . a Jew . . . a Buddhist . . . a Hindu . . . I AM all these things."

The term *New Thought* has become a popular, generalized term. Composed of a very large number of churches, centers, prayer groups, and institutions, this has become a metaphysical movement that reveals the oneness or unity of humankind with Infinite life . . . with the innate dignity, worth, or value of every individual. In fact, and in truth, the emphasis is on the individual rather than on an organizational body or function. But as mentioned, there is nothing new in New Thought. Metaphysics is actually the oldest of all religious approaches. It reveals our purpose to express God,

and the greater measures of the Good: "I AM come to bring you life and that more abundantly." It reveals our identity: "children of the infinite" who are loved and have spiritual value as necessary parts of the Creative Holy (whole) One.

Metaphysics enables and assists us to return to our Divine Source, and ends the sense of separation and feeling of alienation; of wandering in a barren, unfriendly desert wasteland. This approach has always been, is now, and ever will be available to all—patiently waiting our discovery and revelation.

Many thousands have been introduced to New Thought through one or another of its advocates. Its formation was gradual, and usually considered to have begun with Phineas P. Quimby. In a fascinating article in *New Thought* magazine, Quimby wrote about his work in 1837. After experimenting with mesmerism for a period of years, he concluded that it was not the hypnotism itself, but the conditioning of the subconscious, which led to the resulting changes. Although Quimby had very little formal education, he had a brilliant, investigative mind and was an original thinker. In addition, he was a prolific writer and diarist. Records have been published detailing the development of his findings. He eventually became a wonderful student of the Bible and duplicated two-thirds of the Old and New Testament healings. He found that there was much confusion about the true meaning of many biblical passages, which caused misunderstanding and misinterpretation of Jesus Christ.

All through the 20th century, so many inspired teachers, authors, ministers, and lecturers contributed to the New Thought movement. Dr. Charles E. Braden, of the University of Chicago, called these people "spirits in rebellion" because these men and women were truly breaking free from existing dogmatism, rituals, and creeds. (Rebelling at inconsistencies in the old traditions led some individuals to fear religion.) Dr. Braden became discontent with the status quo and refused to conform any longer.

New Thought is an individual practice of the truths of life—a gradual, continuing process. We can learn a bit today, and even more tomorrow. Never will we experience a point where there

is nothing more to be discovered. It is infinite, boundless, and eternal. We have all the time we need—eternity. Many of us are impatient with ourselves, and with what we consider our failures. Looking back, though, we discover that these have been periods of learning, and we needn't make these mistakes again. Progress may seem ever so slow: "In patience, possess ye your soul."

In Dr. Murphy's book *Pray Your Way Through It: The Revelation,* he commented that heaven was noted as being "awareness," and Earth, "manifestation. Your new heaven is your revised point of view—your new dimension of consciousness. When we see—that is, see *spiritually,* we then realize that in the absolute, all is blessed, harmony, boundless love, wisdom, complete peace, and perfection. Identify with these truths, calm the sea of fear; have confidence and faith, and become stronger and surer.

In the books in this series, Dr. Murphy has synthesized the profundities of this power and has put them into an easily understood and pragmatic form so that you can apply them immediately to your life. As Dr. Murphy was a Protestant minister, many of his examples and citations come from the Bible. The concepts these passages illustrate should not be viewed as sectarian. Indeed, their messages are universal and are preached in most religions and philosophies. He often reiterated that the essence of knowledge is in the law of life and belief. It is not Catholic, Protestant, Muslim, or Hindu; it is pure and simple faith: "Do unto others accordingly."

Dr. Murphy's wife, Dr. Jean Murphy, continued his ministry after his death in 1981. In a lecture she gave in 1986, quoting her late husband, she reiterated his philosophy:

> I want to teach men and women of their Divine Origin, and the powers pregnant within them. I want to inform them that this power is within and that they are their own saviors and capable of achieving their own salvation. This is the message of the Bible, and nine-tenths of our confusion today is due to wrongful, literal interpretation of the life-transforming truths offered in it.

I want to reach the majority, the man on the street, the woman overburdened with duty and suppression of her talents and abilities. I want to help others at every stage or level of consciousness to learn of the wonders within.

She said of her husband: "He was a practical mystic, possessed by the intellect of a scholar, the mind of a successful executive, the heart of the poet." His message summed up was: "You are the king, the ruler of your world, for you are one with God."

Joseph Murphy was a firm believer that it was God's plan for people to be healthy, prosperous, and happy. He countered those theologians and others who claimed that desire is evil and urged people to crush it. He said that extinction of our longings means apathy—no feeling, no action. He preached that desire is a gift of God. It is healthy and wholesome to want to become more and better than we were yesterday . . . in the areas of health, abundance, companionship, security, and more. How could these be wrong?

Desire is behind all progress. Without it, nothing would be accomplished. It is the creative power and must be channeled constructively. For example, if one is poor, yearning for wealth wells up from within; if one is ill, there is a wish for health; if lonely, there is a desire for companionship and love.

We must believe that we can improve our lives. A belief—whether it is true, false, or merely indifferent—sustained over a period of time becomes assimilated and is incorporated into our mentality. Unless countermanded by faith of an opposite nature, sooner or later it takes form and is expressed or experienced as fact, form, condition, circumstance, and the events of life. We have the power within us to change negative beliefs to positive ones, and thereby change ourselves for the better.

You give the command and your subconscious mind will faithfully obey it. You will get a reaction or response according to the nature of the thought you hold in your conscious mind. Psychologists and psychiatrists point out that when thoughts are conveyed to your subconscious mind, impressions are made in your brain cells. As soon as this part of you accepts any idea, it proceeds

to put it into effect immediately. It works by association of ideas and uses every bit of knowledge that you have gathered in your lifetime to bring about its purpose. It draws on the infinite power, energy, and wisdom within you, lining up all the laws of nature to get its way. Sometimes it seems to bring about an immediate solution to your difficulties, but at other times it may take days, weeks, or longer.

The habitual thinking of your conscious mind establishes deep grooves in your subconscious mind. This is very favorable for you if your recurring thoughts are harmonious, peaceful, and constructive. On the other hand, if you have indulged in fear, worry, and other destructive concepts, the remedy is to recognize the omnipotence of your subconscious and decree freedom, happiness, perfect health, and prosperity. Your subconscious mind, being creative and one with your Divine Source, will proceed to create the freedom and happiness that you have earnestly declared.

Now for the first time, Dr. Murphy's lectures have been combined, edited, and updated in six new books that bring his teachings into the 21st century. To enhance and augment this original text, we have incorporated material from some of Jean Murphy's lectures and have added examples of people whose success reflects Dr. Murphy's philosophy.

The other works in this series are listed on the second page of this book, but just reading them will not improve your state of being. To truly maximize your potential, you must study these principles, take them to heart, integrate them into your mentality, and apply them as an integral part of your approach to every aspect of your life.

— **Arthur R. Pell, Ph.D.,** editor

•• ••

Preface

*A*ll of us experience times when fear and worry dominate our lives due to global factors such as war, famine, political unrest, or natural disasters; or personal concerns, such as when we or people close to us are besieged with illness, unemployment, overwhelming debt, marital discord, or concern about our children.

These traumas often overwhelm us and remove all joy and happiness from our lives. We cannot always prevent disasters from happening or find immediate solutions to others, but all of us have within us the ability to deal with them so that they won't devastate our lives.

In this book, Dr. Murphy teaches how you can use prayer and meditation to develop the power to solve the problems you face and defeat the depression that usually accompanies them. Pragmatic solutions must still be found, but applying Dr. Murphy's suggestions can often accelerate the process and certainly will enable you to deal with them more effectively.

An illness will still require medical therapy; if you lose a job, you must find another one; if you have legal problems, an attorney can be of aid. Dr. Murphy does not advocate depending on God to cure your illness, find you a job, or solve your legal or other problems, but by turning to God, you can keep up your morale. As he shows over and over again in the examples and anecdotes in his books, God works in mysterious ways and often sends believers solutions to their problems.

In all of Dr. Murphy's writings, he recommends prayers and meditations that have proven to be effective. In this book, he turns to the psalms as a wonderful source of inspiration and help in overcoming worry and fear.

Psalms have been an important part of Judeo-Christian worship for thousands of years. The inner, esoteric meaning of the psalms reveals the Infinite Healing Power within. The Book of Psalms is sometimes called "the Little Bible." It is a treasure-house of spiritual and practical riches—a great source of inspiration and comfort to all men and women in every walk of life.

The Book of Psalms addresses our every possible mood, from the depths of despair to the heights of exultation. In no other single book of the world's holy books will we find so many varieties of experience—spiritual and secular.

There are psalms of gladness, peace of mind, happiness, and joy; they speak to the wonder and glory of creation and humankind's place in the universe. But there are also cries of the broken heart: in times of sickness, injury, grief, humiliation, and reproach; treachery or danger; and betrayal by friends and associates. And psalms also have been written concerning national peril, as well as personal endangerment and risk.

We experience a variety of moods and attitudes as we approach life and God, from self-pity, loneliness, complaints, despair, sadness, humility, longing, vengeance, and smugness to joy, thanksgiving, faith, and spiritual ecstasy.

All these moods and more are addressed in the Little Bible. For this reason, it has been said that every person can discover his or her identity in the psalms—at any given moment, in all circumstances, in every mood: It gives us the sense and feeling that we are indeed a son or daughter of God, a child of the Eternal Spirit, the living presence of God, a necessary and needed expression of Infinite life. The psalms allow us to enter into conversation with our true self, and help us to relate to it. It is we, talking and we, hearing: God speaking through us and in us.

The 150 psalms are, of course, from the Old Testament, which was written in ancient Hebrew and has been translated into most languages. As in any translation, there are variations in what the actual meaning of any word or phrase may be. There are several English-language translations of the Bible. In this book, Dr. Murphy uses the language of the King James Version, probably the most familiar one. He also points out that the words of the Bible are symbolic and should not be taken literally. The meaning of the symbolism is explained in the text.

Psalms are not the only sources for meditation. Several other prayers and meditations are offered in the book that can help the readers in their efforts to overcome worry and restore peace of mind to their lives.

— Arthur R. Pell, Ph.D., editor

•• ••

Chapter One

Overcoming Worry

*P*rolonged worry robs you of vitality, enthusiasm, and energy and leaves you a physical and mental wreck. Healers point out that chronic worry is an underlying cause of numerous diseases such as asthma, allergies, cardiac trouble, high blood pressure, and a host of other illnesses too numerous to mention.

The worried mind is confused and divided, and is thinking aimlessly about a lot of things that aren't true. Worry, really, is due to indolence, laziness, apathy, and indifference; because when you wake up, you don't have to think these types of thoughts. You can think of harmony, peace, beauty, right action, love, and understanding. You can supplant the negative thought with a constructive one.

Your problem is in your mind. You have a desire, the realization of which would solve your problem. But when you look at conditions and circumstances as they are, a negative thought comes to your mind and your desire is in conflict with your fear. Your worry is your mind's acceptance of the negative conditions. Realize that your desire is the gift of God. God is the Living Spirit within you. It's telling you to rise higher in life. It's also saying that there is no power to challenge God, the Living Spirit within you. There is only One Power—not two, three, or four. That Power moves as unity, as harmony and peace; there are no divisions and quarrels in it.

When worry thoughts come to your mind, remind yourself that Infinite Intelligence is bringing your desire, ideal, plan, or purpose

to pass in Divine order. That's supplanting the negative thought. Continue in this attitude of mind, and the day will break and the shadows will flee.

After one of my lectures, one of the attendees asked for my advice. He'd been worried about his health, but after a comprehensive physical exam, his doctor had told him that there was nothing wrong with him physically but that he was suffering from anxiety and neurosis. *Neurosis* is a $25 word for just plain chronic worry. And the word *worry,* when you translate it from its original root, means "to strangle, to choke," which is what that man was doing to himself.

He told me that he was constantly worrying about money, his business, and the future. His vision of success and prosperity was thwarted by his chronic worry, and the fretting consumed his energy. He felt constantly tired and depressed.

I suggested that he have quiet sessions with himself three or four times a day and declare solemnly that the Almighty has given him inspiration and hope and all he need do is tune in to the Infinite and let the harmony, peace, and love of the Infinite move through him . . . I told him to affirm to himself:

God, or the Supreme Wisdom, gave me this desire. The Almighty Power is within me, enabling me to be, to do, and to have. This Wisdom and Power of the Almighty backs me up and enables me to fulfill all my goals. I think about the Wisdom and Power of the Almighty regularly and systematically. And I no longer think about obstacles, delays, impediments, and failure. I know that thinking constantly along this line builds up my faith and confidence and increases my strength and poise, for God hath not given us the spirit of fear but of power, and of love, and of a sound mind.

Sometime later he wrote to me that he continued to do this regularly and systematically. These truths entered into his conscious mind, and then the brain sent these healing vibrations all over his

system. They went into his subconscious mind and, like spiritual penicillin, they destroyed the bacteria of worry, fear, anxiety, and all these negative thoughts. In a month's time, he arrived at that awareness of strength, power, and intelligence that were Divinely implanted in him at his birth. He conquered his worries by partaking of the spiritual medicine of the Supreme Wisdom and Infinite Intelligence locked in the subconscious depths.

On another occasion a concerned mother visited me, saying that she was terribly worried about her daughter who had joined the Peace Corps and was now in a remote and dangerous area in Africa. I gave her a specific prayer to use night and morning for herself and her daughter. A year later, her daughter completed her tour in Africa safely and returned home and married her longtime boyfriend.

Again, the mother came to see me, quite concerned about her daughter. She was now troubled that her daughter may have married the wrong man; however, she admitted that the man was a wonderful husband. When her daughter got pregnant, she was so worried that their child might be born dead or crippled, but her daughter gave birth to a perfect child. She was also fearful about a money shortage in her daughter's home. This woman wasn't really distressed about what she *thought* was bothering her.

Her actual difficulty was that she had an inward sense of insecurity. She was emotionally immature and certainly spiritually immature. If she was spiritually mature, she would have sat down and blessed her son-in-law and daughter, realizing that God was guiding them, there was right action in their lives, Divine law and order were governing them, Divine peace was filling their soul, and God was prospering them beyond their fondest dreams. How, then, could she be worried about them?

She was just an anxious person. Her real problem was that she was not in tune with the Infinite. Her thoughts were not God's thoughts.

When your thoughts are God's thoughts, God's power is with your thoughts of good. It's as simple as that. You must cleanse your mind like you cleanse your own home. If you don't keep the house

in order, all sorts of pesky insects come in, the paint falls off of the walls, and all manner of things begin to happen. The mind is your house. You have to constantly purify it, filling it with truths of God, which crowd out of the mind everything unlike God.

While talking to this woman, I was able to show her that she was the creator of her own worries. She thereupon replaced her inner sense of insecurity with a real feeling of security. I wrote out a special prayer for her to use. It is taken from the 91st Psalm, the great psalm of protection. If you are a nervous person, use this prayer:

> *He that dwelleth in the secret place of the Most High shall abide under the shadow of the Almighty mind. All the thoughts entertained by me conform to harmony, peace, and goodwill. That's discipline. My mind is the dwelling place of happiness, joy, and a deep sense of security. All the thoughts that enter my mind contribute to my joy, peace, and general welfare. I live, move, and have my being in the atmosphere of good fellowship, love, and unity. All the people that dwell in my mind* [people that dwell in your mind are thoughts, ideas, images, feelings, emotional reaction, and so forth] *are God's children, meaning they are God's ideas. I am at peace in my mind with all the members of my family and with all mankind. The same good I wish for myself I wish for my daughter and her family. I am living in the house of God now. I claim peace and happiness, for I know I dwell in the house of the Lord forever.*

She reiterated these truths frequently during the day, and these wonderful spiritual vibrations neutralized and obliterated the disease-soaked worry center in her subconscious mind, which was like a festering psychic wound. She discovered that there were spiritual reserves that she could call upon to annihilate the negative thoughts. As she saturated her mind with these wonderful, spiritual verities, she became possessed by a deep faith in all things good. She is now living in the joyous expectancy of the best.

There are many prayers that can help you overcome worry. Every morning before the day's work, go to a quiet place and identify yourself mentally and emotionally with these truths:

I live, move, and have my being in God [God is the Life Principle in you, and you know very well you are alive; and God is the Progenitor or the Father of all, so all religions of the world say "Our Father"]. *God lives, moves, and has His being in me. I AM the temple of the Living God. God lives in me. I am immersed in the Divine Presence that surrounds me, enfolds me, and enwraps me. My mind is God's mind, and my Spirit is the Spirit of God. This Infinite Being within me is the Only Presence and the Only Power. It cannot be defeated, thwarted, or frustrated in any way. There is nothing to oppose It, challenge It, thwart It or neutralize It. It's Almighty. It moves as unity. There are no divisions or quarrels in It. It is all-powerful and all-wise. It is present everywhere.*

As I unite mentally with this Infinite Power through my thoughts, I know I am greater than any problem. I grapple courageously with all difficulties and problems, knowing they are Divinely outmatched; and whatever strength, power, and creative ideas I need will automatically be given to me by the Divine Intelligence within me. I know that the Infinite lies stretched in smiling repose within me, where all is bliss, harmony, and peace. I am now in tune with the Infinite; and its wisdom, power, and intelligence become active and potent in my life. This is the law of my being, and I know that God's peace fills my soul. I know I can't think of two things simultaneously. That is, I can't think of failure and dwell upon success at the same time in my mind.

Do you shovel out the darkness in your own home? No, you turn on the light, and the light dissipates the darkness like the sun dissipates the mist. And darkness is absence of light. All you have to do is turn on the light in your own mind. You can say, "I dwell in the secret place of the Most High. I abide in the shadow of the

Almighty. I will say of the Lord, He is my refuge and my fortress: my God, in Him will I trust. He covers me with His feathers, and under His wing shall I rest. The truth is my shield and buckler." Isn't that a wonderful thing to say? Isn't it a wonderful thing to affirm? Isn't it a marvelous thing to know? Isn't it a wonderful, wonderful thing to practice it? Repeat these words and all the worry will go away.

A truck driver came to see me. He was panicked because he'd had two bad accidents and knew that if he had one more, he would be discharged from his job. Each time he climbed into the cab of his truck, he quaked with fear. I told him he couldn't fear his journey and bless his trip at the same moment. Therefore, he had to supplant his worry with confidence and a sense of security. He began each trip by blessing himself and his truck as follows:

> *I am Divinely guided in all my ways. Divine love goes before me making joyous and perfect my way. My truck is God's truck. This guides me and directs me in all my movements. Divine law and order govern me in my driving, and I go from town to town freely, joyously, and lovingly. I bless all other drivers on the road. I wish for them health, happiness, peace, and right action. I am an ambassador of God. I know that all the parts of my vehicle are God's idea and function perfectly. I am always poised, serene, and calm. I am always alert, alive, and quickened by the Holy Spirit. This love surrounds me and goes before me, making my way straight, joyous, and perfect. I am always surrounded by the sacred circle of God's eternal love, and Divine love goes before me making straight, joyous, and wonderful my way.*

During the past three years, he has had no accidents, and he has received no citations or traffic-violation tickets. He began to fill his mind with these truths and crowded out of his mind all worry thoughts that had haunted him. He said, "I made it a habit to use that prayer all the time I was on the road. I committed the whole thing to memory. It wasn't mumbo-jumbo. I knew what I was doing

and why I was doing it. I knew that I was implanting these ideas in my subconscious, and whatever is impressed on the subconscious comes forth as form, function, experience, and events. I also knew that the higher vibration of my spiritual thoughts would wipe out the lower vibration."

This truck driver is no longer anxious or fearful. He knows that prayer changes things. This is discipline, of course. Prayer is a habit—a very good one. How did you learn to walk? You made many attempts to walk across the floor. You fell down. You had a thought pattern. You began to move your legs and so forth. Gradually, it became second nature when you walked across the floor. In other words, if you repeat a thought pattern or act over and over again, after a while it becomes second nature, which is the response of your subconscious mind to your conscious thinking and acting. And that's prayer, too.

I was in a store in Wichita a few years ago. The proprietor invited me to come behind the counter, where he showed me a sign over the cash register: "I will fear no evil for thou art with me." (That's from the 23rd Psalm.) He added that the store had been robbed three times, and he had been held up twice with a gun pointed at his head.

After the third robbery, he wanted to sell the store and get into some other trade, but he had so much invested in the store—not only in money, but in the long-term relationships with his customers and his love of the community—that he decided to stay. He prayed hard over it and read and reread his Bible. He was comforted and encouraged by what he read, especially the 23rd Psalm.

The man said, "I think of that sentence of the psalm, and it falls as a blessing on my mind. I have taken this Infinite Presence and Power within me as my partner, and I claim many times during the day that 'the Infinite Intelligence within me is my higher self; It's my senior partner. This Intelligence guides me and watches over me. His power and wisdom are instantly available to me. I am not alone.'

"Now I feel secure because I know that God's circle of love surrounds this store, myself, and all of my customers. I make this

prayer a habit: 'I will fear no evil for thou art with me. Thy rod and thy staff, they comfort me. Goodness and mercy follow me all the days of my life, for I dwell in the house of God forever.'"

The house of God is your own mind. Your mind is where you walk and talk with God, for God is that Supreme Intelligence, that Boundless Wisdom within you. It's locked in your own subconscious depths.

The storekeeper met the problem of anxiety and worry, and he overcame it. During the past four years, he has had no trouble and has prospered beyond his fondest dreams. He realized that his fear was irrational. There is an Infinite Intelligence and Boundless Wisdom, which we call God knocking at the door of your heart. It opens with an inside latch. All you have to do is let it in and contact it with your thoughts. It will lift you up, heal you, inspire you, guide you, open new doors of expression, watch over you, and sustain you. That's the Presence and Power that heals a cut on your finger. If you burn yourself, it reduces the edema and gives you new skin and tissue. It's that which started your heartbeat and watches over you when you're sound asleep.

Now, the Presence is always there whether or not you make conscious use of it. That's why I say that worry is laziness.

An engineer told me how he overcomes all his distressing thoughts. He looks at them as an engineering problem. "When I face a technical problem on the job," he said, "I take it apart and break it into small pieces. Then I ask myself 'Where do they come from? What does each piece signify? How can I adapt it to the entire problem?' With worries I ask, 'Do these worries have any power? Is there any principle behind them?'"

With his cool, rational thought and logical analysis, he dismembers his nagging concerns and realizes that they're shadows in his mind, fallacious and illusionary. No reality, just shadows in the mind.

A shadow has no power! Well, that's what worry is: a shadow in your mind. It has no reality, no principle behind it, no truth behind it. These anxieties are no more than a conglomeration of sinister shadows.

Doctors will tell you that many of their patients fret so much about diseases that they don't have that they suffer the symptoms of that ailment. Doctors call this "psychosomatic." The roots of this word are "psycho," which means of the mind; and "somatic," meaning of the body. What you think in your mind is reflected by the reaction of your body.

A friend of mine, the assistant pastor of a church in Los Angeles, was worried that he had a bad heart. His senior pastor, a man 20 years older than he, had just had a heart attack and was sure that his assistant was also susceptible. He went to see a heart specialist, who took a cardiogram and learned that his heart was normal and that his problem was psychosomatic. The senior pastor's heart attack triggered in him an inordinate concern about his own heart, and he actually experienced spasms in his chest and other symptoms of heart trouble.

The doctor told him: "You should practice what you preach. The cure for your problem is not in my medical books, but in the Book of Books. Read again and again the 27th Psalm. Meditate on it until the false idea is lifted from your psyche, and your soma will respond."

It only took a few weeks. He practiced the great law of substitution by repeating the good idea over and over again until the mind laid hold of the truth, which set him free.

It takes a little work, but you can do it. That's why I said that it's a discipline. It's a willingness to do it. "I'm going to overcome this. I'm going to meet it head-on. It's a shadow in my mind, and I'm not going to give power to shadows." These emotional spasms were caused because the man was obsessed with the idea that he had a bad heart. He didn't, so he was completely healed. He was healed of what? A false belief in his own mind.

Another example of how prayer and meditation can help overcome worry and restore health was brought to my attention when a man with a seemingly well-adjusted and composed personality came to see me. He was very worried and anxious because his personal doctor told him that his blood pressure was over 200, that he should take it easy and relax more. He said to

me, "I can't take it easy. I have too much to do, and the pressure in my organization is terrific." He was really suffering from a long-mounting accumulation of petty frustrations and worries.

I suggested that he begin to apply this simple truth to himself: that he could not be sick forever; that he was here to meet all problems and to overcome them, not run away from them; that he was mentally and spiritually equipped to handle any challenge, regardless of what it was; and that he could meet it head-on, grapple with it courageously, and say, "The problem is here, but Infinite Intelligence is here, too, and knows only the answer."

All conditions, circumstances, and events are subject to alteration. Every created thing will someday pass. The age-old maxim "This, too, shall pass away" is always true. But your mind and Spirit, the personality of you, will never pass away

The first step was that this man had to extract his attention from his ailment and business difficulties and trust the Creative Intelligence within him (which made his body) to heal and restore him. I gave him the following meditation to use several times each day, accompanied by a suggestion that he was to assert absolutely and believe implicitly the following simple truths:

Periodically during the day, I withdraw my attention from the vexations and strife of the world, and I return to the Divine Presence within me and commune with that Creative Intelligence within. I know that I am nourished spiritually and mentally, and God's river of peace floods my mind. Infinite Intelligence reveals to me the perfect idea for every problem I meet. I reject the appearance of things, and I affirm the supremacy of the Presence and Power within me. I am absorbed and engrossed in the great truth that Infinite Intelligence is guiding me, that Divine Right Action reigns supreme. The Miraculous Healing Presence is flowing through me now, permeating every atom of my being. His river of peace flows through my mind and heart; and I am relaxed, poised, serene, and calm. I know that the Divine Presence that made me is now restoring me to wholeness

and perfection. I give thanks for the miraculous healing that is taking place now.

By affirming regularly many times a day in this manner, he succeeded in retrieving his senses from the annoyances and irritations of the day. In a month's time, a medical checkup revealed normal blood pressure. He discovered that his renewed mind restored his body to wholeness. When the strain and pressure of business tend to disturb him today, his motto is: "None of these things moves me." He has that on his desk.

Do things disturb you? If you have no opinion, there is no suffering. You have no opinion about the headlines in the newspaper today? Well, where there is no opinion, there is no suffering. If the cucumber is bitter, don't eat it. If there are briars and brambles on the road you're traveling on, avoid them.

Tune in to the Infinite. By doing so, how, then, could you be disturbed? Aren't you disturbing yourself? Exalt Divine wisdom in the midst of you. Say to yourself: "I will lift up mine eyes into the hills from whence cometh my help."

In a Nutshell

When worry thoughts come to your mind, remind yourself that Infinite Intelligence is bringing your desire, ideal, plan, or purpose to pass in Divine order. That's supplanting the negative thought.

When your thoughts are God's thoughts, God's power is with your thoughts of good. You must cleanse your mind like you cleanse out your own home. The mind is your house. You have to constantly declutter it, filling it with truths of God, which crowd out of the mind everything unlike God.

If you repeat a thought pattern or act over and over again, after a while it becomes second nature, which is the response of your subconscious mind to your conscious thinking and acting. And that's prayer, too.

The house of God is your own mind. Your mind is where you walk and talk with God, for God is that Supreme Intelligence, that Boundless Wisdom within you. It's locked in your own subconscious depths.

All conditions, circumstances, and events are subject to alteration. Every created thing will someday pass away. The age-old maxim "This, too, shall pass away" is always true. But your mind and Spirit, the personality of you, will never pass away.

••· ·•·

Chapter Two

---·•·---

Banish Guilt

*L*ife holds no grudges against anyone. God is the Life Principle within you. It's animating, sustaining, and strengthening you at this very moment. If you're wondering where God is, the Life Principle in you is God. It's the Living Spirit Almighty within you. It's your mind, your Spirit. You are alive with the life of God, for God is life, and that is your life now. Life is forever forgiving us. We must let the scales of superstition fall from our eyes and become aware of simple truths, which have always been known.

Truth has been distorted, twisted, and prostituted beyond recognition. This is why guilt is universal. Psychologists call guilt the curse of curses, yet the Life Principle does not condemn us; we condemn ourselves. In all ages, human beings have been told to banish their sense of guilt; and they've employed various ceremonies and rituals for this purpose. In ancient times, they sacrificed their bullocks and doves to propitiate a God of wrath. When storms came, crops were ruined or a great drought prevailed. The people believed that the gods were angry, and the tribal priest had to give these folks an answer. If he didn't, they'd kill him. Therefore, the priest offered answers that satisfied the superstitious imaginings of such people.

In ancient times and even now in remote parts of the world, people have sacrificed their children to appease the so-called angry gods of fire, flood, and famine. This is somewhat like paying a

gangster, giving him a payoff every week so that he won't throw a bomb into your store.

Now if you burn your hand, life forgives you; reduces the edema; and gives you new skin, tissue, and cells. Life doesn't hold a grudge against you. If you injure your hand, cutting it severely, life forgives you. New cells build bridges over the cut and you have a marvelous healing. Life is always forgiving you. Life is giving and forgiving. If you take some bad food, life forgives you, too, causing you to expel and regurgitate it. Life bears no ill will against you.

We must learn to use the Life Principle the right way and cease going against the flow. When a child is born, it is Universal Life individualizing itself and appearing in your home. The child has no discrimination or discernment and hasn't begun to use its reason as yet. Therefore, he or she is subject to the mood and attitude of the parents.

All children want to follow their own inherent drives. They do not intentionally cause problems, but the father or mother who doesn't understand says, "You little brat. You are a sinner. You are evil. You are a naughty girl. God is going to punish you. You are going to suffer for this." The child is baffled. She cannot reason out what is wrong, as she lacks discernment. Therefore, she feels cut off from love, affection, and security, for that is what the mother represents to her. She feels that her mother is angry, and perhaps reacts by wetting her bed at night. Psychologists say that this is a way of indicating that the child wants to drown her mother in resentment. The child may also react by becoming timid, weak, and inferior, showing a deep sense of unworthiness or rejection.

A young boy might react to a cruel, tyrannical father by becoming hostile, belligerent, and resentful. He knows that his father is a big man, so he suppresses his anger. As such, it becomes a festering sore. Later on he finds himself opposed to authority because he has been against his father all his young life. He gets in trouble with the police, the principal at school, and other symbols of authority. He's always fighting his father, but he doesn't know it because no one has ever taught him how his mind works.

Even the President of the United States is subject to authority; Congress has power over him. We all have to live and adjust to authority, but we must learn to establish control over our thoughts, feelings, and responses. We must take charge of our own mind. When we do take charge of this motley crew in our mind and say, "I am the master; I am going to order my thoughts around," and tell them what to give attention to, then we'll be like an employer ordering employees to execute his instructions.

You must take charge of your own mind and not permit others to govern it for you. Creed, dogma, traditions, superstition, fear, and ignorance rule the mind of the average person. The greatest desert in the world is not the Sahara; it is in the mind of the typical individual. Unexceptional people do not own their own minds at all; their minds don't belong to them. They're often ruled by strong-minded family members or governed by the domination of others.

We must realize that a great sense of guilt stems from what is called conscience. A great number of people think that the voice of conscience is that of God. It is not. Conscience is your inner feeling and the voice of someone else. Often it is the voice of ignorance, fear, superstition, falsehoods, and weird concepts of God.

I knew a boy who feared that God would punish him because he didn't go to church on Sunday. This is the inner voice of superstition and false belief implanted in his subconscious mind by his parents, preachers, or teachers. This boy's belief gave him a sense of guilt, and he felt that he must be punished. When you were young, you were given taboos, restrictions, homilies, and a series of "don'ts." You were, perhaps, told that you were evil, a sinner, and that you would be punished. Perhaps you were told of a lake of fire waiting for you if you didn't believe in a particular creed. The minds of children are contaminated and polluted with all kinds of strange notions and false doctrines.

Children are particularly susceptible to feelings of guilt when they disobey parents or teachers. They're warned that disobedience will lead to punishment—not only by the parents for the specific disobedient act, but by God, Who will punish them for being

naughty. This can be disastrous for some children. It breeds within them a guilt complex that can destroy their lives. It would be far better to explain to children why what they did was wrong, and administer appropriate discipline such as a time-out or a withdrawal of a privilege. Do not invoke the fear of eternal damnation. It's better to tell them that God's love never ceases and will be there to help them live a good life.

Children should never be told that they were born in iniquity and conceived in sin. It's a monstrous lie; it's too stupid for words. They should be taught that they are children of God. As Moses said, "We are all children of the I AM."

God is their real Father, and God is love. God is *your* Father, and that is the Life Principle within *you*. It's the Progenitor of all. It's *our* Father. It's the Father of all the people in this world, for there is only one Life Principle.

The children should also be taught that love can't do anything unloving. Peace can't wish pain, joy can't wish sadness, and love can't do anything that isn't loving. There are a lot of things God can't do: God can't punish you. God can't wish death, for life can't wish death. That would be a contradiction of its own nature.

There is the good conscience where the child is taught the Golden Rule: love of others, respect for parents, and that honesty is the best policy. When a child is tempted to steal, there is that within him or her that cries out, "No, you shouldn't do that; that belongs to someone else!" The mother and father are there to teach the child the difference between rat poison and butter, between the skunk and the cat, between what is right and what is wrong. The child has to go to school. He or she has to learn manners; be indoctrinated properly; and learn what is right, true, noble, and Godlike. The child must learn about universal principles and eternal verities, which never change. They are the same yesterday, today, and forever. Yet how many are taught these qualities today? We all want self-esteem; want to feel worthy; and want to be recognized by our neighbors as honest, sincere, and good.

You want your children and your spouse to love you. You want the respect of the community. When you fall short of expressing yourself in doing the right thing, you feel a sense of guilt and proceed to punish yourself.

Some people have serious doubts about their priorities. On the one hand, they believe that what they're doing is what is best for their families and themselves; but on the other hand, they have qualms about it.

Barbara L. was such a person. She was a very successful real estate sales executive who supervised a staff of seven Realtors and was acclaimed by her company as one of their best producers. She was a single mother of two school-age boys, and she made sure that they were well taken care of. They attended a prestigious private school; and had a full-time housekeeper who prepared their meals, attended to their needs, and drove them to and from school and their many other activities. Barbara often had to work nights and weekends, but she tried to make the time she spent with her sons quality time. When she was home, she talked with them, played games, and helped them with their homework, but she wasn't a happy person.

She told me that she felt so full of guilt that she wasn't a good mother. She said, "I must work long hours on my job. I must be available to show clients houses at their convenience, not mine. I depend on my job to support my kids." This strong sense of guilt had become so great that it was affecting Barbara's health. Her blood pressure had risen well above normal, she had difficulty sleeping, and had frequent digestive problems.

I asked her if her children were doing well. "Oh, yes," she responded. "They're both doing well in school. The older boy is on the baseball team and has many friends. The younger is more interested in music and is doing well with his piano and guitar lessons. They love the housekeeper and are very affectionate with me. I truly believe they're happy."

"If they're happy and doing well, why are you feeling so guilty?" I asked her.

We discussed this, and she said. "My mother disapproves of my lifestyle. She was always a stay-at-home mom and strongly believes that a mother's first priority is taking care of the children. I can't disagree. I could get a less demanding job and be home much more, but I'm making an income that enables my children to have the best education and care they could get. My mother says that God will punish me for not being a good mother, and I'm concerned that she may be right and I don't know what to do."

I explained that God cannot condemn you or punish you. You do it to yourself. If you let other people take control of your mind, you lose the freedom God has given you to make decisions based on your own thoughts. What you're doing is letting your mother's feelings replace your own in your subconscious, and the result is conflict and guilt. Yes, we should honor our parents, as the Bible says, but that doesn't mean that they're always right. What is right for them may not be right for you. You must follow your own heart—that is, your own subconscious mind. You must feed your conscious mind with positive thoughts through prayer and meditation, and it will push out from your subconscious the seeds of guilt sown by your mother. Post the following prayer on your mirror so that you see it every morning when you rise and every night before you retire:

> *The kingdom of God is within me. Infinite Intelligence*
> *will lead and guide me in all my ways when*
> *I turn to It and call upon It.*

Self-condemnation is the most destructive of all mental poisons. It robs you of vitality, enthusiasm, and energy. It may affect all the organs of your body. If you have a glass of dirty water, you may condemn, resent, and curse it indefinitely, but you won't get clean water. However, if you continually pour clean water into the glass, you will have clean water. No matter what you've done in the past—if you've murdered, robbed, cheated, defrauded, or committed all manner of evil—if you stop now and change your

mind and let Divine love, peace, and harmony flood your mind, and if you're sincere in transforming yourself, the past is forgotten and remembered no more.

From the Mind Principle, there is no time or space. If you had misused the laws of chemistry for 50 years and suddenly you studied these laws again and brought forth marvelous compounds, do you mean to tell me that the principle of chemistry would have a grudge against you because you had misused it? Your Mind Principle is the same as that of chemistry. It has no grudge against you. Forgive yourself and walk on.

I've often been asked to provide a comprehensive summary of my concepts on a specific subject by giving my listeners or readers a list of suggestions that synthesize my ideas. Here are ten basic rules on dealing with feelings of guilt:

1. You are not born with a sense of guilt. Guilt is a mental disease and is abnormal and unnatural.

2. What you want must first be conceived in your thoughts and then programmed into your subconscious mind.

3. Conscience is your inner feeling. It is not necessarily based on Truth. It is often the voice of ignorance, fear, superstition, and prejudices implanted in your mind by your parents or by others you look upon as authorities.

4. It's wrong to threaten children by saying, "God will punish you." God punishes no one.

5. Don't let your conscience be your guide. Your true guide is God; He is that Infinite Intelligence that will lead you to live a good ("Godlike") life.

6. Different cultures, religions, and ethnic groups have different concepts of "conscience."

7. What is "Godlike" isn't dictated by any one religion. God knows nothing about creeds, dogma, or sectarian opinions. God is above all.

8. God and God alone should be your spiritual guide.

9. Many people are misled and are full of guilt because they accept as right that which is actually wrong.

10. God wants you to be happy. God's law is the law of health, happiness, peace, order, beauty, good deeds, and prosperity.

In a Nutshell

We must learn to use the Life Principle the right way and cease going against the stream of life. When a child is born, it is Universal Life individualizing itself and appearing in your home. The child has no discrimination or discernment. He or she has not begun to use reason yet. Therefore, the baby is subject to the mood and attitude of the parents.

You must take charge of your own mind, not permit others to govern it for you. Creed, dogma, traditions, superstition, fear, and ignorance rule the mind of the average person. The greatest desert in the world is in the mind of such a person. Average people do not own their own minds at all; their minds don't belong to them. They're often ruled over by strong-minded family members or governed by the domination of others.

Children are particularly susceptible to feelings of guilt when they disobey parents or teachers. They're warned that disobedience will lead to punishment—not only by the parents for the specific disobedient act, but by God, Who will punish them for being naughty. This can be disastrous for some children. It breeds within them a guilt complex that can destroy their lives. Do not invoke the fear of eternal damnation in children. It's better to tell them

that God's love never ceases and will be there to help them live a good life.

If you let other people take control of your mind, you lose the freedom God has given you to make decisions based on your own thoughts. You must follow your own heart—that is, your own subconscious mind. You must feed your conscious mind with positive thoughts through prayer and meditation, and it will push out from your subconscious the seeds of guilt sown by others.

Self-condemnation is the most destructive of all mental poisons. It robs you of vitality, enthusiasm, and energy. It may affect all the organs of your body. If you let Divine love, peace, and harmony flood your mind, and if you're sincere in transforming yourself, the past is forgotten and remembered no more.

•• ••

Chapter Three

The Supreme Mastery of Fear

*T*he most extensive of all the morbid mental conditions that reflect themselves so disastrously on the human system is the state of fear. It may range from the state of extreme alarm, fright, or terror down to the slightest shade of apprehension of impending evil. But all along the line it's the same thing—a paralyzing impression upon the centers of life that can produce a variety of morbid symptoms in every tissue of the body.

Fear is like a poison gas pumped into one's atmosphere. It causes mental, moral, and spiritual asphyxiation, and sometimes death—death to energy, to tissue, and to all growth.

In this chapter we'll explore how fear can keep you from success and what you can do to overcome this blight and turn your thoughts from fear to courage. It starts with a strong belief that you and God are one. The Life Principle is always for you. It heals a cut on your finger. If you take some bad food, It causes you to regurgitate it. It always seeks to preserve you, to heal and restore you.

So, keep telling your subconscious that you are Divine. Your subconscious wants you to say it over and over again, for ideas are conveyed to the subconscious by repetition, faith, and expectancy. Do it again and again and again; and realize that the God Presence is within you and that you are one with It. You are Divine. You are a child of the Living God, heir to all of God's riches. And all the power of the godhead flows to your focal point of attention.

There are plenty of people who are simply afraid to live, scared to death that they will die. They don't know how to dislodge the monster fear that terrifies them, and it dogs their steps from the cradle to the grave.

For thousands of people, the dread of some impending evil is ever present. It haunts them even in their happiest moments. Their joy is poisoned with it so that they never take much pleasure or comfort in anything. It is the ghost at the banquet, the skeleton in the closet. It is ingrained into their very lives and emphasized in their excessive timidity, their shrinking, and their self-conscious bearing.

Some people are afraid of nearly everything. They're afraid of a draft, afraid to eat what they want, afraid to venture out in business matters for fear of losing their money, afraid of public opinion, and more. They have a perfect horror of what their neighbors think. They're afraid hard times are coming; and fear poverty and all manner of natural disasters. Their whole lives are filled with fear, fear, fear.

Fear and worry make us attract the very things we dread. The fear habit impairs health, shortens life, and paralyzes efficiency. Doubt and fear mean failure; faith is an optimist, fear a pessimist.

Fear in all its different phases of expression, such as worry, anxiety, anger, jealousy, and timidity, is the greatest enemy of the human race. It has robbed humankind of more happiness and efficiency, and has made more people cowards, more people failures, or forced them into mediocrity than anything else.

There's no need to fear. Tell yourself that over and over again. Gradually, your subconscious will accept it. And your subconscious will believe it because you believe it in your conscious, reasoning mind. Whatever your conscious mind really believes, your subconscious will dramatize and bring to manifestation. Do not vacillate or equivocate. Your subconscious mind knows when you're sincere. It knows when you really believe; then it will respond.

Tell yourself frequently that God dwells within you, that you are Divine and that Omnipotence is moving on your behalf. Say it to yourself when you're challenged, and whenever you have any kind of trouble or difficulty. The problem is here, but the God

Presence is here, too. Say it to yourself when you're driving your car, when you're going to sleep, and when you're talking to someone. Realize that God is thinking, speaking, and acting through you. And realize that it's always functioning.

When fear comes, say, "Faith in God opens the door of my mind and there is no one there." Realize that you are one with this God Power. You are aligned with It now, and mighty forces will come to your aid. You are one with the Infinite, with life, and with all things.

The Bible says: "Thou shalt compass me about with songs of deliverance. I will fear no evil for Thou art with me. Thy rod and thy staff, they comfort me. Goodness and mercy follow me all the days of my life, for I dwell in the house of God forever." Your mind is the house of God. It's where you walk and talk with the Supreme Intelligence—this Infinite Presence and Power.

When you're fearful or indulge in negative thoughts, you're vibrating at a very low level. When you meditate on a psalm, say to yourself, "The Lord is my shepherd; I shall not want," or "The Presence of God is right where I am," or "I will fear no evil for God is with me," or "I dwell in the secret place of the Most High and I abide in the shadow of the Almighty," or "I will say of the Lord, He is my refuge, my fortress; my God, in Him will I trust," or "Surely, He will cover me with His feathers, and under His wing shall I rest," or "The truth shall be my shield and buckler."

Affirm frequently: "God is guiding me now. The Presence of God is with me." Then you are thinking spiritually. Your thoughts now are God's thoughts, and all the power of God flows through that thought. That's the meaning of "one with God is a majority." For the only immaterial power is your thought, and your thought is creative. Therefore, think of harmony; think of Infinite love flowing through you, vitalizing, healing, and restoring you. These spiritual thoughts are of a very high frequency and are of a very high vibration.

What happens to the evil, negative thoughts—the fear, foreboding, destruction, disaster, earthquakes, and things of this nature? When you say, "Oh, maybe another earthquake will come;

maybe my house will be knocked down," think along these lines:

Say, "God's love surrounds me and enfolds me; the Presence of God is in my home" (which is the presence of harmony, beauty, love, and peace). Divine love saturates the walls, the atmosphere. Wherever you are, whether asleep or awake, walking the streets, or at work, God's love surrounds you, enfolds you, and enwraps you. You are immunized; you are God-intoxicated; you have no fear.

You are not afraid of anything in the past, the present, or the future. You aren't afraid of people, conditions, or events. For the Eternal God is your dwelling place and the everlasting arms of wisdom, truth, and beauty. You are immersed in the Holy Omnipresence. In Him we live and move and have our being. And this God Presence lives, moves, and has His being in us.

Now you are vibrating at a spiritual frequency; and just like you put your finger on a tuning fork, that is the end of the negative or fearful vibration. That is the end of the evil, for evil is a false belief of God, the Infinite One, and the Infinite Goodness of the Infinite One.

When you're full of fear, you have greater faith in evil than in the God Presence. That's shocking but true. Fear is God upside down. You have faith that the sun will rise in the morning; you have faith that you can drive your car; you have faith that you will get an answer to your prayer when you pray for guidance. But many people have faith in the wrong thing. There are people who are looking forward to misfortune. There are people working in offices who are afraid of their jobs. They're afraid they're going to lose their money, and of what is going to happen to them when they grow old, instead of realizing: "I am always in my true place. God is the Source of my supply, and all my needs are met in every moment of time and point of space. God is my instant and everlasting supply, meeting all my needs all the time, no matter where I am. I am always gainfully employed. I am always working for Him, and I live forever."

Why be upset, angry, or fearful as a result of another's remark? Does what others say contribute to your success, your happiness,

your peace, or your failure in any way? No. Their thoughts have no power. Your power is with your thoughts of good. Someone may spread lies about you, and you may say, "Oh, well, they're undermining me; they're telling lies about me," and you feel full of fear and anger. But does their opinion make it so? No. What governs you? Is it your belief or another's belief? Is it your thought or someone else's? Do you own your own mind? Are you permitting others to manipulate you? Who's thinking for you? Are you coming to your own decisions? Are you doing your own thinking?

You are in the kingdom of heaven, which means that you are king over your conceptive realm, which is your own mind. You have authority and dominion over your thoughts, feelings, emotions, and actions. That's why the kingdom of heaven is within you. It's not a place up in the sky where you go; you're already there.

Why make yourself subservient to another's thought? Why not have reverence for your own thought? Your thought is Divine. It is creative. It is of God. The capacity of Spirit is to think. You are a Spirit. When were you not a Spirit? You will always be a Spirit. You are a Spirit now. Have a healthy, reverent respect for your thought, because your thought is your prayer. What you feel, you attract; what you imagine, you become.

Your thought governs you, not another. So stand tall. Stand up straight, and say: "I am one with the Infinite, which lies stretched in smiling repose." The finite alone hath wrought and suffered, but the Infinite lies stretched in smiling repose.

Yes, each time a fear thought comes to you, supplant it and say, "God loves me and cares for me." Say to yourself, "God loves me. The sacred circle of God's eternal love surrounds me. The whole armor surrounds me, enfolds me, and enwraps me. And Divine love goes before me, making straight and perfect my way."

A pilot said to me, "I'm never afraid when I navigate a plane, whether I go north, south, east, or west, for I am a pilot for God. I am flying for Him. And I am as safe in the sky as on the earth. Nothing can happen to me. It's impossible. I'm always surrounded by the sacred circle of God's eternal love."

Robby Wright, a lad who works in my recording studio, is a person of tremendous faith and has a great reverence for things Divine. And whatever he prays for, he gets, because, as he said, "The Source is God. Therefore, whatever I pray for, it already is. Because I couldn't think of it if it were not so." Therefore, whether it's an automobile, or a bicycle, or a trip to Europe, or whatever it is he prays for, he realizes that before he calls, the answer is there. And all of these lad's prayers are answered in Divine order. He never looks to any person, place, or thing. He looks to the Source. That's a smart young man.

So have faith in the goodness of God and the right action of God and the guidance of that Infinite One within you. Have faith in the eternal principles and in the immutable, changeless laws of God. Have faith in your own mind, because any idea that you emotionalize, nourish, sustain, and exalt in your mind by the process of osmosis sinks down into your subconscious, where it dies like a seed and bequeaths its energy to another form of itself. And what is the energy that it bequeaths? It is the joy of the answered prayer. After all, the corn and wheat must die before we have a harvest. The apple seed must die before we have an apple.

Likewise, your desire is a gift of God. Therefore, God does not mock you. You say, "God, Who gave me this desire, reveals the perfect plan for its development." And you contemplate the end. Faith is your attitude of mind. Faith is your thought. Whatever you impress in your subconscious is expressed on the screen of space. Nowhere in any holy book in the world does it say you have to have faith in Catholicism, Buddhism, Judaism, Hinduism, Shintoism, or any "ism." You have faith in the creative laws of your own mind. You have faith in the goodness of God in the land of the living. You have faith that there's an Infinite Intelligence that responds to your thought. It will respond to an atheist, agnostic—anybody. And before you call, the answer is there. It was always there.

Faith is your attitude of mind. It's what you expect, what you're focused on. The things that you are vividly imagining will come to pass. Some people are afraid of old age. Age is not the flight of

years; it's the dawn of wisdom. Some are afraid of death. There is no reason to fear death. Death is simply a new birth; that's all it is. You are alive, and your life is God's life. You are alive now. God is life eternal. Because God lives, you live. God cannot die; therefore, you cannot die.

Realize that God is your employer, and the God Presence is always taking care of you. The great dancer says, "I dance for Him." The great singer says, "God sings in majestic cadences through me." He commands that internal power and wisdom. He calls upon it and it answers him. Naturally, he gets honors. He gets emoluments. He gets the praise of other people, but he doesn't seek it. He turns to the Source, and all these things are added to him.

Seek ye first the kingdom of God, and all these things, like honors, wealth, and everything else, will be added to you automatically. You will never want for anything. When someone makes a negative statement about you, begin to dwell on the fact that you "will fear no evil, for Thou art with me. Thy rod and Thy staff, they comfort me. Perfect love casteth out fear, for fear hath a torment. He that feareth is not made perfect in love."

Fearful people are always very selfish. They're wrapped up in themselves. They're hugging the shore. Love is always outgoing. It is an emanation. Fear is turning within in morbid introspection, believing someone is going to hurt you, that evil spirits can possess you. All this is ignorance. Ignorance is the only sin, and all the punishment is the consequence of that ignorance. Ignorance is the only devil in the world.

When you believe in external powers, you deny the One True Cause, which moves as a unity. It is the Life Principle within you, forever seeking to express Itself as love, bliss, joy, and right action. When we are afraid, we are selfish in the wrong way. Fear is a morbid introspection. Cease building a wall around yourself, saying, "I'm going to get hurt." Realize God is, and all that exists is God. Realize that the love of God surrounds you, enfolds you, and enwraps you. Say to yourself, "God walks and talks in me. I know I am one with my Father, and my Father is God. I have faith

in God; therefore, I fear not." Fear not, little flock, for it is your Father's good pleasure to give you the kingdom.

Realize that you're surrounded by Divine love and that God's power is with your thoughts of good—that you're immersed in the Holy Omnipresence. God is with you.

The fear of the Lord is the beginning of wisdom. When you learn the laws of electricity, you're very careful how you apply them, because you know the consequences. You know what will happen if you put your hand on a naked wire or cause a short circuit. You learn the theories about insulation and conductivity, resulting in a healthy respect and reverence for these laws. And you will follow the nature of the principles.

Likewise, when you learn the principles of chemistry, you have a very healthy respect for the combination of chemicals and their atomic weight because you know the disastrous consequences of mixing things together when you do not know the results. For instance, if you mix nitric acid and glycerin, you will have a powerful explosive.

Fear is a reverence, a healthy respect. You have a healthy respect for the law of your mind when you learn the consequences of misusing it, because your mind is a principle. Nothing can give you peace but the triumph of principles, Emerson said. You have a healthy respect for the fire, so you don't put your finger into it.

Similarly, when you know that your mind is a principle, like the principles of chemistry and physics, you will have a very healthy respect for the subconscious mind. A principle doesn't change. God is the Living Spirit within you. It's Infinite Intelligence, Boundless Wisdom. It's the Only Cause, Power, and Substance in the world. It's Supreme and Omnipotent. There is nothing to oppose it, nothing to challenge it, nothing to vitiate it. If there were two powers, there would be two wills. There would be chaos everywhere. There would be no order, symmetry, or proportion anywhere.

When you think God's thoughts, God's power is with your thoughts of good. You can tune in to the Infinite. The only immaterial power you know is your thought. In the beginning was

the word. The word was with God, and the word was God. The word is a thought expressed. When you have discovered the power of your thoughts, you have discovered God in that sense; because your thought is creative, not because it is *your* thought, but because it is thought. You can demonstrate that, of course, under hypnosis.

You can put a finger on a person's neck and say, "This is a red-hot poker." That person will get a blister. So you know very well that your thoughts become flesh; they become manifest in your life. And you'd better have a healthy respect for your thoughts.

Water runs downhill. It expands when frozen. It takes the shape of any vessel into which it is poured. These and many other characteristics determine the principle by which water operates. We learn that it runs downhill. Your mind operates in the same way. If you think good, good follows; if you think evil, evil follows. Evil is the misuse of the law, a misinterpretation of life. There is only One Power: That's the Living Spirit Almighty, which is undifferentiated, undefined . . . the Self-Originating Spirit.

Your mind is creative. That is, the thought in your mind is creative. Therefore, if you think good, good follows; if you think evil, evil follows. If you say, "The Infinite Healing Presence can heal me now," It will respond to you. You can say, "Infinite Intelligence guides and directs me and watches over me in all my ways." Faith is an attitude of mind. Faith is the use you make of your mind. Therefore, realize that fear is a thought in your own mind created by yourself. It has no reality; it's a shadow in your mind. The thing you are afraid of does not exist. Fear is faith in the wrong thing. It is faith upside down. Fear is God upside down. It's a twisted, morbid concept of life.

Fear can also cause real physiological effects. Just the same as if a boy were in a chair and you told him a bogeyman was downstairs with a black bag and was going to take him away because he was a bad boy. He's frozen to the chair. He gets white and rigid. Yet, there is no reality to the thought. Take him downstairs and point out to him that there is no bogeyman; he is free of the fear. But it had the same physiological and physical effect as if it were real.

Basil King, who wrote *The Conquest of Fear*, says that he was going blind. He was a young man—depressed, dejected, and fearing blindness and old age. He said he recalled something that a teacher said years ago. The Life Principle (God) in you is indestructible, invulnerable, and eternal. It always brings about the expedient, which is an answer to the particular need of any person. He used to think that Nature was cruel and raw and that evil abounded in the world. He had strange concepts of God. I might say that good and evil are the movements of your own mind relative to the One Being Who is forever whole, pure, and immaculate.

It's the use that you make of the power. How do you use electricity? You can use it to kill a person or fry an egg. How do use nitric acid? Well, you can blind a person with it, or you can paint a Madonna on a windowpane with it. You can use water to drown a child or quench his thirst. Surely, these things are not evil. The forces of nature are not evil. The Living Spirit is the God Presence in you. How are you using it?

This man who was going blind said he used to think that Nature was cruel and raw and that God was punishing him, and so on. Then he began to think the Life Principle within him had overcome every obstacle in the world—whether it was a flood, volcanic eruption, war, or some other type of destruction. The Life Principle goes on, invulnerable and eternal. You can't destroy life; life just is. You are alive. Your life is God.

The Life Principle gives fur to the animals in the north; It gives them hair in the temperate zone. It covers others with shells to preserve them. Others are given a poisonous fluid that they emit when attacked. It takes care of all forms of life, such as those that came out of the sea. It gave them legs, made them stand upright, and gave them wings to fly in the air. Always the Life Principle met the particular need.

When our ancient ancestors met the tiger, they were frozen with fear. Gradually, the dawn of reason, imagination, and memory came to their aid. There was a time when humans had no memory.

Later, they began to think, and this Power within them responded to their thoughts.

Basil King, in meditating and musing on the Power within him, discovered that Life or Nature is not cruel, but when he combined or united with this Principle in thought, mighty forces came to his aid. He no longer believed in three old men sitting on a throne: Father, Son, and Holy Ghost. But he perceived that God was the Life Principle. The Trinity is your Spirit, mind, and body. And the mind is the priest, or the intermediary, between the Invisible and the visible; namely, your own thought. Therefore, the Spirit responds to the nature of your thought.

The average person has pigeonholed this God Presence and brings Him out on the Sabbath; holidays; and occasions of death, birth, and marriage. But the rest of the time, the God Presence is put away in a corner. Some people are afraid to use the term *God.* Others look askance when God is mentioned, as they begin to think of God in terms of religious connotations because each has a different concept of Him. God is your mind, your Spirit. God is your thought, too. Because your thought is creative, you have a healthy respect for It. Think of harmony, peace, love, right action, and beauty. Think of an Infinite Healing Presence. Know that the sacred circle of God's Eternal Love surrounds you.

Think of a circle. Imagine that you are in the midst of the circle. That's a circle of love, peace, harmony, and power. Then nothing will touch you. You are immunized. You are God-intoxicated. You are always in the sacred center of God's Eternal Love.

So, Basil King discarded all the sentimental connotations associated with the name of the Deity. He began to realize that God was the Life Principle within him, operating through him. When he united with this Infinite Intelligence, mighty forces came to his aid. He found that this Creative Intelligence was the answer to every problem. He said, "This realization was the beginning of the process of casting out fear, which was blinding me and paralyzing me."

You cannot conquer fear until you come back to the fact that there is only One Power, One Presence, One Cause, One Substance.

Therefore, you'd better get it straight in your cranium that the minute you give attention to externals, you are denying the One Presence and the One Power. A scientific thinker does not make a created thing greater than the Creator; therefore, get it clear and straight in your mind that never again will you give power to any person, place, thing, condition, circumstance, star, sun, moon, weather, water, or anything in this universe to harm, hurt, or bless you. You simply recognize that there is only One Creative Power: That is the Spirit and the mind in you. It's Almighty, Over All, Through All, and In All. It's the Only Cause. It's Supreme and Omnipotent. There's nothing to oppose It.

Will you tell me what can oppose Omnipotence? Is there something? Produce it. Show it to me. Let me look at it. It has no reality. It's a shadow in your mind. Fear is a conglomeration of sinister shadows. You are fighting a shadow in your mind. You are the creator of your own fears. These fears have no reality.

Come back, therefore, to the One Presence and the One Power. When you reject and refuse to believe that any person, place, thing, condition, or circumstance can hurt or harm you, then you are on the way. That's your great rejection. Then comes the great affirmation:

> *I am God, and there is no God beside me. From the rising of the sun to the setting of the same, there is none else. I am the Lord, thy God. My glory you shall not give to another, neither shall you give my praise. I am the Lord, thy God, that brought thee out of the land of Egypt, out of the house of bondage. There is no other God before me. I am, and there is none else.*
>
> *And the Lord is my light and my salvation. Whom shall I fear?*
>
> *The Lord is the strength of my life; of whom shall I be afraid? For in time of trouble He will hide me in His pavilion. In the secret of His tabernacle He shall hide me. He shall set me up upon a rock—the rock of truth—the same yesterday, today, and forever.*

Are you standing on that rock? It's All-Powerful, All-Wise, the Ever-Living One, the All-Wise One, the All-Knowing One. You are the Trinity yourself. You are the triangle, and you are the circle. The triangle is the Spirit, mind, and body. You are this being. There is only One Power, One Presence, and Its Source is Love. It has no opposition. It is the Life Principle. It has overcome every opposition in this world and goes on conquering. There is nothing to oppose It. It is Omnipotent.

Thoreau wrote that we are born to succeed, not fail. You were born to win. How could the Infinite within you fail? Meditate on this.

Do not look for flattery from others. Do not look to others for promotion or aggrandizement. Turn within and realize that success is yours, harmony is yours, right action is yours, and beauty is yours. And when you establish the mental equivalent in your mind, there is no person, place, thing, or any power in the world that can prevent you from promotion, recognition, expression, or achieving your goal, for the Infinite cannot fail. You are a Spiritual being. You are one with the Infinite. The Infinite cannot fail. You don't want dominion over other people. You want dominion over your own thoughts, feelings, actions, and reactions. And you want that now.

Many have faith in evil powers that will bring harm to them. Others have faith in a hell, a lake of fire waiting for them. All of this, of course, is utter nonsense. Faith is an attitude, an expectancy. Some expect to be passed over for promotion. Whatever you deeply expect, of course, you will experience. How can you believe in a good future if you fear death and torment? You cannot. There is only One Power.

Do not think that God is cruel and He is punishing you, that God has created a hell for you because you have erred, when you couldn't help yourself anyway. All humans have to err, because that's the only way we are going to grow and expand. It's impossible for anybody to banish fear if you've been indoctrinated in a fear of the future and the afterlife—if you've been taught that God is a God of fear. But God is a God of love.

In order to banish abnormal fear, you have to come back to the fundamental truth that there is but One Power. The Lord, thy God, is One Lord, One Power. Not two or three, or a thousand. Just one. It moves as unity. It is all love, all peace, all harmony. Align yourself with that and all fear will go away.

When we're fearful or indulge in negative thoughts, we're vibrating at a low level. When we meditate on the Psalms and say, "The Lord is my shepherd; I shall not want," or "The Presence of God is right here where I am," or "I dwell in the secret place of the Most High and God is guiding me now," we are thinking spiritually. We are vibrating at a higher level at a spiritual frequency. And just as when we place a finger on a tuning fork, it is the end of the negative vibration. This is the end of the evil, because evil is a false belief about God and the Infinite Goodness of the One Who Forever Is.

You have the capacity to easily destroy and neutralize fear by simply changing the thought. Fear depresses, suppresses, and strangles. If it were indulged in, it would change a positive, creative mental attitude into a nonproductive, negative one, and this is fatal to achievement. The effect of fear, especially when it has become habitual, is to dry up the very source of life. Faith that replaces fear has just the opposite effect upon the body and brain. It enlarges, opens up the nature, gives abundant life to the cells, and increases brainpower.

Fear works terrible havoc with the imagination, which pictures all sorts of dire things. Faith is its perfect antidote, for while fear sees only the darkness and the shadows, faith sees the silver lining, the sun behind the cloud. Fear looks down and expects the worst; faith looks up and anticipates the best. Fear always predicts failure; faith predicts success. There can be no fear of poverty or failure when the mind is dominated by faith. Doubt cannot exist in its presence. It is above all adversity.

A powerful faith is a great life-prolonger because it never frets; it sees beyond the temporary annoyance, the discord, the trouble; it sees the sun behind the cloud. It knows that things will come out right, because it sees the goal that the eye cannot see.

You can cast out fear. You can affirm boldly by repeating:

I have absolute trust in the God Presence within me. I expect the best. I know that only good can come to me. Divine love in me casts out fear. I am at peace. I see the Presence of God everywhere. I am absolutely fearless. God, or the Divine Presence, is with me always. It made me, created me, and sustains me. It is the Invisible Life Principle within me. It loves me and cares for me, for it is written: "He cares for me." If God be for me, who can be against me? I know that one with God is a majority. This heals and frees me from all sense of fear. Only God's thoughts come to me. These thoughts continually unfold, bringing me harmony, joy, peace, and success. I am surrounded by Divine love. I think rightly on all occasions. God's Power is with my thoughts of good. The love, the life, and the truth of God flow through me now. I am immersed in the Holy Omnipresence. The Infinite Ocean of Peace always surrounds me. I am full of Divine understanding. Divine love goes before me, today and every day, to make straight, perfect, and joyous my way.

In this meditation, you're sending the messengers of peace, love, harmony, right action, and beauty into your subconscious mind. And these messengers fulfill your orders. They are faithful messengers. You will discover that all your ways are pleasantness and all your paths are peace.

You are one with your Father within, and your Father is God. He said, fear not, little flock, for it is your Father's good pleasure to give you the kingdom. And that kingdom of God is within you. The love, the light, and the glory of God surrounds you, enfolds you and enwraps you. The Divine Presence governs you now. You love to work with others. You love to represent and express God's ideas.

So, affirm boldly:

God's ideas unfold within me bringing me harmony, health, peace, and joy. I will fear no evil for Thou art with me. Thy rod

*and Thy staff they comfort me. I know goodness and mercy
follow me all the days of my life, for I dwell in the house of God
forever. I dwell in the secret place of the Most High. I abide in
the shadow of the Almighty. I will say of the Lord: He is my
refuge, my fortress, my God; in Him will I trust. He covers me
with His feathers, and under His wing shall I rest. The truth of
God is my shield and buckler. His angels watch over me. They
bear me up lest I dash my foot against a stone, for God is love
and He cares for me.*

In a Nutshell

Fear is like a poison gas pumped into one's atmosphere. It causes
mental, moral, and spiritual asphyxiation, and sometimes death—
death to energy, death to tissue, and death to all growth.

Fear and worry make us attract the very things we dread. The
fear habit impairs health, shortens life, and paralyzes efficiency.
Doubt and fear mean failure; faith is an optimist, fear a pessimist.

Do not let yourself be subservient to another's thoughts. Have
a healthy, reverent respect for your thought, because your thought
is your prayer. What you feel, you attract; what you imagine, you
become.

Your thought governs you, not another. So stand tall. Stand up
straight, and say, "I am one with the Infinite, which lies stretched
in smiling repose."

Fearful people are always very selfish. They are wrapped up
in themselves. Love is always outgoing. It is an emanation. Fear is
turning within in morbid introspection, believing someone is going
to hurt you, that evil spirits can possess you. All this is ignorance.
Ignorance is the only sin, and all the punishment is the consequence
of that ignorance. Ignorance is the only devil in the world.

Realize that fear is a thought in your own mind created by
yourself. It has no reality; it's a shadow in your mind. The thing
you're afraid of does not exist. Fear is faith in the wrong thing.

Fear is faith upside down. Fear is God upside down. It's a twisted, morbid concept of life.

God is the Life Principle. The Trinity is your Spirit, mind, and body. And the mind is the priest, or the intermediary, between the Invisible and the visible; namely, your own thought. Therefore, the Spirit responds to the nature of your thoughts.

All humans have to err, because that's the only way we are going to grow and expand. It's impossible to banish fear if you've been indoctrinated in a fear of the future and afterlife—if you've been taught that God is a God of fear. But God is a God of love.

In order to banish abnormal fear, you have to come back to the fundamental truth that there is but One Power. The Lord, thy God, is One Lord, One Power. Not two or three or a thousand. Just one. It moves as unity. It is all love, all peace, and all harmony. Align yourself with that and all fear will go away.

•• ••

Chapter Four

The Healing Power of Love

There is only one love. It is pure, perfect, undefiled, approving, abundant, and generous. It never changes nor wavers nor weakens. It is God. We love because God first loved us. God is the source of love. Love frees and gives; it is the Spirit of God. You practice love when you have an emanation of goodwill. It's an outreaching of the heart, wishing for every person what you wish for yourself, such as health, happiness, peace, and all the blessings of life. Whatever you think and feel, you also create in your own life, in your own body, and in your own circumstances. This One Power has no opposition. It is the Omnipotent Life Principle that has overcome every opposition in this world. It is forever victorious.

This is the basic truth of every religion of the world during all the ages of time. The heightened expansive awareness of this essential nature of a supreme, intelligent, and loving Presence has been expressed and iterated by every inspired leader of whom we have knowledge. All have insisted that just as the sun shines equally on the rich and the poor, the strong and the weak, the intelligent and the ignorant, the holy and the blasphemous, God's absolute love shines on and is radiant within all people.

No one is excluded from the love of God, nor is anyone forgotten, neglected, or lost in Divine love. It is omnipresent, omniscient, and all-inclusive. Everybody who begins to live in the conscious awareness of absolute and holy love will experience a

definite response of Divine love within—no matter where, when, or what is taking place around them—no matter who they are.

God's love responds to everyone as a liberating, lightening of the heart. It is a higher awareness of consciousness, which heals and makes us whole again.

You must have a healthy, reverent, wholesome respect for the Divinity within you, which shapes your ends. The Bible tells us: "Love thy neighbor as thyself." By "neighbor," it means the closest thing to you, which is the Living Spirit Almighty—closer than breathing, nearer than hands and feet.

Love in the Bible is giving all your loyalty, devotion, and recognition to the Divine Presence within you. Emerson said, "I, the imperfect, adore the Perfect." So put it first in your life. Then you will automatically respect the Divinity in others. You can't honor the Divinity in another if you don't honor it in yourself. How could you? That's what "Love thy neighbor as thyself" means, for the self of you is the neighbor, the closest thing to you.

This is not egotism, egoism, self-aggrandizement, or narcissism. Not at all. It's having a healthy reverence for the God Presence within you, which created you and the whole world. Surely, if you don't honor and exalt that in yourself, how can you honor it and exalt it in your wife, husband, son, daughter, or anybody?

Some people are unsure what is meant by "love" in the Bible and other religious writings. We're taught to "love" everyone— good and bad alike. "Love" here means to see the presence of God everywhere, present in everything, the life energy of humankind— saint and sinner alike.

Let's reconsider the intent of the word *love* and lift our minds above what the world generally considers to be Divine love. It is the pure essence of being that joins and binds in harmony the universe and everything in it. It is the greatest harmonizing principle we know. It is the universal solvent. It is a love that shines on the just and the unjust; Divine love loves for the sake and joy of loving.

Love in the Divine sense is an act of compassion and mercy, and our every attempt to practice Divine love is effective at some time,

in a certain way. Granted, we are not perfect, but we can become committed to practicing and living according to the Golden Rule and the law of love.

Murray L. was a successful business executive. He was respected and admired by his employees, his customers, and his community. He came to me one day, very upset. "I have been chosen by our Chamber of Commerce as "Man of the Year." It is a great honor, but I have to give a speech at the presentation. I'm absolutely terrified when it comes to public speaking. What can I do?"

I suggested that he go to a quiet place three or four times a day where he would not be disturbed. He should sit comfortably in an armchair and relax his body to the utmost. This physical inertia would render his mind more receptive to his affirmations. Then I told him to say the following aloud:

I am completely relaxed and at ease. I am poised, serene, and calm. At the presentation I will make a fine speech; I will be calm and collected. I will present my message clearly and with confidence. The audience will be friendly and receptive and enjoy my speech. I will do this because God is within me, and He gives me the strength and courage I need. My message is God's message. My speech is God speaking through me. The audience congratulates me. I am at peace in my mind.

Murray did this each day prior to the presentation. When he stood on the dais facing his audience, he was confident and at ease. He spoke flawlessly and was given a standing ovation.

When you mentally and emotionally unite with honesty, integrity, justice, goodwill, and happiness, you love God, because you love that which is good. You're loving God when you're fascinated, absorbed, and captivated by the great truth that God is One and Indivisible, and there are no divisions or quarrels in It. To love God is to give your allegiance, devotion, and loyalty to the One Power, refusing to recognize any other power in the world. When you definitely recognize and completely accept in your mind

that God really is Omnipotent in the most practical, literal, and most matter-of-fact manner, you are loving God, because you're loyal to the One Power.

Sit down quietly at times and think over this vital, interesting, fascinating, and greatest of all truths: that God is the only Power, that everything we can become aware of is part of His self-expression.

A young mother approached me after one of my lectures. She told me how afraid she was of hurting her children. She said, "I have a very bad temper. I'm easily upset, and even when my children do trivial things that annoy me, I scream at them and sometimes hit them. The poor kids are afraid of me, and I'm afraid that someday I'll really hurt them."

I told her, "You must cleanse your subconscious mind of anger. It's not easy, but you must replace the anger that may have been inculcated in your mind when you were a child by parents or teachers or others in authority. Several times a day, when the children are at school or away, go to a quiet place and repeat the following meditation:

God's love fills my soul. God is with me now. Free me from the thoughts of anger that have permeated my mind. My children are good. They want to be loved, not punished. Divine love flows through me to them. God's love for me will help me control my temper and will sink deep into my subconscious mind so that my actions will reflect this love.

It didn't take long. God's Power captivated her imagination. It filled her through and through. She became entranced with the idea of being a good mother. This love caused her to persist in her efforts to control her anger. This, truly, is love. Soon the feelings of anger went away; it was swallowed up in love, because love and anger cannot dwell together.

The Bible says: "By this shall all know that you are my disciples: If you love one another." God is absolute love. Hence, it follows that

before the appeal is made, the answer is given. The love of God flows through you now. You are surrounded by the peace of God. All is well.

Affirm boldly: "Divine love surrounds me, enfolds me, and encompasses me. This Infinite love is inscribed in my heart and written on my inward parts. I radiate love in thought, words, and deeds. Love unifies and harmonizes all the powers, attributes, and qualities of God within me."

Love means joy, peace, freedom, bliss, and praise. Love is freedom. It opens prison doors and sets free all the captives.

Everyone represents Divine love in operation. I salute the Divinity in the other. I know and believe that Divine love heals me now. Love is the guiding principle in me. It brings into my experience perfect, harmonious relationships. God is love, and those who dwell in love dwell in God, and God in them. You must believe that the love, the light, and the glory of God surrounds you, enfolds you, and enwraps you. And into whatsoever house you enter, first say, "Peace be unto this house."

Affirm boldly:

My mind is flooded with the life, the love, and the truth of God. Whenever my attention wanders away, I bring it back to the contemplation of His Divine Presence. I enter into the secret chamber within myself. It is my own mind where I walk and talk with the Infinite. I am in the heavens of my own mind because I am at peace. I am perfectly quiet, calm, serene, and poised. Peace be within thy walls and prosperity within thy palaces. For my brethren and companions' sake, I will say, "Peace be within thee."

I live in the house of the Lord, my God. I seek only the good. I am living in His kingdom. I feel and sense the Divine atmosphere of peace, love, and joy. I stir up the gift of God within me. I know that I and my Father are one. I sense and feel the reality of this. His life flows through me now. I know that in this heaven where I live, move, and have my being all my prayers are answered. I am at peace. The dove of love has whispered in my ear, "Peace

be still." For God is the Only Presence and the Only Power and the Only Presence here now. And all the rest is but shadow. In Him we live, move, and have our being. God's love, life, and truth move in me now.

Fear thoughts, worry thoughts . . . negative thoughts of any kind will not hurt you unless you entertain them for a long period of time and emotionalize them deeply. Otherwise, they won't hurt you in the slightest. They're potentially troublesome for you, but as yet, they're not actualized. Your fears cannot be actualized unless you emotionalize them, thereby impressing your subconscious mind. Whatever is impressed on the subconscious mind is impressed and expressed on the screen of space. So into whatsoever house ye enter, first say, "Peace be unto this house." For God is love, and those that dwell in love dwell in God and God in them.

You are dwelling in the secret place of the Most High, because your mind is a secret place. No one knows what you're thinking or planning, so you're thinking on whatsoever things are true, whatsoever things are lovely, whatsoever things are just, whatsoever things are pure, and whatsoever things are of good report. If there be any virtue, if there be any praise, think on these things. For you are what you think about all day long. For as you think in your heart, so you are, so do you experience, and so do you become. Under His wings you shall trust. His truth is your shield and buckler.

In a Nutshell

There is only one love. It is pure, perfect, undefiled, approving, abundant, and generous. It never changes nor wavers nor weakens. It is God. We love because God first loved us. God is the Source of love.

God's love responds to everyone as a liberating, lightening of the heart. It is a higher awareness of consciousness, which heals and makes us whole again.

Love in the Divine sense is an act of compassion and mercy, and our every attempt to practice Divine love is effective at some time, in a certain way. Granted, we are not perfect, but we can become committed to practicing and living according to the Golden Rule and the law of love.

To love God is to give your allegiance, devotion, and loyalty to the One Power, refusing to recognize any other power in the world. When you definitely recognize and completely accept in your mind that God really is Omnipotent in the most practical, literal, and most matter-of-fact manner, you are loving God, because you are loyal to the One Power.

Faith is an attitude of mind. It's a way of thinking. You have faith if you have a mental image of accomplishing something wonderful, and if you sustain it with expectancy and confidence, your subconscious mind will bring that to pass.

If you want to conquer fear, you have to come back to the truth that there is only One Power, Indivisible, and One Source of love. When you know that, when you align with It, you can't be fearful; you can't worry. This Power has no opposition. There is nothing to oppose, challenge, vitiate, or thwart It. It is the Life Principle. It has overcome every opposition in the world. It's Omnipotent and All-Powerful.

The love, the light, and the glory of God surrounds you, enfolds you, and enwraps you. The Divine Presence governs you now. You love to work with others. You love to represent and express God's ideas. So, affirm boldly: "God's ideas unfold within me, bringing me harmony, health, peace, and joy.

·•· ·•·

Chapter Five

--- • • • ---

The Inner Meaning of the 23rd Psalm

The Lord is my shepherd; I shall not want.
He maketh me to lie down in green pastures: he leadeth me
besidethe still waters.
He restoreth my soul: he leadeth me in the paths of righteousness
for his name's sake.
Yea, though I walk through the valley of the shadow of death,
I will fear no evil: for thou art with me; thy rod and thy
staff they comfort me.
Thou preparest a table before me in the presence of mine enemies:
thou anointest my head with oil; my cup runneth over.
Surely goodness and mercy shall follow me all the days of my life:
and I will dwell in the house of the Lord forever.

This is the 23rd Psalm. This is probably the most frequently repeated psalm from the Judeo-Christian Bible. Many people of all faiths meditate on the great truths of this psalm. They get marvelous results. As you focus your attention on these truths, absorbing them into your mentality, you're meditating in the true sense of the word, because you're appropriating more of your Divinity, the Divine Presence that dwells deep within all people.

Meditation determines your destiny. We're always meditating. Your thoughts and feelings control your destiny. Meditation is as real and as natural as digestion, assimilation, and breathing.

In Las Vegas I met a woman who suffered from shock. She'd lost her voice, but the doctors could find no infection, no affliction of any kind, when examining the throat and the vocal organs. At my suggestion, she began to practice what I call *real meditation*. Her son was coming home from Vietnam in a few weeks, and she sat still and quiet and imagined that she was embracing him and welcoming him home, saying all the things that a mother would say. She did this for about ten minutes, two or three times a day. She gave attention to a selected goal, an objective. At the end of two weeks, her son came home, knocked at the door, and she welcomed him. She began to talk naturally. That's real meditation. She gave attention to her voice, to the fact that she was talking, and to the fact that she was welcoming him. It was a mental and spiritual drama taking place in her own mind.

The Lord is my shepherd. The *Lord* means God, the Living Spirit Almighty, in particular, your awareness and knowledge of this Infinite Presence and Power within you. The shepherd takes care of the sheep, and the Divine Power will take care of you. As you turn to this Indwelling Presence, Its nature is to respond to you.

You are told: *I shall not want.* This means that you will never want for evidence of the fact that you have chosen God as your shepherd. Shepherds watch over their sheep. They love them and care for them. They examine the field where they graze and eradicate locoweed, which would harm the sheep. They lead them to the shade and guide them single file over the steep ravine to water, where they're refreshed. At night they examine the sheep's nostrils to see if there are any needles or other irritants embedded therein. If so, they pluck them out and pour some soothing oil upon them. They also examine their feet, and, if injured, administer kindly to them with whatever medication or treatment is appropriate.

Shepherds love their sheep. All of this is symbolic, of course, and very significant, indicating to all of us that if we choose God as our shepherd, and God is the Living Spirit within us, the Supreme Intelligence, the Life Principle, then we will not want for any good thing.

Before we get an answer to our prayer, we must first possess our desire in consciousness. We must establish the mental equivalent. We do this by thinking of what we want with interest and feeling, and by giving it our attention. Gradually, by osmosis, it sinks into our subconscious mind and becomes a conviction.

Our consciousness represents the sum total of our acceptances and beliefs, both conscious and subconscious. Our state of consciousness is the way we think, feel, and believe, and whatever we give mental consent to. That's the Only Presence, Power, Cause, and Substance in your world. When you discover that, you have discovered God within you. In other words, your desire must be deposited in your subconscious mind.

The ancient Hebrews said, "To be is to have." If I try to obtain what I want by external means, the Bible says, I am a thief and a robber. My state of consciousness is the door to all expression. This consciousness is the way you think, feel, and believe. It is done unto you as you believe, the way you believe. I must possess the mental equivalent of whatever I want to be or possess in this world.

Let's take a simple illustration. You want to be healed, and you affirm over and over again: "I am healed." These mechanical statements aren't enough. You must enter into the joy of feeling that you're healed. You must realize that there is an Infinite Healing Presence that created you from a cell. It knows all the processes and functions of your body. It heals a cut in your finger and reduces the edema of a burn. It restores you. The tendency of all life is to heal. This must be a conviction based upon the silent inner knowing of the soul.

To be wealthy, you must assume the *feeling* of being wealthy and realize that God, or Spirit within you, is the Source of the entire world—the Source of the hair on your head, the bread on your table, the shoes that you wear, the ground that you walk on, the air that you breathe, the sun that shines, and the stars that come nightly to the sky. Then wealth will follow based upon your knowledge, awareness, feelings, and understanding.

The sheep are the noble, dignified, Godlike ideas that bless us. Our conviction of good is the shepherd that watches over the sheep. Our dominant state of mind always rules in the same manner as a general commands the army. We call our sheep by name when we enter into the consciousness of them having, being, or doing the thing we long to have, to be, or to do. If we sustain this consciousness, it gels and crystallizes within us, and our desires are manifested.

The sheep will not follow strangers, but will flee from them, for they don't know the voice of strangers. The strangers are the thoughts of fear, doubt, condemnation, jealousy, envy, or anxiety that enter the mind. These ideas delay our healing or prosperity and postpone our demonstration . . . because these thoughts are the voice of strangers.

For example, if there were 20,000 sheep in a corral and ten shepherds, and they came in the morning to lead the sheep out, they would say, "Follow me." All the sheep of each shepherd would know his voice, and they would follow their own shepherd. But if a stranger said, "Follow me," there would be no response. This simply means that when you have the mood or the feeling of being what you long to be, and you know that there is an Almighty Power backing you up and moving in your behalf, then that ideal that you want to bring to pass will come to pass, and the light will shine upon your ways.

It is idle to pray that the Infinite Healing Presence is making you whole and perfect, and at the same time be resentful or fearful that you cannot be healed. If you believe that circumstances, conditions, age, events, race, or lack of money can prevent you from attaining your objective, you are, in biblical language, a thief and a robber, because you are robbing yourself of the joy of the answered prayer. There is nothing to oppose the Infinite, and the Infinite Spirit gave you the desire. The desire is good; therefore, know that Infinite Spirit gave you this desire and will reveal the perfect plan for its development in Divine law and order.

The seed you deposit in the ground has its own mathematics and mechanics in it. The oak is the realized potential of the acorn,

but you must first deposit the acorn in the soil. And the seed is faith, because you understand the Divine law. And the seed is your desire—a new invention, a new book, or a wish to become greater than you are. You must believe that you already are what you long to be. To believe is to be alive to the truth.

•●•

Many people meditate. In India, for example, they give you a word to repeat over and over again. Doing so quiets the mind and concentrates your thoughts. Various people use Sanskrit words such as *Om, Ayim,* or *Sharim.* You may prefer to use a word or phrase more meaningful to you, such as *insight, peace, love,* or *I am.* Any word or phrase will do. Even a term such as *Coca-Cola,* if repeated over and over, will help create a quiet mind. Your blood pressure will drop and your pulse will become normal. But such words will not help you grow in a spiritual way. You could grow spiritually by repeating, "Divine love fills my soul" or "God's peace fills my mind." You must know what you're doing. To say an idle word and not know the meaning of it doesn't accomplish very much.

So many people meditate. Some people meditate on negative things such as financial losses, the blowout on the lonely road, ill health, or bad decisions they've made. That is meditation of a very negative nature, and because you're giving those thoughts your full attention and devotion, they sink into your subconscious mind and you magnify them. Then you bring all these things to pass in your own life.

Meditate on whatsoever things are true, lovely, noble, and Godlike. To meditate is to eat all these truths, to cogitate, to give your attention to the Divine, and to focus on the One Presence. Sir Isaac Newton was asked how he accomplished great things. He said, "I intend my mind in a certain direction." In other words, he focused on a solution, the way out, the happy ending.

You're told that meditation is for the purpose of redirecting your mind to Godlike ways so that Divine law and order may

govern all of your activities in all the phases of your life. There is nothing mysterious about meditation. You're always meditating— but perhaps not always constructively. Shakespeare said, "All things are ready if our minds be so." The Bible says that the works were finished from the foundation of the world. All this means is that we should open our minds and hearts and accept the gifts of God proffered to us from the foundations of time.

We should reorder our minds and ask ourselves the simple question: *How is it in God and heaven?* Heaven is that Infinite Intelligence in which you live and move and have your being. God is Spirit, and that Spirit is in you. The answer to that is: All is bliss, harmony, joy, love, peace, perfection, and all this indescribable beauty.

That's the reality of you, the All-Wise One, the All-Powerful One, the All-Knowing One within you. No matter what you seek, it already is. Why wait for love? God's love is within you. Say, "God's love fills my soul." Peace is. You don't wait for it, do you? "God's peace fills my soul."

The joy of the Lord is your strength. Power *is*. The Almighty Power *is* within you; It's timeless and spaceless. Harmony *is*. God is Absolute Harmony. The harmony of God is in your mind, in your body. The answer to every problem is within you now. For God is the timeless, spaceless Being within you, that Living Spirit Almighty.

No matter what you seek, it already is. Why wait for it? If you say, "Someday I'll be happy," the world won't give you happiness; you need to give it to yourself. If you're seeking guidance, affirm: "Infinite Intelligence knows the answer, the way out. Even before I ask, as I call on the Supreme Wisdom, I know that Its nature is to respond to me. I will clearly recognize the answer when it comes. I know that it comes clearly into my conscious, reasoning mind, and I recognize it instantaneously. It's impossible for me to miss it."

Having done so, dismiss it from your mind, knowing that you have turned your request over to the Infinite Intelligence in your subconscious, and inevitably the answer will come. You know when you've really turned it over because your mind is at peace and you don't subsequently deny what you've already affirmed and decreed.

He maketh me to lie down in green pastures. I am writing this chapter in Laguna Hills, California. A letter arrived in the mail yesterday from a woman in Hawaii telling me that she meditated on these words. For about a half an hour, three times a day for a week, she focused all her attention on this promise of Psalm 23. She began to look at it from all angles—its inner meaning and how it applied to her. She stated that in her meditative mood and in her reflection of these words, the phrase meant peace of mind, contentment, tranquility, abundance, and security.

The vision of a cow lying down in the field chewing the cud came clearly to her, symbolizing the meditative process of her own mind. In chewing the cud, the cow is absorbing, digesting, and transforming everything eaten into milk, tissue, bone, muscle, blood, and so forth. Likewise, she was digesting, ingesting, and absorbing these truths until they, too, became a part of her. So as the cow chews on the clover, it goes from one stomach to another, and then comes up again into the mouth of the cow; and it chews it again and again to a fine consistency, and lo and behold, the cow has the nourishment to produce milk.

That's meditation. The ancients said, "You can eat the cow because it chews the cud and divides the hoof. It's clean unto you." Dividing the hoof is getting a clear understanding of what the truths of God are, separating your mind from that which is false—knowing, therefore, what the truth is. Then you absorb, digest, and give your attention and devotion to these truths. Then you are chewing the cud, and these truths become a part of you like an apple becomes your bloodstream. That's meditation. It's practical; it's down to earth.

I knew a woman whose finances were in bad shape, and she was in danger of losing her lovely home. The mine in which she had invested a large part of her money suddenly collapsed, and her son was missing; no one could find him. As she continued to meditate, at the end of a week she received notice from an attorney that a large sum of money had been bequeathed to her by a distant relative on the big island of Hawaii. This solved her financial

problem, and she was able to make satisfactory arrangements with all concerned. Then her son returned home. He'd run away to Canada thinking that there were greener pastures there. He was wiser on his return and established peace within himself.

This was real meditation of a very constructive nature. The woman appropriated these great truths mentally, and they became a living part of her, the same way that a banana or a piece of bread becomes a part of your bloodstream after being eaten. She quietly devoted her mind to a certain passage of the psalm and dwelled on the profundity of its meaning and its healing power. She decided to lie down mentally with these truths and experience all-around harmony in her life.

He leadeth me beside the still waters. The shepherd in the Bible is a symbol of the guiding, healing, protective power of the Divine Presence within you. You are a good shepherd when you know and believe that God, or the Supreme Intelligence, is the only Presence and Power, Cause, and Substance within you. This is the Power that enables you to walk and lift a chair; it's an unseen Power. When this conviction is enthroned in your mind, you will be Divinely directed and blessed in countless ways because the nature of Infinite Intelligence is responsiveness.

He restoreth my soul. When you choose God, or the Supreme Intelligence, as your shepherd, you will sing the songs of triumph; or, to put it in Emerson's words, your mental attitude will be "the soliloquy of a beholding and jubilant soul." For prayer is the contemplation of the truths of God from the highest standpoint. You are recognizing the Infinite Spirit within you, and you know that there will be a response when you call upon It. It's impersonal. It responds to the atheist and the agnostic. It responds to everybody. Call upon It and It answers you. It's no respecter of persons. It knows nothing about Islam, Judaism, Christianity, Buddhism, Shintoism, or any specific creed.

Love belongs to all. The law is always impersonal. Furthermore, you recognize that the Power is one and indivisible. As you recognize this, you reject all fear and false beliefs of the world.

Whatever fears, frustrations, and misguided beliefs were deposited in your subconscious mind can be obliterated and expunged, because you're claiming boldly that the Infinite ocean of life, love, truth, and beauty is saturating your subconscious mind— cleansing, healing, and transforming your whole being into the Divine pattern of harmony, wholeness, and peace. It's similar to pouring distilled water into a bottle of filthy water. After a while, the moment comes when the last drop of dirty water is removed. That's called prayer, filling your mind with the truths of God, and crowding out of your mind everything unlike God.

Once you acknowledge the supremacy of the Supreme Healing Power and the Creative Power of your own thought, you have the Lord as your shepherd, and you have restored your soul.

He leadeth me in the paths of righteousness for his name's sake. Go within. Close your eyes. Become still and quiet, and gently affirm that the wisdom of God anoints your intellect and is always a lamp unto your feet; it's always a light upon your path. Claim that Divine love goes before you, making straight, happy, joyous, and prosperous your way. Look to the Infinite Presence at all times; and think, speak, act, and react from the standpoint of the Divine Center within you. Realize, know, feel, and claim that the Infinite Spirit is your guide, your counselor, your boss, and your senior partner, and that Divine right action governs you at all times.

Affirm boldly:

From now on I think right because I think from the standpoint of eternal verities and principles of life. I feel right. I do right. I act right. And everything I do is in accordance with the eternal principles of Divine law and order, heaven's first law. I know that the name of the Infinite means the nature of the Infinite, which refers to the fact that the God Presence is the Ever-Living One, the All-Powerful One, the All-Knowing One, the Self-Renewing One, the Boundless One. And He is Omnipresent

and Omniscient, and is also the omni-action of the Infinite. You
know that the Infinite and His love saturate your whole being;
whatever you do will prosper.

So, realize that the Infinite is within you. It's called the Ever-Living One, the All-Wise One, the All-Knowing One, the Self-Renewing One, the One who lives in the hearts of all people. It is older than night or day, younger than the newborn babe, brighter than light, darker than dark, beyond all things and creatures, yet fixed in the hearts of everyone. And from it the shining worlds flow forth. The whole world comes forth from the One Presence and the One Power. So, It is you. You came forth from the Infinite, also. The whole world is a creation of the Infinite.

In the Upanishads, the mystic teachings of the Hindus, it says: "God thinks and worlds appear." So, the whole world, modern science says, is a thought of the One, the Beautiful, and the Good. The whole world is also mathematically ordered by a Supreme Intelligence, so scientists can predict the return of Halley's comet to a split second. It is a Divinely ordered universe, so the astronauts, before they left Earth, could calculate mathematically that they could walk out in space. And, of course, they could. They had faith—not in a human or a corporeal personality; or a creed, a dogma, or a church—not at all. They had faith in the Creative Laws of Mind, and principles that never change; it is the same yesterday, today, and forever.

Engineers have faith in the principles of mathematics. When they build bridges, they conform to universal principles of stress and strain, the curvature of the earth, and other things. They calculate the whole project mathematically. Navigators flying through the Pacific may not know where they are, but by "shooting the stars," they calculate the location, and the latitude and longitude. Likewise, when you're lost or confused, you can shoot that great star within you, the I AM, the Presence of God, the Om of India. It's the Living Spirit Almighty. Contact that. It's All-Wise. It created the whole world.

Realize that Infinite Intelligence knows the answer, guides and directs you, leads you, and reveals the answer to you, for It knows *only* the answer. This is why you read: Before you call, I will answer. Before you call, the answer is there, waiting for you, for the Infinite will do nothing for you except through you. The Infinite works on a cosmic scale, and you're an individual. You're free to choose; you have volition, choice, and initiative. You have the freedom to become a cutthroat or a holy person. You're not compelled to be good, not compelled to be honest, and not compelled to express love. You're not compelled to be successful. You have freedom of choice. You can choose from the kingdom of God within you. You can choose harmony. You can choose right action, which is the principle of life. You can choose beauty, love, inspiration, abundance, and security. You can choose from the Infinite Resources within you, from that Infinite Presence and Power that is All-Wise and knows all. You have volition and choice and initiative.

Your state of consciousness is the only God you'll ever know. Your state of consciousness is the way you think, feel, and believe, and what you give mental consent to. There is no other Cause, Power, or Substance in this world.

Therefore, if you're wise, you'll begin to believe in the goodness of God in the land of the living, in the guidance of God, the harmony of God, and the love of God. And you realize that your sheep are the lovely, noble, Godlike states you wish to embody. And they'll follow you as you begin to feel that you now are what you long to be, that you're now doing what you love to do. If you're a singer, you're now the great singer; and God is singing in majestic cadences through you. As you continue, God in the midst of you will bring it to pass.

Yea, though I walk through the valley of the shadow of death, I will fear no evil: for thou art with me; Thy rod and thy staff they comfort me. Wherever you go, walk the earth with the awareness of peace, love, and goodwill to all. Suppose you go to a hospital to see a sick

friend and you're taking with you the mood of love, peace, and goodwill. Well, that's a wonderful way to visit a sick person. Your mental and spiritual atmosphere will bless this person. And when you pray for this individual, never identify with symptoms, pains, aches, or corporeal conditions. Realize that the Presence of God is where the sick person is; and realize that the vitality, wholeness, and perfection of the Infinite are now being made manifest to the loved one. Then you see the loved one as the loved one ought to be. The person should be home; you don't see that person in the hospital as being sick, wan, and weak. You're fastening that sickness on the person. You're also creating it in your own mind. It doesn't make any sense.

If you're praying for wholeness, vitality, perfection, peace, and harmony, and for the miraculous Healing Power to flow through the person, visualize that person home, vital and alive. Your image must agree with your affirmation. This is why so many people don't know how to pray and this is why many do more harm than good. It's because they're identifying with the sickness, condition, tumor, or whatever it might be. Or they look at the medical chart and say, "It's terrible; he hasn't got a chance," and so forth. That's no way to pray.

Your mental and spiritual atmosphere can bless the person if you have the right attitude. Give the person a transfusion of faith, confidence, trust, and love. Tell the person that the Miraculous Healing Power is within him or her; and give that person a transfusion of grace, love, power, and wisdom, thereby nourishing him or her with confidence and a belief in the Infinite Healing Presence. God is life; that is your life now. Do that whenever you visit a hospital or a sick person. Give that person a transfusion of life, love, and beauty.

God is life, and that is your life now. So, life cannot die; that would be absurd. Why talk about death? There is no death. It's a shadow. A shadow has no reality. In other words, how could life die? How could God die? God was never born and will never die; water wets It not, fire burns It not, wind blows It not away. It has no beginning or end. It's the Life Principle within you. How in

the name of heaven could life become death? It's absurd! So-called death is an entry into the fourth dimension of life, and you go there every night in your sleep. That's where you go when you're called "dead." Your journey is from glory to glory, from wisdom to wisdom—ever onward, upward, and Godward.

There is no death. If a lightbulb goes out, do you say, "That's the end of electricity," or do you insert another bulb? Electricity *is*. It was here before Jesus, Moses, Elijah, Mohammed, or Buddha walked the earth. So was the idea of the principle of radio, television, submarines, or airplanes. They could have used these things, but the idea didn't come to them. They didn't think it was possible. They were human, like all of us. They were born, like all of us. It may be that some appropriated more Divinity than others. They were all born, like all of us, for all humans are children of God. What else could they be? There is only One Life, One Spirit. We are all children of the One. That's why all religions of the world say, "Our Father." We have a common Progenitor, the Life Principle.

That's why, when you radiate love, peace, and goodwill to another, you are selfish because you are blessing yourself. When you hurt another, you hurt yourself. Objectively, we are all one; subjectively, we seem to be somewhat different—just like the various countries in the world. Above the ocean, they all seem to be different. Underneath there is a unitary wholeness. They are all connected deep down in the ocean. Likewise, we are all one. To hurt another is to hurt yourself; to bless another is to bless yourself. When you radiate love, peace, and goodwill to all those where you are working and to all those people in this country and every other country, you are selfish because you are blessing yourself.

There is no end to the glory that is humankind. The journey of your loved one is ever onward, upward, and Godward. You can't be less tomorrow than you are today. Life goes not backward nor tarries with yesterday. Tell me honestly: If someone is lost up in the air, do you go up there and say, "This is where he was born" or "This is where he passed on"? No, you don't. Likewise, if many people were lost in an ocean catastrophe, do you go out in the

ocean and post a little sign saying, "This is where they were born" or "This is where they died"? All these things are lies. All graves are lies, because there's no one who died anyplace and there's no one buried anyplace. Do you think that Eisenhower is buried someplace, or President Kennedy? That's absurd! No one is buried anyplace. There are no graveyards except the graveyards you make in your own mind. The earthly remains may be interred, but the real person lives on.

If something happens to a piano and it's burned up, is that the end of music? Music just *is*. It transcends all instruments. You have bodies to Infinity. You'll never be without a body. You have a body now. That's why the wise and spiritually illumined person today never visits a graveyard, because there's no one there. They asked of Socrates: "Master, where will we bury you?" He looked at them, laughed, and said, "Bury me anyplace if you can catch me." How could you bury someone anywhere? That's too stupid for words. You have bodies to Infinity, a fourth-dimensional body. You'll never be without a body; you couldn't be. You have it now. And the body undergoes dissolution; it becomes grass, hail, and snow; but there is no one buried anyplace. To go to a grave is to identify with lack, limitation, cessation, and misery; and you create graveyards in your own mind and bring on all manner of disease. Never do it.

Give the love in your heart to your loved ones. They are right where you are. They are around you, separated by frequency only. In other words, wake up. You have another body. You have it now. It's rarefied and attenuated, enabling you to pass through solid matter. You will meet your loved ones; you will grow in wisdom, truth, and beauty. The little child whose life was snuffed out in the womb still grows and expands as a grace note in the grand symphony of all creation. It will be a beautiful girl or boy when you meet it in the next dimension, for life is growth. Life is newness and expansion. Actually, you go there every night, as I said, when you go to sleep.

If, for example, you're afraid of death, the afterlife, judgment day, and things of that nature, then you're being governed by

ignorance, delusion, and by false beliefs of all kinds. For God has not given us the spirit of fear, but of power, love, and a sound mind. Death, in biblical language, is ignorance of the truth. That's the only death there is. We die only to the illusions of the world, to the creeds and dogmas of the world, to the fears and the false beliefs of the world.

Every prayer is a death. You must die to what you are before you can live what you long to be. You must die to the belief in poverty and resurrect a God of opulence in your own mind. Death in biblical language is ignorance of the truth of God. Ignorance is the only sin, and all the misery and suffering in this world is the result of ignorance. Buddha discovered that thousands of years ago. He asked Brahma the cause of all the suffering and misery in the world; and Brahma (which means God) answered him: Ignorance. Teach the people the truth and set them free. That's the answer he got, and that was 5,000 years B.C.

Thy rod and thy staff they comfort me. They asked Moses: What do you have in your hand? He said, the rod. And he threw it on the ground and it became a serpent, crawling. Do you crawl on the ground? Do you resurrect the Divinity within you? Do you realize that one with God is a majority? Do you realize you that you can think of the Infinite now? That It moves on your behalf? Or do you crawl along the ground, governed by your five senses? You catch it by its tail, you know. Moses smote the rock, and lo and behold, the water came forth. Then that rod swallowed up all the false rods of the Egyptians.

The rod is the Power of God, the Wisdom of God. When you touch that Power, call upon It. It responds to you, and all the rods of the Egyptians (meaning ignorance, fear, and false beliefs) are swallowed up. So, the staff represents your authority and ability to use it.

To meditate and think about the Omnipotence and Omniscience of the Infinite Presence brings your mind to an inner state of quietude and passivity. Think of a beautiful, quiet lake on a mountaintop and how it reflects the heavenly lights, such as the stars and the moon. Likewise, when your mind is still

and quiet, you will reflect the heavenly truths and lights of God. The quiet mind gets things done. When your mind is still, quiet, and receptive, the Divine idea or solution to your problem rises to your surface mind. That is the guidance and intuitive voice of the Infinite Presence and Power.

When the lake in the mountain is disturbed, it doesn't reflect the lights of the heavens above. When your mind is quiet, the answer comes. A quiet mind gets things done. Claim that Infinite Intelligence is guiding you now, and give thanks for the joy of the answered prayer. The Power is omnipotent; there is nothing to oppose It. How could you have peace unless you've discovered the Power? Peace comes on the heels of your discovery of the Infinite Presence and Power. There is nothing in the world to oppose It. It's omnipotent and all-powerful. Otherwise, works have no meaning. There is no power in the stars, suns, moons, voodoo, or anything of that nature. That is all based on ignorance. A scientific thinker doesn't give power to the created thing; he gives power to the Creator.

Thou preparest a table before me in the presence of mine enemies. The enemies are your own thoughts, your fears, your self-condemnation, your jealousy, your envy, your doubts, your anger, and resentment and ill will. These are real enemies, but they are in your own mind. When fear thoughts come to your mind, supplant them with faith in God and all things good. When prone to engage in criticism and self-condemnation, the most destructive of all mental poisons, supplant these thoughts immediately with this great truth: "I exalt God in the midst of me, mighty to heal."

A young lady was making false allegations against her uncle, hoping to break a will so she could get some of the money bequeathed to him. He was angry and fighting the matter in his mind, making a nervous wreck of himself. However, when he saw what he was doing, he ceased fighting the matter in his mind and began to feed himself spiritually with the great truths of the Infinite, which, of course, are in meditation. Meditation is simply to ponder upon, to consider with purpose, to get interested in, to get fascinated about, and to get absorbed in a certain truth

so it becomes a part of you. That's all it means. There is nothing mysterious about it.

The uncle began to think of the great truths of the Infinite. He contemplated peace, harmony, and Divine right action. There is a principle of right action; there is no principle of wrong action in the world. He realized that there was a Divine, harmonious solution. He stopped giving power to her. She had no power. She was full of greed, avarice, and false beliefs. Of course, the whole thing was dissolved, and the judge dismissed the woman's claim. The uncle realized that an Infinite law of justice, truth, love, and harmony reigned.

A medical doctor, a close friend of mine, said to me recently that the publicity given to the wives of two prominent politicians in Washington who had developed breast cancer caused a great deal of fear. A number of women flocked to him for tests to see if they, too, had cancer. He added that he felt that fighting cancer, tuberculosis, heart disease, and so forth through propaganda on the screen, radio, and in print does more harm than good because what we fight in our mind we magnify. He pointed out that the constant fear of cancer on the part of these women would ultimately create precisely the thing they fear.

You should fight nothing. Think instead of love, harmony, health, peace, and right action. Walk in the consciousness of God's love, peace, wholeness, and perfection. You will automatically rise above these false beliefs, fears, and propaganda of the mass mind.

There is a prayer used in India by many people, which the young boy in a spiritually oriented family is taught: "I am all health. Brahma is my health." *Brahma* is a Hindu word for "God." As the young boy sings this to himself many times a day, it becomes a habit. As he is impressionable and malleable, he gradually builds up immunity to all sickness and disease instead of being taught that the night air gives him pneumonia, that God is going to punish him, that he's a bad boy and is going to get the measles and the whooping cough, and that he'll never amount to anything. That's what some kids are taught today. They're like little animals.

Your children grow in the imagery and likeness of the dominant mental climate of the home. Teach them the Golden Rule and the law of love. Teach them to respect the Divinity within themselves and to respect the police officer and the teacher, and they'll respect their father and mother, too. Realize that there is nothing in God's universe to fear. Cease giving power to the created thing. Stop being ignorant. Give power to the Creator. The whole universe is for you; nothing is against you.

Thou anointest my head with oil. Oil is a symbol of light, healing, praise, and thanksgiving. This means that the Infinite Healing Presence is now functioning on your behalf, and the wisdom of God anoints your intellect. You are consecrated with Divine love. You have put gladness in your heart. God has anointed you with the oil of gladness.

One of the most wonderful ways to get an answer to your prayer is to imagine that you're addressing the Infinite in the silence of your soul. Lull yourself to sleep with the words "Thank you, Father," over and over again, until you get the feeling of thankfulness. You don't change the Infinite by begging or beseeching, by prayer, or by anything; but when you enter into the mood of thankfulness, you are rising high in your mind to the point of acceptance, and the good things of life begin to flow to you.

You are thanking the Infinite for the answer to your prayer. As you do so, you carry a thankful attitude to the deep of yourself, to the point of acceptance. You don't create harmony, peace, love, or beauty; you don't create anything. All these things *are,* and God never changes. God doesn't change Himself because you are a Catholic, Protestant, Jew, Muslim, or Hindu, or because you belong to some religion or denomination. That is utter nonsense! You rise to the point of what's true of God. As you claim that and believe it, then your prayer is answered. But you don't change God by your prayer. That's superstition and gross ignorance.

My cup runneth over. The cup is a symbol of your heart, which, by contemplation, you can fill with the great truths of God. As you contemplate the beauty, the glory, and the wonders of the Infinite,

you will automatically generate a feeling of love, peace, and joy, which fills your heart with ecstasy and rapture. You are able to pass that cup. You are able to say to others: "Drink ye all of this." Drink of love, wisdom, power, and beauty. How can you drink of it except that you have it? You can't give what you don't have.

So, the cup is your heart. It's not a fancy teacup or some antique vessel in a British museum. This is metaphoric; it's a mystical cup. It belongs to all of us. You will find yourself exuding vibrancy, cordiality, geniality, and goodwill to all as you fill your soul with love. Your subconscious magnifies exceedingly what you deposit in it. Therefore, you find that your good is pressed down, shaken together, and running over with the fragrance of the Infinite. You will find that God's love has completely dissolved everything negative in your subconscious, and you are as free as the wind. And goodness and mercy will follow you all the days of your life because you *dwell in the house of the Lord forever.*

As you continue to meditate and absorb these truths, you will discover that all things are working together for good. Divine love goes before you, making happy and joyous your way. The harmony, peace, and joy of the Lord flow into your life, and you find yourself expressing your talents at the highest possible level. You will discover that you become what you contemplate. When meditating on the truths of God, you will find that all your ways are pleasantness and all your thoughts are peace.

I will dwell in the house of the Lord forever. You are a temple of the Living God now. You are dwelling in God now. You are dwelling in heaven now, for heaven is the Infinite Intelligence in which you live and move and have your being. A kid of seven can understand that. God dwells within you and walks and talks in you. You dwell in the house, which is your own mind, when you regularly and systematically remind yourself many times a day that the Infinite Spirit is your guide and your counselor and that you are being constantly inspired from On High. Then you inhabit it. You look upon God as your Father, your Source of supply. You know that you will never want for any good thing in life, because He loves you and cares for you.

The tabernacle of God is with humankind. He will dwell with them; they shall be his people. And God, Himself, shall be with them and be their God. You are now rooted in the Divine. You are at home with God. He gives you rest and security. You are relaxed, at peace, and completely free from fear. For where you are, God is; and you dwell with God forever. You are on a journey on the celestial ladder that knows no end. Every night of your life you go to sleep with the praise of God forever on your lips; and your journey is ever onward, upward, and Godward—from glory to glory, from octave to octave, from wisdom to wisdom, from power to power, from beauty to beauty, for there is no end to the glory that is yours now and forevermore.

In a Nutshell

Meditation determines our destiny. We are always meditating. Our thoughts and feelings control our destiny. Meditation is as real and as natural as digestion, assimilation, and breathing.

God is the Living Spirit within, the Supreme Intelligence, the Life Principle. We will not want for any good thing if we choose the Supreme Intelligence as our guide and counselor.

Meditate on whatsoever things are true, lovely, noble, and Godlike. To meditate is to eat all these truths, to cogitate, to give your attention to the Divine, to focus on the One Presence.

The shepherd in the Bible is a symbol of the guiding, healing, protective power of the Divine Presence within you. You are a good shepherd when you know and believe that God, or the Supreme Intelligence, is the only Presence and Power, Cause, and Substance within you.

Close your eyes. Become still and quiet, and gently affirm that the wisdom of God anoints your intellect and is always a lamp unto your feet; it's always a light upon your path. Look to the Infinite Presence at all times; and think, speak, act, and react from the standpoint of the Divine Center within you. Realize, know, feel,

and claim that Infinite Sprit is your guide, your counselor, your boss, and your senior partner, and that Divine right action governs you at all times.

If you're afraid of death, of the afterlife, of judgment day, and things of that nature, then you are being governed by ignorance and delusion and by false beliefs of all kinds. For God has not given us the spirit of fear, but of power, love, and a sound mind. Death is the ignorance of the truth. That's the only death there is.

The tabernacle of God is with humankind. He will dwell with them; they shall be His people. And God, Himself, shall be with them and be their God. You are now rooted in the Divine. You are at home with God. He gives you rest and security. You are relaxed, at peace, and completely free from fear. For where you are, God is; and you dwell with God forever.

•• ••

Chapter Six

The Protective 91st Psalm

The book of Psalms is called "The Little Bible." It's a treasure-house of spiritual riches. Reading and meditating on these wonderful poems to God have helped people throughout history find peace, inspiration, and comfort. Of the 150 psalms in the holy scriptures, I've chosen the three that, I believe, are most helpful in overcoming fear and worry. In the preceding chapter, we examined the first of these, the 23rd Psalm, often called the great, protective psalm. Later in this book we'll discuss another helpful meditation, the 139th Psalm.

Now let's read and study the 91st Psalm, which is a great source of inspiration and comfort to men and women throughout the world. Millions of people from all walks of life meditate on it, and it has saved them from all manner of trouble. Many turn to this psalm of protection for healing in all sorts of emergencies. First, read it to get its essence, and then reread it aloud. Take one verse at a time. Savor it, dwell upon it, give it your attention and devotion, and think about it from all angles. Consider the meaning of each verse and know that these great truths are sinking down into your subconscious mind and will be resurrected in your daily life. Just like you deposit seeds in the ground, plant the words of the psalm in your mind and their power will grow and be magnified.

Psalm 91

*He that dwelleth in the secret place of the Most High shall abide
    under the shadow of the Almighty.*

*I will say of the Lord, He is my refuge and my fortress: my God;
    in him will I trust.*

*Surely He shall deliver thee from the snare of the fowler, and
    from the noisome pestilence.*

*He shall cover thee with his feathers, and under his wings shalt
    thou trust: His truth shall be thy shield and buckler.*

*Thou shalt not be afraid for the terror by night; nor the arrow
    that flieth by day.*

*Nor for the pestilence that walketh in darkness; nor for the
    destruction that wasteth at noonday.*

*A thousand shall fall at thy side, and ten thousand at thy right
    hand; but it shall not come nigh thee.*

*Only with thine eyes shalt thou behold and see the reward
    of the wicked.*

*Because thou hast made the Lord, which is my refuge, even
    the most High, thy habitation;*

*There shall no evil befall thee, neither shall any plague come
    nigh thy dwelling.*

*For he shall give His angels charge over thee, to keep thee
    in all thy ways.*

*They shall bear thee up in their hands, lest thou dash thy
    foot against a stone.*

*Thou shalt tread upon the lion and the adder: the young lion
    and the dragon shalt thou trample under feet.*

*Because he hath set his love upon me, therefore will I deliver him:
    I will set him on high, because he hath known my name.*

*He shall call upon me and I will answer him: I will be with
    him in trouble; I will deliver him and honor him.*

With long life I will satisfy him and show him my salvation.

When you are fearful or worried, reread the psalm aloud. Recite it slowly and quietly and you will dissipate, neutralize, and obliterate the fear. You can meditate on the Only Presence and Power. God is all there is, and God is the Living Spirit within—the Only Power, Presence, Cause, and Substance. You can meditate on the fact that God is guiding you, God is with you, there is right action in your life, and One Power is moving through you. Then you are meditating, and mentally eating these great truths.

To meditate is to give your attention and devotion to certain truths. Think about them from all angles so that you ingest and absorb them, and they become a living part of you. That is real meditation. Then you demonstrate what you have been meditating on.

You *dwelleth in the secret place of the most High*. This means that God, the Living Spirit Almighty, is within you. The secret place, of course, is not up in the sky, but within you, where you are dwelling upon these great truths. You contact the Infinite with your own thought. The kingdom of God, Intelligence, Wisdom, and Power are all within you. You enter into the closet, shut the door, and pray—and the Father "which seeeth in secret shall reward thee openly." This simply means that you shut the door of your senses; turn your attention away from the problem, difficulty, lawsuit, or whatever it is; and focus all your attention on the Infinite Intelligence and the wisdom and the power within you. Realize that It is flowing through you and responding to your prayer. Whatever you claim and feel to be true will come to pass. You will be rewarded openly.

To abide under the shadow of the Almighty means to live enveloped in God's love. As you claim and recognize your Good, it comes to you. *Draw nigh to God, and He will draw nigh to you.*

You are immersed in the Holy Omnipresence, and the Overshadowing Presence watches over you at all times. Realize that God's love surrounds you as you dwell in the impregnable fortress of the secret place and as you contemplate the Presence of God where you are. Then you are rendered impervious to all harm. You are invincible and invulnerable in this fortress. No one can lay siege

to it, for one with God is a majority. If God is for you, who can be against you? For there is only One Power. It's the Almighty Power.

Shade in the Middle East, where the Bible was written, represented protection from the sun. The shade or shadow, of course, was a sanctuary, the cooling refuge of a great rock in a weary land. People walking or riding their camels through the desert would look for a rock to protect them from that broiling sun beating down upon them.

He that dwelleth refers to anyone in contact with the Infinite within. The psalmist speaks of the Almighty, the One Power, the All-Powerful One, the Ever Living One, the All-Wise One, the All-Knowing One. There is nothing to oppose, thwart, or vitiate It. It's the Self-Renewing One, and with God all things are possible.

Dwelling in the secret place simply means that you are constantly thinking of the Infinite Presence and Power guiding, directing, watching over, sustaining, and strengthening you, realizing It's your guide, counselor, adjuster, troubleshooter, and paymaster. It's the healing agency within you, and you are always looking to It for guidance and for right action. *In Him we live, and move, and have our being.* God lives, moves, and has His meaning in us.

Think about this Presence frequently during the day. Realize that you are dwelling in the Infinite now. Regularly and systematically, claim: "Infinite Intelligence guides, directs, and watches over me." Make a habit of this and you could be said to dwell in that secret place of the most High.

Many people pray when they get sick or when trouble comes, but if you pray regularly, you will avoid problems. Meditate regularly on this psalm and it will charge your mental and spiritual batteries.

To meditate, as I said, means to give your attention to the great truths of God. Absorb them, digest them, and let them sink into your soul. *I will say of the Lord, He is my refuge and my fortress: my God; in Him will I trust.* The Lord is God, as the psalmist says, the Sovereign Power, the Living Spirit Almighty. There is only One Power, not two or three. You trust this Presence, which means that you give It your allegiance, loyalty, and recognition, knowing there

is no other. The minute you give power to any created thing on the face of the earth, you cease to worship the One Who Forever Is. Then you are giving greater power to the created thing than to the Creator, which is absurd, of course.

You trusted your mother when you were young. She had you in her arms, and you knew she wouldn't throw you into the fire. You looked into her eyes, and you saw love there. And all the love in the world is a faint reproduction of that Infinite ocean of God's love. God is Pure Spirit. There is no other power.

Affirm frequently: "I am inspired from On High. God loves me, for it is written: *He careth for me.* As you constantly claim that God is the Only Presence, Power, Cause, and Substance guiding, directing, governing, and sustaining you, your conviction in the Living Spirit Almighty will grow.

Your subconscious mind accepts the dominant of two ideas. Therefore, this dominant conviction that God's love and peace are saturating your mind and heart will govern all your lesser thoughts, actions, and reactions, and you will lead a charmed life. You trust the Infinite regardless of appearances, for He never fails. The mere fact that you are meditating on this psalm indicates that you have faith and trust the Presence and the Power. Your faith and confidence is in God's healing love instead of the ailment, the negative condition, or the impending lawsuit.

You are told: *Surely, he shall deliver thee from the snare of the fowler, and from the noisome pestilence. He shall cover thee with his feathers, and under his wings shalt thou trust: his truth shall be thy shield and buckler.* Here is a definite assurance that your prayer will be answered in ways you know not of, for as the heavens are above the earth, so are my ways above your ways, and my ways are not your ways.

The snare of the fowler and the noisome pestilence could mean deception, trickery, or someone trying to undermine you; or it could also mean fear of the flu, a virus, or something of that nature. You are, however, to have no fear or doubt, for you have received the Divine antibody and the conviction of God's love and guidance surrounding you at all times.

Under his wing shalt thou trust. This phrase is, of course, symbolic. God is the Living Spirit without face, form, or figure. *Wings* mean "protection." The hen gathers her chickens under her wings to protect them, and so do other mother birds.

His truth shall be thy shield and buckler. God is truth and all-powerful, and the realization of your desire today is the truth that will set you free. If you are sick, health will free you. If you are poor, wealth will release you from your problems. If you are in prison, freedom will be your savior.

One with God is a majority. The joy of the Lord is your strength. If God be for you, who can be against you? *Thou shalt not be afraid for the terror by night; nor for the arrow that flieth by day.* Night means darkness. Fear is a shadow in the mind created by your own thoughts and generated by you. The things that frighten you do not exist, for they are only shadows in your mind. Most fear comes from the idea that external things are causative, which is a big lie. An external condition is an effect, not a cause, and everything is subject to change. As you change your mind, you change your body and your environment.

You are told that your enemies are of your own household. The enemies are fear, doubt, resentment, and hostility. These are of your own mind, generated by you. You are the creator of your worry and fear. You can instead contemplate God's love, peace, harmony, and right action, and your fear will go away. When fear comes, affirm: "God's love fills my soul. God's peace floods my mind." Then your apprehension melts away. What happens to the darkness when you turn on the light? Darkness is the absence of light. Turn on the light in your own mind and affirm: "God loves me and cares for me."

The *arrow that flieth by day* is any negative thought—the propaganda, the news, the headlines, and things of that nature. The term can also refer to sickness, problems in the office, or inharmonious human relations. Day means light, and night means darkness, as I said. In other words, when the sun is shining you can see things better than when the night comes. In the light you are aware of the problem and you can meet it head-on. The problem is

there, but God is there, too, and God knows only the answer. God is the Infinite Intelligence within you, not an anthropomorphic being up in the skies or a glorified sort of man. That characterization is absurd and childish. That's living in the jungle.

The *pestilence that walketh in darkness* could refer to some subconscious resentment, suppressed rage or anger, or prejudice. Prejudice means pre-judgment. I have judged something before I know anything about it. Prejudice means that I'm down on what I'm not up on. Pestilence may also refer to some poisonous pocket in the subconscious mind, like jealousy or the green-eyed monster. It's one of the most destructive mental poisons there is. Envy is another poison.

Most difficulties are caused by subconscious patterns of false religious beliefs, such as guilt. Guilt is called the curse of curses. Nobody is punishing you but yourself, for life never punishes. You are passing judgment and punishing yourself. Forgive yourself and you are forgiven, for Life always forgives.

Feed your subconscious mind with life-giving patterns and you obliterate all the negative patterns, for the lower is subject to the higher. Suppose you had a pail of dirty water in your home and you began to pour clean water into it. The moment comes when you have clear, pure water. That's prayer. Filling your mind with the truths of God, you crowd out of your mind everything unlike God, so you won't be afraid of the pestilence that walketh in darkness, nor for the destruction that wasteth at noonday.

If people are plotting against you, trying to undermine you or sell you a shady deal of some kind, they are the pestilence that walketh in darkness. But you can dispel any negative activity that threatens your welfare by realizing that the love, light, and glory of the Infinite surrounds you and enfolds you. The pestilence will dissolve because faith in God and all things good will protect you.

God's love saturates your whole being; therefore give all your allegiance to the One Power, not to other men or women, because if you give power to other humans, you'd say, "They are gods." You would be making them greater than God. Wouldn't that be

absurd? Wouldn't you be unjust to yourself? Wouldn't it be a form of insanity to give power to other people?

I know a detective who, every morning of his life, says, "Thou art my hiding place; thou hast preserved me; thou shalt compass me about with songs of deliverance." He has said this so frequently—at night prior to sleep and in the morning before he goes to work—that his soul is saturated with it, and he has built up an immunity. He has been shot at and has had grenades thrown at him, but somehow he has always escaped injury.

Nothing ever will harm him because he has built up this immunity by saying to himself, "Thou art my hiding place; thou hast preserved me; thou shalt compass me about with songs of deliverance." You have that deliverance, also, and there is only One Power that delivers you—not two, only one.

A thousand shall fall at thy side, and ten thousand at thy right hand; but it shall not come nigh thee. As you fill your mind with the eternal truths of God, you will crowd out of your mind everything unlike the One Who Forever Is. Your spiritual thoughts destroy the negative thoughts. One spiritual thought destroys ten thousand negative thoughts, and you can also neutralize all the negative patterns in your subconscious mind. The "ten thousand at thy right hand" are the negative thoughts. If you are thinking constructively, harmoniously, and peacefully, these negative thoughts come in and out but find no pastures. They have no effect upon you.

Only with thine eyes shalt thou behold and see the reward of the wicked. This verse refers to the need to stay detached from the problems of the world. Of course you realize that there is a lot of evil in the world. There is no principle of evil, but people commit evil. There is crime and sickness, and we experience man's inhumanity to man. The jails and hospitals are full of people: psychotics, schizophrenics, sex maniacs. People commit murder. Surely, they do all these things. You are aware of that, but you say: "Well, I'm not going to get involved, agitated, perturbed, and excited because I might get ulcers, high blood pressure, or something else."

If you get terribly agitated, you could get a stroke, you know. That's no way to live. Where there is no opinion, there is no

suffering. You are not responsible if a person is psychotic or a hardened criminal. When you walk in the consciousness of God's love, peace, and harmony, you contribute to the peace and harmony of the whole. You radiate the sunshine of His love, and the whole world is blessed because you walk this way. But if you go forth with anger, rage, hate, and all the rest of it, you are pouring out more mental poisons on the mass mind and are contributing to the negativity of the world.

Where there is no opinion, there is no suffering; where there is no judgment, there is no pain. Let your opinion lie still. Maintain a calm, peaceful mind. What good would a doctor be without a peaceful mind and steady hand when operating? What good could an emotionally disturbed and agitated psychologist offer you? Preserve your peace, inner serenity, and tranquility; and stay in tune with the Infinite, and then you can help the world. The mind at peace gets things done.

Only with thine eyes shalt thou behold and see the reward of the wicked. This verse also tells us that when people misuse the law, the law punishes them. The wicked means those who are bewitched or using the law negatively. *Vengeance is mine: I will repay, saith the Lord.* Fret not about evildoers or the workers of iniquity. They shall be cut down. The law takes care of people if they are misusing it.

Exalt God in the midst of you. The law of the Lord is perfect. The mills of the gods grind slowly, but they grind exceedingly fine.

Because thou hast made the Lord, which is my refuge, even the most High, thy habitation; there shall no evil befall thee, neither shall any plague come nigh thy dwelling. God dwells within you, walks and talks in you. By keeping in tune with the Infinite, no evil shall befall you. This is a definite promise of the response of Infinite life and love.

Turn to the Divine Presence as your refuge by constantly claiming: "God loves and cares for me." Do it regularly so that it becomes the frequent habitation of the mind, which performs a miracle. The promise in the Bible is always a law. The Infinite Intelligence always responds to you.

I will set him on high, because he hath known my name. With these words, the psalmist states that God will be with us in times of trouble. The *name* means the nature of Infinite Intelligence, which is responsiveness. As the Bible says, if you ask for bread, I will not give you a stone; if you ask for a fish, I will not give you a serpent. You get a response according to the nature of your request. It's a law like Boyle's law, Roman law, or any other law. Whatever you impress is expressed. That's the law of mind.

He shall give his angels charge over thee, to keep thee in all thy ways. *Angel* comes from "Angelus," a messenger of God. These messengers can be ideas, monitions, feelings, or flashes of illumination coming into one's mind.

At one of my lectures, a man told me that one day he was driving along the road and suddenly stopped. He said, "I didn't know really why, but I was compelled to, and I turned off the main road." He said, "Immediately, a drunkard came around the corner. He was going 80 miles an hour and was right in my lane. If I had kept driving, a collision would have taken place, and both of us probably would have been killed."

This man, before he gets in the car in the morning to go to work, reads the 91st Psalm out loud three times. It is a great protective psalm. Then the angels, the guiding principle within him, or the wisdom of his subconscious mind, prompted him. It was sort of a compulsion within him, and he followed the lead. He didn't suppress or reject it, and he didn't keep on driving. He responded.

The angel is the Angelus, the guiding principle or the idea that pops into your mind and directs you in your relationships with people. It also steers you in your diet, work, investments, and activities. Say, "Infinite Intelligence guides me in all my ways." If you are eating the wrong kinds of food, it leads you to stop choosing items that contribute to your weight problem. The One Presence also directs the hands of surgeons when they operate. Declare: "God is guiding me now." It can also help you to say the right thing at the right time. If you are wondering what to say to

a person, say, "Infinite Spirit reveals to me the right words for this occasion," and the words will be given to you instantly.

When the con man tries to sell you something that doesn't exist, asks you to take your money out of the bank to invest with him, or tells you that you can earn 20 percent interest if you buy into his "fantastic business," you might wonder why he doesn't tell all his relatives about these so-called great opportunities. Why doesn't he take the 20 percent himself? Why does he come to you? It's because he thinks you are gullible and that he can brainwash and make a fool of you. If you are saying, "God is guiding me in all my ways; the light shines in me," immediately you will have an inner feeling and a silent knowing of the soul that the whole thing is phony, and you won't give him a dime. The Infinite Almighty is watching over you, protecting you from fraud.

Claim that the angels will watch over you. They don't have wings but are an intelligence, wisdom, and power within you that responds to you. They are a predominant hunch, an inner feeling, and an idea that wells up in your mind.

Thou shalt tread upon the lion and adder: the young lion and the dragon shalt thou trample under feet. The lion is that great obstacle, confusion, or problem. The lion might be the so-called incurable disease. There are incurable people but there are no incurable diseases. There are certain people who are absolutely convinced that they can't be healed, and according to their belief it is done unto them. You are told that Daniel was saved from the lion's den by turning to the light within, meaning that Supreme Intelligence that knows only the answer and knows the way out. It can provide a solution to the most complex problem in the world. You may be in a lion's den of obstacles or difficulties. You say, "Look at all these bills. I can't pay them." Instead, turn to the God Presence within; don't think of the bills or your worries, and don't think of any sum of money or any particular date. Go to the Source and say: "God is the Source of my supply, and all my needs are met at every moment of time and point of space. God's wealth is circulating in my life, and there is always a surplus."

The adder in the psalm means a complex, a hidden fear. It could also be a symbol of mental illnesses such as multiple personality disorder, schizophrenia, paranoia, and so forth. The lion is ferocious, of course, and pitiless, but it confronts you directly. It doesn't hide like a snake in the jungle, striking you when you don't expect it.

The lion and the adder are both complexes, a group of negative thoughts charged with fear, hidden in the recesses of the subconscious mind.

As you claim the Presence of God, Divine love, peace, and harmony saturate your mind and your heart. The lower is subject to the higher, love casts out hate, peace casts out pain, and joy casts out sadness. Then you are cleansing the stable that has been dirty, perhaps for many years. Divine love, peace, and the miraculous Healing Power go straight to the roots of the trouble and you are redeemed.

Great peace have they which love thy law: and nothing shall offend them. It is done unto me as I believe, and all things are ready if the mind be so. And according to my faith is it done unto me. *And I will restore health unto thee, and I will heal thee of thy wounds,* saith the Lord. *Call upon me and I will answer you. I'll be with you in trouble. I'll set you on High because you have known my name.*

Today, of course, much emphasis is placed on subconscious fixations and compulsions. However, the real trouble is in your conscious mind, for there is no error in the subconscious that is not under the control of the conscious mind. Surely, these problems are in the subconscious, but they can be controlled and eliminated. The subconscious is subject to the conscious mind. Your feelings are subject to your thoughts. Even if false beliefs or religious dogmas were foisted upon you when you were a child, you can still obliterate them by changing your opinions and beliefs now. You can begin to believe in a God of love and drop the concept of a devil with hooves and horns.

Your old fear abides because you still hold a philosophy that sustains it. If you believe in a power other than the Infinite, then you are in trouble. This false idea is the root of all fear and mental

illnesses. When you disabuse your mind of this error, you have cut the pipeline that nourishes the neurotic tendencies in your subconscious mind. Prayer is a great changer of all things, because it alters your consciousness, which makes all things. Don't beg an anthropomorphic being in the sky to create a miracle for you. Recast your thoughts. There is only One Power, which is Spiritual. It is your own consciousness. Realize that It is sovereign and supreme.

As the love, light, and glory of the Infinite flow through you in transcendent loveliness, you will dethrone, exorcise, and banish all the tormentors in your mind. Then you are treading on the lion and the adder, and trampling the dragon under your feet. It's a magnificent truth.

Because he hath set his love upon me, therefore will I deliver him: I will set him on high, because he hath known my name. Love is not an emotion or a sentiment. When you tune in to the Infinite, you realize that it is all-powerful. It is all love, light, truth, and beauty. When you give your loyalty to this Presence and Power and insist on harmony, you will accept nothing less. You will not compromise but instead will insist on health, peace, and well-being. When you give all your allegiance and loyalty to the One Power, then you are said to love God.

As the Bible says, if you love me . . . keep my commandments. The mere fact that you pray, turn to the Infinite, and read the Psalms, looking for their inner meaning, indicates your love and recognition of the Almighty. It means your mind is pure, because you are giving allegiance to the One Power, not two or three.

I will set him on high, because he hath known my name. The *name* is the nature of something, and the nature of the Infinite is omnipotence. It's all-powerful, boundless love, infinite intelligence, and absolute harmony. It's all-wise. If It's all-powerful, nothing can challenge It. When you know the name or nature of the Infinite and call on It, you are set on high—that is, above difficulties and problems. This knowledge assures you your freedom, because you know the nature of the One Presence is to respond. To know the God Presence is to know It is supreme and omnipotent. There is no doubt in your mind about it. It's the only Power there is.

He shall call upon me, and I will answer him: I will be with him in trouble; I will deliver him, and honor him. With long life will I satisfy him, and show him my salvation. The answer is known even before you call upon God. It is known in the Divine mind, which knows all things. It's the All-Wise One, the All-Knowing One, the Self-Renewing One. The modern scientist knows that before you call, the answer is there. It doesn't make any difference whether it's a mathematical, geological, or physics problem. The answer is known to the Infinite Intelligence. Therefore, you contemplate the answer, knowing that it will flow through you.

I will deliver him, and honor him means that deliverance will come—the solution to your problem—because you recognize the Divine as supreme and omnipotent. You recognize Its nature as responsiveness.

With long life will I satisfy him, and show him my salvation. A long life means a life of peace, harmony, joy, wisdom, and understanding. You may live to be 90 or 100 years of age, but if half the time is spent in a hospital with pains and aches, that's not a long life in spiritual terms. A long life is one of peace, harmony, creativity, and joy. It's the life abundant.

Salvation is a solution to your problem, no matter what it is. Your prayer conforms to the Divine will when it is constructive, blesses you, and conforms to Universal Principle. A wonderful prayer would be:

> *I dwell in the secret place of the Most High, and I abide in the shadow of the Almighty. As I contemplate God in His glory and His wonders within me, I abide in the shadow always, because I know God's love surrounds and enfolds me, making straight, beautiful, and joyous my way. The Lord, the Spiritual Power, is sovereign and supreme, the Only Power. It responds to my thought and therefore is my refuge and my fortress. This Spiritual Power inspires, heals, strengthens, and restores my mind and body. It is God. It is beneficent. It is a kindly Power, and I trust it completely. It responds as mercy, love, inspiration,*

and beauty. This Divine Power covers me with its feathers of love, light, and peace. It is wonderful. I completely reject the negative thoughts of the world, the arrow by day. God's love dissolves the fear patterns of my subconscious, the terror by night. I know I am secure in the invisible hands of God. I always vibrate with the mind of God, and all is well. I am completely free from fear of accidents or hostile activities—the pestilences that walketh in darkness—because I know I am immunized and God-intoxicated. I have received the Divine antibody, the Presence of God, in my heart. The thousands of negative thoughts and suggestions of the world are destroyed consciously and subconsciously, for God walks and talks in me, and I live in the joyous expectancy of the best. God's ideas, impulses, intuition, and guidance have complete charge over me, and I am safeguarded in all my ways: in health, right activity, self-expression, and Divine companionship.

By contemplating the Presence of God, you tread upon the lion and the adder, the obstacles and complexes of all kinds. The Presence of God is the presence of peace, harmony, joy, love, abundance, light, and truth. Your salvation, or solution, is revealed to you as you think of the Infinite, the only Presence, Power, Cause, and Substance. All the Divine forces hasten to minister to your eternal joy. That Lordly Presence is your shepherd, and you sing the song of the jubilant soul, for you have chosen God as your guide, counselor, and way-shower. You are always in the shadow of the Almighty. Divine Intelligence rules and guides you in all your ways. You shall never want for peace, harmony, or guidance, because God's wisdom governs you. You lie down in green pastures always, since God is prospering you beyond your fondest dreams. You find yourself beside the still waters as you claim the infinite peace of God floods your mind and your heart. Your emotions (waters) are still and calm. Your mind is serene and it reflects God's heavenly truths and light. Your soul is restored. Think of God's Holy Presence within you all day long, the Infinite that lies

stretched in smiling repose. It's the Infinite Presence and Power, the Living Spirit Almighty. You walk the paths of righteousness through your devotion and attention to God's eternal verities. You know there is no death, for you fear no evil. God has not given you the spirit of fear, but of love, power, and a sound mind.

The banquet table of God is always set before you. It is the secret place of the Most High, where you eat of the great nourishing truths of God and where you walk and talk with the Infinite. You eat these nourishing truths as you contemplate the bread of peace, love, faith, and joy. You say: "My faith is in God and all things good. I believe in the goodness of God in the land of the living. I believe in the guidance of God, and God is guiding me now." Then you are spreading the banquet table in your own mind and you are eating the truths of God. You say, "I am inspired from On High; the Spirit of the Almighty moves on the waters of my mind." The meat that you eat is the Omnipotence of God; the wine that you drink is the essence of joy; and the bread that you eat is the substance of peace and well-being. *Lord, ever more give us this bread.*

The wisdom of God anoints your intellect and is a light upon your path. Your cup (your heart) is truly a chamber of God's Presence. It runneth over with love and joy. You mentally dwell on goodness, truth, and beauty. You are dwelling in the house of God at all times.

Forgiveness must take place within your heart and mind to be the real thing. To *forgive* means to "give for." Give yourself the feeling of love and goodwill, instead of the mood of anger, resentment, or hatred. Your mental attitude governs your experience. Keep your mind clear, poised, serene, and calm, and full of the expectancy of the best. If you resent another, you are giving too much power to that other and you are hurting yourself. Remember, *I will say of the Lord, he is my refuge and my fortress: my God; in him will I trust.* You turn to the God Presence. That is your Source of all blessings. Don't look to somebody else. God is the Source of guidance, prosperity, peace, and harmony. Why would you look to another? Why would you say, "He's blocking my good"? Why would you

have resentment? You see, this law does away with all cause for resentment, because you can go to the Living Spirit within you and claim your good. Believe in the reality of this Presence and Power; It will respond to you. You have the unqualified capacity to go within yourself and claim health, happiness, peace, abundance, and security. To forgive, therefore, is to change your thoughts. Forgive yourself and release the guilt.

Why should you be jealous of anyone? Why be envious? You can go to the eternal Source. Where did the other person get what you desire? You can go to the Source of all and claim it, too. It's impersonal and does not discriminate. It will respond to you, too.

Call upon the Almighty One and It will answer you and deliver you from poverty, pain, sickness, confusion, and trouble. It will lead you out. Pray for the person who bothers you wholeheartedly, sincerely, and lovingly. Surrender the other person to God. This is one way, too, of getting rid of the lion and the adder—the complex within you. If there is some suppressed rage, resentment, or poisonous pocket in your subconscious, this is a wonderful way to get rid of it. For example, if you have resentment against a former spouse, say, "I surrender that person to God completely. The peace of God fills his soul. He is inspired and blessed in all ways." Anytime you think of him, say, "I released you. God be with you." After a while you'll meet that person in your mind, and you'll be at peace.

If you are seething over something someone did, tread upon the adder by filling your mind with love and say, "God's love fills my soul. I surrender that person to God completely. I wish for that person health, happiness, peace, and all the blessings of life." For the other is yourself, and what you withhold from another, you withhold from yourself. Then wonders will begin to happen in your life, because the person, you see, is not out there. The person is a thought-image in your mind. It is browbeating, intimidating you, and robbing you of vitality, enthusiasm, and energy, making you a physical and mental wreck. And who is it hurting? The other person is in the Mediterranean, dancing under the midnight stars on a beautiful ship. Look at what you're doing to yourself and just forgive.

Resentment is the quickest way in the world to get old and to establish mental and spiritual trouble in your mind and body. It is also a surefire way to become depleted—to be a mental and physical wreck. Stop robbing yourself of vitality, enthusiasm, and energy. Realize that God's love fills your soul and God's peace floods your mind. You will say of the Lord, "He is my refuge and fortress: my God; in Him will I trust. He will deliver me from the snare of the fowler and from all negativity, for I walk and talk with Him." Then wonders will begin to happen in your life.

Realize that the Lord is your pilot. You shall not drift, for angels watch over you to keep you safe on your way. Mariners, naval officers, and pilots use the Guiding Principle to protect and lead them through the storm, turbulence, and lightning, too. Say to yourself:

> *The Lord is my pilot. I shall not drift. He lighteth me across the dark waters. He steereth me in the deep channels. He keepeth my log. He guideth me by the star of holiness for His name's sake. Yea, though I sail with the thunders and tempests of life, I shall dread no danger, for thou art with me. Thy love and thy care, they shelter me. Thou preparest a harbor before me in the homeland of Eternity. Thou anointest the waves with oil. My ship rideth calmly. Surely, some light and starlight shall favor me on the voyage I take, and I will rest in the port of my God forever.*

Angels have charge over thee. *They shall bear thee up in their hands lest thy dash thy foot against a stone.,* They protect you from hurting yourself in any way. The Guiding Principle watching over you prevents you from stumbling and making the wrong decision. The *Lord doth go before thee* when you drive. Have faith and confidence and God's wisdom will guide and govern you in all ways. This awareness is the Lord or the dominant conviction that goes before you. Your conviction of God's Presence is strong and mighty, and you know the spiritual atmosphere in which you dwell goes before you making straight, beautiful, joyous, and happy

your way. Know that whenever you travel by bus, train, airplane, automobile, or whatever means of conveyance you use, God's love and intelligence protects you on your journey.

All the highways and byways of your world are controlled by God, making the skies above and the earth beneath a highway for your God. Angels are ideas, impulses, monitions, and flashes of illumination that come into your mind. They will bear you up and protect you, lest you dash your foot against a stone and make any error or mistake. Claim it, believe it, and make a habit of it.

Saturate your mind with this psalm, interspersed, of course, with the 23rd. Realize that God's circle of love is always around you, watching over, sustaining, and strengthening you. The Lord is your light and your salvation, whom shall you fear? The Lord is the strength of your life; of whom shall you be afraid? This is the Lord spoken of in the 91st Psalm, the Lordly Power, the God Presence that is always your refuge. Turn to Him. *Draw nigh to God, and He will draw nigh to you.*

You are ever joyous, active, and energetic. You are always calling upon this Presence and It is always answering you. It's giving you the right words for the occasion. It's inspiring, guiding, and revealing to you truths you never knew before. It's delivering you from all sorts of problems. It's honoring you, exalting you because you are here to grow and expand. You are always passing on God's ideas to other people, giving them peace, joy, and happiness. *In thy presence is fullness of joy. In Him there is no darkness at all. My peace I leave you; my peace I give you. Not as the world giveth, give I unto you. These things have I said unto thee, that my joy might remain in you, and your joy might be full.*

The joy of the Lord is your strength. You are always cheerful, free, and full of happiness. You have dominion over all things in your world. You sense and feel your oneness with God, life, the universe, and all things. You meditate on whatsoever things are true, lovely, wonderful, and Godlike. Realize that you are a child of God, and the children of God shouted for joy. Above all things, realize now that you are dwelling in the secret place of the Most

High, and you abide in the shadow of the Almighty. You are always watched over by the overshadowing Presence, because you are thinking of God. And to think of God is the greatest prayer in all the world, for God is the Infinite, the only Presence, Power, Cause, and Substance—the Ever-Living One, the All-Wise One, the All-Knowing One, and the Self-Renewing One. When your thoughts are God's thoughts, no evil shall befall you. A promise in the Bible, you see, is the law. And the law never changes. It remains the same yesterday, today, and forever. Then you say of the Lord, "My God; in Him will I trust." Where is your confidence today? Is your confidence in the law of the Lord? Place your confidence in God, in the goodness of God in the land of the living, in the guidance of God, the abundance of God, the love of God, the peace of God, and the justice of the Infinite. That's where your faith is; that's where your confidence is; that's where your trust is. He never fails. And *He shall cover thee with His feathers and under His wing shalt thou trust.* And the truth of God shall be the shield and buckler. Wherever you go, you lead a charmed life, for the spell of God is always around you. And God's love surrounds, enfolds, and enwraps you. God walks and talks in you.

No matter what the problem is, no matter what the difficulty is, you will call upon the Almighty Spirit and It answers you. It will be with you in trouble. It will deliver you and honor you. With long life will It satisfy you and show you the solution to all problems and show you Its salvation.

So, think of this God Presence. Dwell in that secret place. Contemplate the Ever-Living One, the All-Wise One, the All-Knowing One, the Self-Renewing One, ever the same in my inmost being, eternal, absolutely one, whole, complete, perfect, indivisible, timeless, changeless, and ageless; without face, form, or figure; that silent, brooding Presence fixed in the hearts of all people.

In a Nutshell

When you are fearful or worried, reread the psalm aloud. Speak it slowly and quietly, and you will dissipate, neutralize, and obliterate the fear.

Realize God's love surrounds you and that the impregnable fortress is within you as you dwell in the secret place, as you contemplate the Presence of God where you are. Then you are rendered impervious to all harm.

Affirm frequently: "I am inspired from On High. God loves me, for it is written: He careth for me." As you constantly claim that God is the Only Presence, Power, Cause, and Substance—guiding, directing, governing, and sustaining you—then after a while your belief will become your Lord, master, and dominant conviction.

As you fill your mind with the eternal truths of God, you will crowd out of your mind everything unlike the One Who Forever Is. Your spiritual thoughts destroy the negative thoughts. One spiritual thought destroys ten thousand negative thoughts, and you will also neutralize all the negative patterns in your subconscious mind.

Love casts out hate, peace casts out pain, and joy casts out sadness. So, Divine love, Divine peace, and the miraculous Healing Power go straight to the roots of the trouble; then you are redeemed.

The wisdom of God anoints your intellect. It is a lamp unto your feet; it is a light upon your path. Your cup (your heart) is truly a chamber of God's Presence. It runneth over with love and joy. You mentally dwell on goodness, truth, and beauty. You are dwelling in the house of God at all times.

••· ·••·

Chapter Seven

Why Did This Happen to Me?

*W*hen life does not go as planned, when misfortune strikes or one is unhappy with the cards one is dealt, we often hear the complaint, "Why did this happen to me?" There's no easy answer to this universal question.

To accept the trials and tribulations all humankind faces, it's necessary to think in a new way and to consider the eternal verities and principles of life—in the same manner that mathematicians think about the principles of mathematics and electricians apply the principles of electricity. Electricians understand how electricity flows, and they use the laws of conductivity and insulation in wiring your house.

In the same way, your mind is a principle, and you think from the God center within. You think about things that are true, just, lovely, pure, honest, and of good report. There's a principle of harmony, not discord; a principle of beauty, not ugliness; a principle of joy, not sadness; a principle of love, not hate. There's also a principle of wholeness and perfection, but not one of sickness. If there were, no one in the entire world could ever be healed.

Realize that when your thoughts are completely free from fear and worry, you're thinking from the standpoint of the Divine center within you; and God speaks, thinks, and acts through you. Therefore, speak in words of wisdom, truth, and beauty; and in words of harmony, health, and peace. Think from the God center within.

Millions of people do not think; they think that they think, but they're mistaken, because true thinking (we're talking about constructive thinking) is completely free from fear, and all fear is based upon external factors, which are an effect, not a cause.

You must remember that if we don't think for ourselves, someone else will do our thinking for us. If you don't choose your own thoughts, who's going to choose them for you? Newspapers? Headlines? The mass or collective mind? We're all subjective and part of the mass mind. We're all in telepathic communication with each other. The people in this world are all extensions of ourselves.

If you don't think constructively, harmoniously, and peacefully, the mass or world mind will do your thinking for you. This mass mind believes in tragedy, misfortune, sickness, disease, and accidents; and it indulges in hate, murder, and all sorts of things. Is that the kind of mind you want thinking through you and in you?

If you don't do your own thinking, these negative vibrations, or thoughts of the mass mind, move in upon you; reach a point of saturation; and precipitate as accident, misfortune, sickness, and disease. Explosions in mines, airplane crashes, and tragedies are occurring daily. It isn't that people are evil or bad because their submarine goes down in the ocean, their home is flooded, or their children are hurt in accidents. These calamities are a result of collective negative thinking.

So we say it's necessary to keep "prayed up." You keep prayed up when you fill your mind with the truths of God, which crowd out of your mind everything unlike God. *Remember ye not the former things, neither consider the things of old; but this one thing I do. Forgetting the things that are behind, reaching forth unto those things that are before. I press toward the mark for the prize.*

The Bible says, "Whatsoever a man soweth, that shall he also reap." This means that if we plant thoughts of peace, harmony, health, beauty, and prosperity, we shall reap accordingly. If we sow thoughts of sickness, lack, strife, and contention, we shall reap these things. We must remember that our subconscious mind is like the soil. Whatever type of seed we plant in the garden of our

mind will grow. Whatever your conscious mind really believes, your subconscious will bring to pass.

Unless you do your own thinking, you'll be controlled by the mass mind, which believes in misfortune, sickness, calamities, and tragedies of all kinds. If you don't cleanse your own mind, the world mind will not cleanse it for you. You must, therefore, do your own thinking.

True thinking is completely free from fear, worry, and anxiety, because you're thinking from the God center within. When your thoughts are God's thoughts, God's power is with your thoughts of good.

What happens to your home when you go away for three or four months? Rats, mice, and other pests come in. The paint falls off the walls and everything goes wrong in the house because there's no one living there to take care of it. You have to clean your mind like you scour your house or shampoo your hair—regularly and with careful attention.

Whatever we really believe with our conscious mind, our subconscious brings to pass. A chaplain in a hospital in Massachusetts told me that she commonly had patients who lamented, "Why did this happen to me? What did I do to deserve this? Why is God angry with me? Why is God punishing me? I go to church regularly. I'm a charitable person, and I'm kindhearted. I must have done something wrong that I don't know about. That's why I'm so ill."

The chaplain reported that in many cases, she prayed with patients and helped them change their beliefs. "I helped them realize that the body is spiritual and that when they changed their minds, they changed their bodies," she said. They began to cease giving power to the sickness in their thoughts. She taught them to pray: "The Infinite Healing Presence is flowing through me as harmony, health, peace, wholeness, and perfection. God's healing love indwells every cell of my being. I am made whole, pure, relaxed, and perfect."

She taught them to repeat this prayer frequently, knowing what they were doing and why they were doing it. The conscious mind

was writing these truths down in the patients' subconscious and, as a result, many of them made miraculous recoveries. Whatever you impress or inscribe in your subconscious will come to pass.

The law of life is the law of belief. What do you believe? To believe is to accept something as true and to live in that truth. We should live in the joyous expectancy of the best. We should believe in the goodness, guidance, harmony, and healing power of God to make us whole, pure, relaxed, and perfect. If you fear sickness, you attract it. The law of the Lord is perfect. You can't think one thing and produce another. Trouble of any kind is nature's alarm system telling us that we're thinking wrongly. Nothing but a change of thought can set us free.

There is a law of cause and effect operating at all times. Nothing happens to someone without his or her mental consent and participation. OSHA, the U.S. federal government agency responsible for occupational safety, investigates the causes of industrial injuries. They're particularly concerned about companies where frequent injuries occur. In addition to their engineering staff, who examine the facilities for physical defects that may cause accidents, safety experts with training in psychology interview the workers—not just the injured persons but all the workers in the plant. They often learn that accidents happen when employees are emotionally upset. In companies where workers have dogmatic and domineering bosses, resentment of the boss leads to negative thoughts in the workers' minds, which results in carelessness and accidents.

Misfortune, accidents, and tragedies of various kinds are signs of mental and emotional disorders that have broken out into manifestation. We must train our minds to think in a new way, to turn back to God and align our thoughts and mental imagery with the Infinite life, love, truth, and beauty of God. Then we become channels for the Divine.

Still your mind several times a day and affirm slowly, quietly, and lovingly: "God flows through me as harmony, health, peace, joy, wholeness, and perfection. God walks and talks in me. God's spell is always around me. Wherever I go, God's wisdom governs me in

all my ways. Divine right action prevails. All my ways are ways of pleasantness, and all my paths are peaceful. God's love surrounds, enfolds, and enwraps me. I'm surrounded by the sacred circle of God's eternal love, and the whole armor of God surrounds me."

As you dwell on these eternal verities, you will establish patterns of Divine order in your subconscious mind, and whatever you impress in the subconscious mind is expressed on the screen of life. You will find yourself watched over at all times by an Overshadowing Presence—your Heavenly Father Who responds to you when you call upon Him. The Bible says, call upon me in the day of trouble and I will deliver you. I'll set you on high because you hath known my name.

One of the corollaries of the great law of suggestion is this: Whatever you suggest to another, you are also suggesting to yourself, because you are the only thinker in your universe. You are always under the law of your own thought. This is the basis of the Golden Rule, which also tells you to treat your enemies well and to pray for those who spitefully use you. In other words, never wish misfortune on anyone on the face of the earth. You do so at your own peril because whatever you are thinking about someone else, you are also creating in your own mind, body, circumstances, and pocketbook. That's a simple truth.

Radiate love, peace, and goodwill to everybody. Don't judge. With what judgment ye judge, ye shall be judged. Your judgment of the other is your judgment of yourself. That's the conclusion and verdict in your own mind. Many people suffer from sickness, disease, accidents, and misfortune because they do not think constructively. They're letting the mass mind, or the law of averages, govern them. They're not bad people, but they refuse to think for themselves. They don't keep prayed up and don't neutralize the mass mind.

If you read the newspapers in the morning and listen to the radio or TV at night, you hear about murder, rape, hate, jealousy, and all sorts of tragedy. Reporters tell you about all the bad things that have happened. They don't tell you about any of the good things.

If you do not keep prayed up and if you do not think for yourself, the mass mind does your thinking for you. You must therefore ask yourself: "Am I thinking constructively, harmoniously, and peacefully?" Of course, you answer that question yourself. You are what you think about all day long. For as we think, so we are, so do we become, and so do we express. That's the whole law. Whatever you sow in your mind, so shall you reap.

All of us are in the mass mind or the great psychic sea. The mass mind believes in sickness, accidents, death, misfortune, and tragedies of all kinds. If we do not do our own thinking, the mass mind will do our thinking for us. Gradually the thoughts of the mass mind impinging on our consciousness may reach a point of saturation and precipitate as accident, sudden illness, calamity, heart attack, and so-called tragedies that happen in the air and at sea. The majority of people do not think; they think they think.

You are thinking when you differentiate between that which is false and that which is real. To think is to choose. How many people are thinking? You have the capacity to say yes and no. Say yes to the Truth of Being and reject everything unlike God or the Truth.

If the mental instrument could not choose, you would not be an individual. You have the ability to accept and reject; you can think about those things that are true, lovely, noble and Godlike all day long. There is nothing in the entire world to stop you from thinking constructively, harmoniously, and peacefully. You are thinking when you know that there is an Infinite Intelligence that responds to your thoughts and that no matter what the problem is, as you think about a Divine solution and the happy ending, you will find the subjective wisdom within you responding and revealing to you the perfect plan and showing you the way to go. Everywhere you go today, the suggestions of people in your office, home, and neighborhood—and on the radio and televison—are playing upon the subtle receptivity of your mind. Whether you know it or not, these impressions are going down into your mind and are muddling and befouling it.

Every morning and every night, sit down and read your Psalms. The 1st, 23rd, 27th, 46th, and 91st are particularly helpful. These are marvelous truths. Psalms are songs of God. You are here to cleanse your mind, to govern and care for it just as you cleanse your body. Cleanliness is next to Godliness. We should give attention to things that are lovely and noble—to eternal verities, the principles of life. We should also discipline our thoughts. Inattention, negligence, apathy, and listlessness pay dividends, but they are negative dividends, aren't they? You have to give attention to what is true, noble, and of God.

Over the years many people with medical problems have come to me for advice. Some had truly serious problems; others had trivial ailments. In all cases I strongly recommended that they seek professional medical help. I am not a doctor, nor am I a "healer" in the sense that the prophet Elisha, Jesus, and others have been. But often I find that the true problem is not medical, but spiritual.

One of the strangest cases brought to my attention was that of a woman who had suffered a series of illnesses over a period of time. She told me, "God has it in for me. I'm a sinner. This is why I'm being punished." She also told me that she had gone to a man who hypnotized her and read her past. He attributed her illnesses to a life she had previously lived, in which she had been an evil person who had harmed many people. As she had not been punished in that life, she was now suffering for the sins she had committed then, he told her.

Of course that was nonsense. It only made things worse.

I explained to her an age-old truth: There is but One Power, called God, the Living Spirit Almighty. Not two, three, or a thousand. It is the Creative Intelligence in all of us that created us. This Power becomes for us what we believe it to be. To the forward, I am forward; to the pure, I am pure. If you think and believe there is a God of love, then the God of love will respond to you and become a loving being to you. If you think that God is punishing you and that you must suffer, according to your thought and belief it is done unto you. But in reality you are punishing yourself. As the

Bible says, it is done unto him as he believes. For as a man thinketh in his heart, so is he.

This woman was seeking justification and alibis for her suffering. She was looking outside herself instead of realizing that the source of her illness was always in her deeper mind and that nothing happens to the body unless there is a pattern in the subconscious mind

I asked her to look inside herself and determine if there was something in her past about which she felt a deep sense of guilt. She confessed that she had had a love affair with a married man a few years ago and that she felt guilty and should be punished. With guilt comes fear and apprehension. And with fear comes punishment. She felt that she should be punished, and she was punishing herself.

Guilt is the curse of curses. It's one of the most destructive of all emotions and cannot have a constructive outlet. These negative emotions get snarled up in the subconscious mind and come forth as illness and disease. This unresolved remorse was the psychic wound behind her illnesses. I helped her realize that God was not punishing her but that she was punishing herself with her own thoughts. My explanation was the cure: She forgave herself, and she sat down for 20 minutes several times a day and said, "God's healing love saturates my soul, and I forgive myself for harboring these negative, destructive thoughts." When she ceased to condemn herself and began to claim that the Infinite Healing Presence was saturating her whole being and that God dwells in every cell of her body, her illnesses disappeared. As she decided to forgive herself, God's healing love healed her. Her illnesses abated; and she was soon back to living a full, healthy, productive life.

Your subconscious assumptions, beliefs, and convictions dictate and control all your conscious actions. Your subconscious beliefs impel, propel, and compel. Whatever you sow, you reap. Your thoughts and feelings create your destiny.

You are what you think about all day long. If you fail to think constructively, wisely, and judiciously, then someone else, or the mass mind, will do your thinking for you, and perhaps make

a complete mess of your life. If you believe that God is Infinite goodness, boundless love, absolute harmony, and pure wisdom, the God Presence will respond accordingly by the law of reciprocal relationship, and you will find yourself blessed in countless ways.

Whether a force of life is good or bad depends on how you use it. Atomic energy is not evil; it is good or bad depending on whether you use it to power a city or create a deadly bomb. You can use electricity to kill someone or to vacuum the floor. You can use water to quench a child's thirst or drown him. You can use nitric acid to paint a beautiful Madonna on a windowpane or to blind a person. The wind that dashes a ship on the rocks can also carry it to safety. Good and evil are, therefore, in our minds. It is the human mind that determines the use of the forces and objects in the world.

No matter how long you might have used your mind in a negative and destructive manner, the minute you begin to use it the right way, the right results follow. Remember not the former things, nor consider the things of old. *This one thing I do: forgetting the things that are behind, reaching forth to the things that are before, I press toward the mark for the prize.*

The prize, of course, is health, happiness, peace of mind, joy, and all the good things of life. Think good, and good follows; think evil, and evil follows. The minute you enthrone in your mind Godlike ideas and eternal verities, they generate their own fragrance. Then your heart becomes a chalice for God's love, and the brain and the heart unite in accord based on eternal verities. Then all your ways will be pleasant, and all your paths will be peaceful.

Nothing happens by chance. It's a universe of law and order and, therefore, everything happens according to the law of cause and effect. There is a cause behind everything. However, we don't always see the cause operating in a given instance and attribute it to chance, coincidence, or accident.

Charles R. was afraid that he was losing his vision. He went to an ophthalmologist and learned that he did not have cataracts or glaucoma or any of the usual symptoms leading to blindness. Further tests found no medical evidence of incipient blindness,

yet in fact his vision was slowly but surely dimming. The medical profession today understands that psychic factors play a definite role in all disease. Disease is the lack of peace, equilibrium, and serenity. It's impossible to have a healthy mind and a sick body.

A healthy mind is a healthy body. Nothing happens in the body unless the equivalent is in the mind. There's no doubt that visual problems can be brought on by workings of the mind. Emotional reactions can cause the involuntary muscles to twist the eyeball out of shape. Treating the mental and emotional factors of the individual rather than just concentrating on the eyes may reveal the basic emotional factor, the reason why the subconscious mind is selecting an ailment that tends to shut out everything except the immediate surroundings.

In my conversations with Charles he constantly complained about his mother-in-law, who was living in his home. He vehemently stated, "I can't stand the sight of that woman." He was full of suppressed rage. His emotional system, which could not stand the strain any longer, selected the eyes as a scapegoat. The explanation was the cure in this case. He was surprised to learn that negative emotions, if persisted in, snarl up in the subconscious mind and, being negative, must have a destructive outlet.

The commands to his subconscious mind were negative: "I hate the sight of her. I don't want to see her anymore." I explained to him that the subconscious mind takes you literally. His statements were accepted by his subconscious mind, and the subconscious looked upon that as a request and proceeded to bring on loss of vision.

He and his wife agreed that it would be best if his mother-in-law lived elsewhere. They arranged for her to move to a senior-citizen facility not too far away. However, simply moving her to another residence would not solve the problem entirely. Charles had to erase his hatred of his mother-in-law from his mind. At my suggestion, he prayed for her by releasing her to God and wishing for her all the blessings of heaven. He did it in a very simple way. He said: "I surrender my mother-in-law [mentioning her name] to God completely. I radiate love, peace, and goodwill to her. I wish for her all the blessings of heaven. I mean this. I'm sincere. I decree

it. It shall all come to pass, and the light of God shall shine upon her ways."

As he continued to pray, I explained to him that he would know he had completely accepted her when he could meet her in his mind without feeling a sting. He would no longer sizzle. His vision began to improve almost immediately, and soon his eyesight was restored to normal. The ophthalmologist looked at his eyes and said, "You solved your problem"—and he *had* solved his problem. He could meet his mother-in-law in his mind and there was no sting there. He no longer sizzled.

In the beginning of this chapter, I stated that you should concentrate your thoughts on those things that are true, lovely, noble, and Godlike. Think about these things, because you are what you think about all day long. Our life is what our thoughts have made it. You don't want the irrational mass mind thinking in you, do you? No, you don't. If you do not think for yourself, you must ask yourself who is manipulating your mind now. Ask yourself: Do I own my own mind? Do I come to my own decisions? Am I thinking clearly, according to Godlike patterns?

You cannot dodge or circumvent the law of mind. It is done unto you as you believe. Years ago the English sailors blamed scurvy on the salted meat they ate exclusively—hardtack and so on. Then someone told them to eat some limes and lemons, full of vitamin C, and of course they were healed. But you see, their scurvy had been due to ignorance, carelessness, indifference, and stupidity. It was a void in the mind, because all the islands and all the countries they visited in their long voyages were full of oranges, apples, limes, lemons, and all kinds of citrus fruits. So where was the lack? The lack was in the mind. The sailors' mistake was carelessness, indifference, and apathy.

People often erroneously attribute their ailments to the atmosphere, the weather, malpractice, evil entities, germs, viruses, and poor diets. Most of us have no doubt that an invisible virus can make us ill, but we don't always believe in the Invisible Presence and Power called God, Which created us and created the whole world.

We pollute the air with strange notions and false doctrines. If we believe that by sitting near an electric fan, we can catch a cold or get a stiff neck, that belief, when accepted, becomes our master and ruler and causes us to experience a cold. Millions of people sit under fans all over the world without getting a stiff neck or cold. The fan is harmless. Millions of people go out in the night air and don't get a chill or pneumonia—ever. Maybe your mother said that when you get your feet wet and you don't dry them and put on new socks, you'll catch your death of cold or pneumonia. Nonetheless, millions of people get their feet wet without getting sick. The water never said, "I'll give you pneumonia, a chill, or a fever."

According to your belief, it is done unto you. According to your faith, it is done unto you. Your faith should be in the goodness of God in the land of the living; in the guidance, healing power, and abundance of God; and in the fact that an Infinite Intelligence responds to you when you call upon It.

Your faith can be used in two ways. You can have faith in an invisible virus to give you the flu, or you can have faith in the invisible Spirit within you to flow through you as harmony, health, peace, guidance, and right action. The God or Spirit in you cannot be sick. What is true of God is true of you, because the word *individual* means the Indivisible One. That's the Living Spirit Almighty within you. The Bible says: "Ye are Gods; and all of you are children of the Most High." Believe that you are a child of the Living God. Believe that the Living Spirit within you is the God Presence, Which can't be sick.

Emerson said that fate is "a name for facts not yet passed under the fire of thought; for causes which are unpenetrated." The soul (the subconscious mind) contains the event that shall befall it, for the event is only the actualization of its thoughts. What we pray for is always granted.

The devil in the Bible means ignorance, misunderstanding, or misapplication of the law. It means a false concept of God, life, and the universe. Actually, it means God upside down—a twisted, morbid, diabolical concept of the God of love. There's no being with hooves, horns, and a tail. This comes out of our

distorted imagination. Not willing to admit that the evil is within ourselves, we postulate that it is outside ourselves. Surely, God is Omnipresent, which means that God must be present in us too.

A man told me, for example, that he was wounded in the jungle and he prayed that someone would come and rescue him. He said: "There was another man who was hunting in that jungle who had a sudden feeling that he should change his course. He did so and came and administered to my wound and helped me get back to safety." The man who was wounded was praying for help, and the man who was out hunting changed his course. He had an intuitive feeling, a perception. It was the Infinite Intelligence guiding the hunter to become the wounded man's rescuer, but it was the One Being operating in both men.

It is done unto you as you believe, and a belief is a thought in the mind. No external power or evil entity is trying to lure or harm you. People are constantly attributing their ailments to the atmosphere, the weather, or even someone practicing black magic against them. However, no person has any dark power over you. The Power of God is in you. One with God is a majority. If God is for you, who can be against you?

Spell *live* backward and you have *evil*. That's living life backward. Evil is the inversion of the Life Principle, Which is God. God moves as Unity and seeks to express Himself through you as beauty, love, joy, peace, and Divine order. The will of God for you is a greater measure of life, love, truth, and beauty—something transcending your fondest dreams.

Realize, therefore, that God is guiding you and that there is right action in your life. Read and meditate on the 91st Psalm, (see Chapter 6) and realize that you dwell in the secret place of the Most High, that you abide in the shadow of the Almighty. You'll say of the Lord: *He is my refuge and my fortress; my God, in Him will I trust. He covers me with His feathers; under His wings shall I trust.* Just like the hen gathers the chickens together to protect them, so does that Heavenly Father in you surround you with the invisible arm of God's love, rendering you impervious to all harm. You become immunized and God-intoxicated because you've received the Divine antibody.

The false idea in your mind is called the adversary, the devil, Satan, and so on. The devils that torment you are enmity, strife, and hatred; they are devils created by you. They drive some people insane. If you put gangsters in charge of your mind, what do you expect? If you fail to believe in the goodness of God and a God of love, you may turn to beliefs in a so-called devil, which is the source of your pains, aches, and misfortune.

God, the Living Spirit Almighty, doesn't judge or punish; He can't. Good and evil are the movements of one's own mind. It is very primitive thinking to believe that God is punishing us or that a devil is tempting us.

Your state of consciousness is always made manifest. This consciousness is the way you think, believe, and feel—whatever you give mental consent to. There is no other cause in the world. Men, women, and children are constantly testifying to one's state of mind, mental attitudes, convictions, and beliefs.

We must remember that the majority of people do not discipline, control, or direct their thinking and mental imagery along Godlike channels. Their failure to think constructively and harmoniously from the standpoint of the Infinite One means that they leave their minds open to the irrational mass mind, which is full of fear, hate, jealousy, and all kinds of negative happenings and destructive thinking.

There is a story of a man who had been fired from his job by a cruel and mean boss. He made up his mind to shoot his former employer. Every day the man waited behind a shed near the factory for the boss to pass by. To avoid being caught, he planned to wait for a time when nobody else was near.

On the third morning, when he was moving stealthily behind the shed, the disgruntled man stumbled and his rifle went off. A bullet pierced his heart and he killed himself.

People call that an accident, but it was no such thing. He had murder in his heart. In the Ten Commandments we are told, "Thou shall do no murder." It doesn't say, "Thou shalt not kill." That is a commonly held belief because of an early mistranslation of the

original Hebrew, which stated, "Thou shall do no murder." The Bible also tells you that murder is of the heart.

When you hate and resent and are full of hostility and resentment, you are murdering love, peace, harmony, discernment, kindness, and everything that's good. As you continue to hate and resent, these negative emotions reach a point of saturation in your subconscious mind and are precipitated as cancer, a bullet, a fatal accident, or something else. There are no accidents. A gun is harmless—it's just a piece of metal. It doesn't do any harm to anybody. It's the mind behind the instrument that kills. You can kill with a stone, a knife, or a club. There are a thousand and one ways, but the stone is harmless and the club is harmless. This man had had murder in his heart for a long time, and his subconscious responded accordingly.

The Bible says, "No man can come to me unless the Father who sent me draws him." The father of everything is your thoughts and feelings. The union of your conscious and subconscious mind, your thought and feeling, is the cause of your destiny—of every single thing in your world. Whatever your conscious and subconscious minds agree on comes to pass. Any idea that you dwell on must come to fruition.

The Father is your state of consciousness, your own creative power that brings all things to pass in your world. No experience comes to you unless there's an affinity in your own mind. Two unlike things repel each other. Harmony and discord do not dwell together. Therefore, if you believe that the whole armor of God surrounds, enfolds, and enwraps you; and that the harmonizing, healing power of God takes care of you, you can't be on a train that gets wrecked, a plane that catches on fire, or the path of a bomb. If you walk and talk with God, and believe that God is guiding you and that the law of harmony is always governing you, then you cannot become the victim of a disaster, because, as I said, discord and harmony do not dwell together.

It would be naive to assume that changing one's beliefs from negative to positive can cure all illnesses and disabilities. There are,

indeed, organic and physical causes for most ailments. However, a significant proportion of health problems are psychosomatic. It is these that changes in thought can reverse. I have heard about examples of this in many countries, and I have been instrumental in helping many people by providing them with prayers and meditations to help program their subconscious minds to bring them back to health.

Guilt, worry, and fear are the psychosomatic equivalent of germs and viruses. By replacing thoughts of guilt, worry, and fear with thoughts of faith, confidence, and forgiveness, healing is accelerated.

Most cases of healing are not at all dramatic. These include insomnia, allergies, headaches, or digestive disorders. In other instances, major maladies such as tumors, paralysis, depression, coronary disease, or psychological breakdowns may be healed through a change in thinking.

When afflicted, we tend to blame others. It may be another person: "I've been cursed by an enemy." It may be your family history: "I come from a weak genetic background." It may be Divine retribution: "I'm being punished by God."

As shown earlier in this chapter, the real cause lies within you. It is you, and only you, who has control of your thoughts. Others may influence you, but only you can make the decision about what will be accepted by your conscious mind and seep down into your subconscious.

Let us cease blaming others. Let us instead look within for the cause of all. Believe in God and God's goodness, love, and guidance, and you will find that all your ways will be pleasant and all your paths will be peaceful, because you are belief expressed.

People ask me about children. They say that children don't know how to pray and that some are caught in a fire, drowned at sea, and become the victims of other tragedies. I respond that children are under the watchful eyes of their parents and that God gave love to all fathers and all mothers, to the lion and the lioness, and to all animals. God's love dwells within the father and mother,

and it is their mission to cause that child to grow in the image and the likeness of the Divine Presence of God.

The child cannot yet discern and reason; therefore, the parents mold the consciousness of the child. A child is subject to the atmosphere in the home and grows up adopting the emotional climate that prevails. You therefore need to realize that the child is God's child and that God's love fills his or her soul; it's growing in wisdom, truth, and beauty. God planted His love in fathers and mothers that they might lead their children through the darkness of the night and through the vicissitudes of life into a realization of God's Holy Presence—to teach them that the love of God is flowing through them in transcendent loveliness. Children brought up to believe that God is love, and that His love enfolds, surrounds, and enwraps them, will grow in a magnificent way, and God will be with them all the days of their life.

In a Nutshell

When your thoughts are completely free from fear and worry, you are thinking from the standpoint of the Divine center within you; and God speaks, thinks, and acts through you. Speak, therefore, in words of wisdom and harmony, truth and beauty, and health and peace.

If you do not think constructively, harmoniously, and peacefully, the mass mind will do your thinking for you. The mass mind believes in tragedy, misfortune, sickness, disease, accidents, hate, murder, and all sorts of unhappy occurrences. If you don't do your own thinking, these negative vibrations, or thoughts of the mass mind, move in upon you; reach a point of saturation; and precipitate as accident, misfortune, sickness, and disease.

The law of life is the law of belief. If you fear sickness, you attract it. If you focus on good health, you will be healthy. The law of the Lord is perfect. You can't think one thing and produce another. Trouble of any kind is nature's alarm system, telling us

that we are thinking wrongly. Nothing but a change of thought can set us free.

There is no worse suffering than a guilty conscience, and certainly none more destructive. Stop condemning yourself and begin to accept that the Infinite Healing Presence saturates your whole being, that God dwells in every cell of your body.

It is done unto you as you believe, and a belief is a thought in the mind. No external power or evil entity is trying to lure or harm you. No person has any negative power over you. The Power of God is in you. One with God is a majority. If God is for you, who can be against you?

Guilt, worry, and fear are the psychosomatic equivalent of germs and viruses. By replacing thoughts of guilt, worry, and fear with thoughts of faith, confidence and forgiveness, healing is accelerated.

•●· ·●•

Chapter Eight

Prayer Is the Key

*A*re you consumed with fear or worry? From time to time all people face problems that dominate their lives. Some of our worries are unfounded, as we get upset about things that are unlikely to occur or are figments of our imagination. But often the problems are real and imminent. We worry about debts we can't pay, our health or the health of a loved one, our jobs, or our investments.

The first step in overcoming these worries is to take pragmatic actions to correct the problem. However, we must also program our minds so that we have the confidence to work through the problems and restore and maintain a positive outlook on life.

There is one key to accomplishing this: prayer and meditation.

What is prayer? Your every thought and feeling is your prayer. Every thought tends to manifest itself unless it is neutralized by a thought of greater intensity. Prayer is conscious contact with the Infinite Intelligence within you. It's based upon the spiritual premise that there's a Supreme Intelligence within us that becomes the thing we desire. Effective prayer is a sustained, affirmative attitude of mind. Once your desire is completely accepted subconsciously, it's fulfilled automatically as part of the creative law.

There's an Infinite Intelligence operating in your subconscious mind that responds to your conscious mind's thinking and imagining. You must come to a definite decision in your conscious mind. You must decide what you want to know, then trust the

deeper mind to answer you. When you turn your request over to your subconscious mind, you should do so with the absolute conviction that it has the know-how of accomplishment and that it will respond to you according to the nature of your request.

When you have reached a conviction, your mind accepts the idea completely and cannot conceive of the opposite. When your belief is total, you have truly impressed your subconscious mind, and it will respond accordingly.

The Bible says, "Ask and it shall be given you; seek, and ye shall find; knock, and it shall be opened unto you. For everyone that asketh, receiveth; and he that seeketh, findeth; and to him that knocketh, it shall be opened. What man is there of you whom, if his son asks bread, will he give him a stone? Or if he ask a fish, will he give him a serpent?"

The Bible tells you that when you ask for bread, you will not get a stone but the embodiment of your request. Keep on asking, seeking, and knocking until you receive a response from your subconscious mind, the nature of which is responsiveness. Become enthusiastic. Feel and know that there is a solution to every problem, a way out of every dilemma, and that there are no incurable conditions. There are people who believe that they are incurable, and of course it's done unto them as they believe. But with God, all things are possible.

We all seek serenity in our lives. Serenity is our strength in God—the healing, protective Presence within and around us. Serenity is the higher awareness of the Presence of God that enables us to remain utterly calm and poised regardless of the turmoil, turbulence, and confusion that are rampant in the world around us.

Serenity is within the reach and grasp of all of us. It's our refuge and fortress in times of trouble and constant change. When we look to the outer or world conditions for stability and sustenance, we look in vain. The outer world only offers us false evidence about what is real.

Worries and fears destroy your serenity. It can be restored if you pray effectively, changing your mind to conform to the

eternal verities, which never change. You do not beg, supplicate, or beseech. To do so is to attract more lack and limitation, because you're thereby denying that your good is already given to you, for God is the giver and the gift. No matter what you seek, it already is, because everything comes forth from the Infinite. You simply reorder your mind and align yourself with the truth.

When the Nazi army marched into Vienna in March 1938, Vicki W. faced a major crisis. Although she was Catholic, she had recently married a Jew. The Nazis declared all marriages between Jews and gentiles void. Her family pleaded with her to accept the Nazi-ordained annulment and come home to them. Her husband, fearful that she would share his fate, urged her to do the same. He said, "I don't know what will happen to me. You'll be better off if you leave me."

Vicki prayed, "I love my husband. I want to stay with him, to raise a family with him, and I know the dangers. We may be forcibly separated, sent to concentration camps, and even killed. Please God, give me the strength and wisdom to make the right decision."

She said this prayer each morning at church and again each evening at home, and she refused to leave her marriage. Meanwhile, her husband put all of his efforts into attempting to find a way to leave Austria. They were frustrated over and over again, but her prayers kept them from losing hope.

After working through the bureaucratic red tape, and with the help of her husband's relatives in the United States, they at last obtained visas to come to America. They left Austria just weeks before the Nazis clamped down on Jews trying to emigrate.

Vicki and her husband settled in Los Angeles and raised a fine family. Prayer helped her through this and other crises in her life.

Most people do not have to face such life-threatening situations, but do worry about their day-to-day problems. A common source of worry is discord in the home or at work. Prayer can help. You can claim that the absolute harmony of the Infinite One reigns supreme in your mind, and in that of the other person or persons. This prayer of the absolute harmony of the Infinite will bring about

results. Rearrange all your thoughts, imagery, and responses on the side of peace and harmony. If you see hatred in another, practice knowing that Divine love dissolves everything unlike Itself in the mind and heart of that person, and also in your own mind and heart. This is effective prayer.

What is true of the Infinite is true of you. To know this is the truth that sets you free. If you do not know the answer to a perplexing problem, claim that the wisdom of the Infinite reveals the answer to you, and you will receive it. God is the name for that Infinite Presence and Power within you. Where Divine love, peace, harmony, and joy live, there's no evil, harm, or sickness.

The cure for all your problems is to practice the Presence of God, which means to fill your soul with Divine love, peace, power, harmony, and right action. If you believe in sickness, disease, and failure, you will always manifest your beliefs. The great truths of the Infinite are available to all, just as the sun shines on both the just and the unjust, and rain falls on both the good and the evil. All that's necessary is faith in God. Faith in its true meaning is the practice of the Presence of God.

From the earliest times, people have asked why we have wars, famines, disasters, and ill health. These are given to us that we might mature within ourselves and achieve a state of serenity within ourselves. All the problems, vicissitudes, and vexations we experience cause us to wake up and become mature.

The problems of life do not exist in conditions or circumstances, but in the minds of men and women. This idea is not popular with those who desire to hear only how mistreated and abused they are; however, for those who want to heal themselves and their lives, it's a blessing to know that the Presence within them says, "You are greater than you may now know!"

The majority of individuals claim that society, the world, or their parents and family are responsible for their misery and unhappiness. This isn't true. The wisdom of the Presence within says: "You're responsible for triumph and achievement. You have aspired to higher understanding and you know a better way!"

One of the greatest and most liberating triumphs is the knowledge and wisdom that there are certain things that you cannot change and that you don't have to try to. All that's required is that you change your perceptions and convictions. Everyone has a God-given privilege to be as he or she is. Let them go to find their highest good in God. The weight of the world will fall from your shoulders! You are not responsible for the world. Heal yourself and let go of the belief that you are responsible for the ills and evils of the world.

Allow everyone, including your children, to find themselves. You've done your best to give them a sense of ethics and morality—no one can do more than that. Let them go and release them to God. Heal yourself of the messianic complex and the perception that you're responsible for everything. You are not! You cannot save the world.

You're only responsible for yourself. Change yourself and your world (the world) will change for the better. Your positive change contributes to the good of the world. The alternative is to wait for the entire world to change. Why weary and exhaust yourself further? What has it accomplished?

Serenity is spiritual maturity. It's achieved following the realization that God, the Father within and of all, is in charge of the universe and the world. "The Father within doeth the works." Taking charge of yourself—and only yourself—provides serenity in the face of change. It may sound callous to state these ideas, but it isn't. It's pragmatic and effective.

Some years ago I listened to a sales manager talk to his staff. He said, "The first thing you do is find a prospect. The second step is to get that person's attention and interest. The third step is to win his or her confidence and create a desire. The fourth step is to close the sale." The process that leads to a successful sale can also be applied to successful prayer.

Are you sold on the Infinite? Do you believe implicitly that God, the Infinite Intelligence in you, can heal you? This is your first step in making prayer work for you. It can solve your problem; wipe away all tears; and set you on the high road to happiness,

freedom, and peace of mind. The second step is to get the attention and interest of your Higher Self. If you believe implicitly that there is a Healing Presence within you, you are selling yourself to your Higher Self. Give your attention to the Infinite and Divine love. Believe that God Who made you can heal you. Be sincere and honest. Give all power and allegiance to the Infinite. You must give allegiance and recognition to no other power. Then and only then are you selling yourself to the Infinite.

Begin to use your mind in the right way. Refuse to give power to anything but the Living Spirit Almighty within you. Then you eliminate false beliefs from your mind and touch the Presence of the Infinite, resulting in an instantaneous healing.

In other words, the first step in praying effectively is complete allegiance, devotion, and loyalty to the Only Presence and Power within you. This Power created you, and It can heal you. Second, you must definitely, absolutely, and completely refuse to give power to any external thing or any other power but the Infinite. You should not give power to the phenomenalistic world—or to any person, place, or thing. Third, whatever difficulty or sickness you may face, turn away from the problem and affirm feelingly and knowingly: "God is, and this Infinite Healing Presence flows through me now, vitalizing, energizing, and healing my whole being. Infinite love flows through me as right action and Divine freedom."

The fourth step is to give thanks for the happy solution. Rejoice and say: "Father, I thank Thee for the perfect answer. I know it's God in action now. I've mentally touched the border of His garment, and I've pinpointed the whole reaction of the Infinite Power. It's wonderful."

Turn to the Divine Presence and remind yourself of that Infinite ocean of peace, absolute harmony, wholeness, beauty, boundless love, and limitless power. Know that the Infinite Presence and Power loves and cares for you. As you pray this way, fear will gradually fade away. Turn your mind to God and His love. Feel and know that there is only One Healing Power and Its corollary. There is no power to challenge the action of the Infinite.

Quietly and lovingly affirm that the uplifting, healing, strengthening power of the Healing Presence is flowing through you, making you whole. Know and feel that the harmony, beauty, and life of the Infinite are made manifest in you as strength, peace, vitality, beauty, wholeness, and right action.

If you pray about a heart condition, don't think of the diseased organ. This wouldn't be spiritual thinking. Thoughts are things. Your spiritual thought takes the form of cells, tissue, nerves, and organs. Thinking about a damaged heart or high blood pressure tends to create more of what you already have and don't want. Cease dwelling on symptoms, organs, or any part of the body. Simply focus on the Infinite Healing Presence within you, flowing through you as beauty, love, harmony, joy, wisdom, power, and strength—then you are really glorifying God in your body.

Live joyously in the world, but don't succumb and eat and drink of its ills and travails. Extract every sense of joy and pleasure within it. The providence, love, and protection of God are all around. Open your eyes to see them, and your heart to receive them. Your heart will be fulfilled and serene with the unchanging, eternal love of God.

In a Nutshell

Your every thought and feeling is your prayer. Every thought tends to manifest itself unless it's neutralized by a thought of greater intensity. Prayer is conscious contact with the Infinite Intelligence within you. Effective prayer must be based upon the spiritual premise that there's a Supreme Intelligence within us that becomes the thing we desire.

There's an Infinite Intelligence operating in your subconscious mind that responds to your conscious mind's thinking and imagining. When you turn your request over to your subconscious mind, you should do so with the absolute conviction that it has the know-how of accomplishment and that it will respond to you according to the nature of your request.

If you're experiencing discord with another person, rearrange all your thoughts, imagery, and responses on the side of peace and harmony. If you see hatred in another, practice knowing that Divine love dissolves everything unlike Itself in the mind and heart of that person, and also in your own mind and heart.

All that's required and asked of you is that you change your perceptions and convictions and know that everyone has the God-given privilege to be as he or she is. Let them go to find their highest good in God. The weight of the world will fall from your shoulders! You aren't responsible for the world. Heal yourself and let go of the idea that you are responsible for the ills and evils of the world.

Know that the Infinite Presence and Power loves and cares for you. As you pray this way, fear will gradually fade away. Turn your mind to God and His love. Feel and know that there's only One Healing Power and Its corollary. There's no power to challenge the action of the Infinite.

•●· ·●·

Chapter Nine

Sleep Soundly

*W*e spend about 8 out of every 24 hours, or one-third of our lives, sleeping. Many people believe that the body repairs itself when we sleep. New cells grow to replace worn-out ones, and nerves and organs revitalize themselves. If we eat prior to sleeping, the food is digested and assimilated. Also, our skin secretes perspiration and our nails continue to grow while we're sleeping.

Most important, our subconscious mind never rests or sleeps. It's always active, controlling all our vital forces. In sleep, the conscious mind is creatively joined to the subconscious. The healing process takes place more rapidly while we're asleep because there's no interference from the conscious mind. Quite often, answers to the problems that have been on our mind all day are given to us when we're sound asleep.

He who watches over all of us neither slumbers nor sleeps. Go to sleep every night, therefore, with the praise of God on your lips. Sleep is indispensable to your perfect spiritual development.

It's generally accepted that all human beings need a minimum of six hours of sleep to be healthy. Most people need more. A lack of sleep causes you to become irritable, moody, and depressed. Medical researchers investigating sleep and sleep deprivation point out that severe insomnia has preceded psychotic breakdown in some instances. Remember, you're spiritually recharged during

sleep, and adequate sleep is essential to experiencing joy and vitality in life.

In some studies of sleep deprivation, subjects have been kept awake for as long as four days. These tests have given scientists astonishing new insights into the mysteries of sleep. They now know that the tired brain craves sleep so much that it will sacrifice anything to get it. After only a few hours of sleep loss, fleeting "stolen" naps called *lapses* occur at the rate of three or four an hour. Each lapse lasts just a fraction of a second. Sometimes the lapses are periods of blackness, but other times they're filled with images or wisps of dreams.

As the hours of sleep loss mount, the lapses occur more frequently and last longer. Even if sleep-deprived subjects are piloting an airliner in a thunderstorm, they still can't resist these few priceless seconds of sleep. It can happen to anyone, as many who have fallen asleep at the wheel of a car can testify.

Sleep deprivation affects human memory and perception. Many sleep-deprived subjects in the studies were unable to retain information and perform tasks efficiently. They were totally befuddled in situations requiring them to hold several factors in mind and act on them, as pilots must when they skillfully take into account wind direction, air speed, altitude, and glide path to make a safe landing.

For example, the opportunity George G. was offered seemed fantastic. A friend who was a brilliant engineer was starting a new company in the rapidly growing Internet industry, and George had great confidence in his technical skills. The investment required was $50,000—practically all the money George had in his portfolio. He pondered over whether to accept. Success would make him a millionaire, but failure would wipe him out.

Prior to going to sleep the night before the decision had to be made, he prayed as follows:

The Creative Intelligence of my subconscious mind knows what's best for me and reveals to me the right decision, which

blesses me and all concerned. I give thanks for the answer, which I know will come to me.

George repeated this simple prayer over and over as a lullaby prior to sleep. In the morning he had a persistent feeling that he should not make the investment. The temptation to take the risk was great, but he chose to follow his feelings and declined the offer. He watched the company start up and begin to flourish, but only a few months later the entire dot-com boom ended, and his friend's company collapsed.

George's conscious mind knew the objective facts about the Internet company, but the intuitive faculty of his subconscious mind saw the failure to come and guided him to the right decision.

If you suffer from insomnia, just dwell upon these wonderful words from the Psalms. Psalm 4 says: "I will both lay me down in peace and sleep; for Thou, Lord, only makest me dwell in safety." And Psalm 121 says: "He that keepeth Israel shall neither slumber nor sleep." In the book of Proverbs, it says: "When thou liest down, thou shalt not be afraid . . . thy sleep shall be sweet."

As you fall asleep, repeat to yourself, "I will lay me down in peace to sleep, for Thou, Lord, maketh me dwell in safety." You will be amazed what a wonderful, peaceful sleep you will have.

Relax and let go. What you're seeking is your desire, the ideal, and the thing closest to your heart. Realize that God gave you that desire. Say, "I go off to sleep and I completely accept it, and I walk in the light." Accept the reality of your desire as you go to sleep. Assume that you now have what you long to possess and that you're now experiencing that which you long to feel. You go off into the deep of sleep and you impregnate your subconscious mind.

If you repeat the word *peace* to yourself, chanting "Peace, peace, peace . . . ," you will fall asleep, too. Or you can repeat the word *sleep* to lull yourself to sleep. Just say this one word silently to yourself and you will fall into the deep of sleep.

Sleep is a state of oneness. If you have difficulties sleeping, when you close your eyes every night, say to yourself, "I sleep in

peace. I wake in joy. I live in God." Or say, "I sleep for eight hours in peace. I wake in joy. I live in God." Then lull yourself to sleep by repeating the word *peace* or *sleep.*

The following prayer helps give confidence, peace, and comfort. Repeat it each night when you lie down:

> *Eternal God, grant that we may lie down in peace and raise us up to life renewed. Spread over us the shelter of Your peace; guide us with Your good counsel; and for Your name's sake, be our help.*
>
> *Shield us from hatred and plague; keep us from war, famine, and anguish; subdue our inclinations to evil. O God, our guardian and helper, our gracious and merciful ruler, give us refuge in the shadow of Your wings. Guard our coming and going, that now and always we have life and peace.*

In my book *The Power of Your Subconscious Mind,* I tell the story of how a marvelous answer was given to a man during a two-minute nap. His name was Ray Hammerstrong, a worker in a steel mill in Pennsylvania. A faulty switch in a newly installed bar mill that controlled the delivery of straight bars to the cooling beds wasn't working properly and was delaying production. The engineers worked on the switch but couldn't solve the problem.

Hammerstrong thought a lot about the problem and tried to figure out a new design that might work, but couldn't come up with a solution. One afternoon he lay down to take a nap. Before sleeping, he began to think about the answer to the switch problem. He had a dream while he was sound asleep in which a perfect design for the switch was portrayed. When he awoke, he sketched his new design according to the outline in his dream. His visionary catnap won Hammerstrong a check for $15,000, the largest award the firm had ever given an employee for a new idea.

You're often instructed in your sleep and given solutions to your problems. So is the scientist, and so is the chemist. You're the master of your thoughts, emotions, and responses to life. When

you pray, become a good executive. Learn to delegate and turn your request over to your subconscious mind with faith and confidence. Know in your heart that you've given your request to the deeper mind, full of wisdom and intelligence. You will receive an answer, for it's written in the Bible: "In quietness and confidence shall be your strength."

Never go to sleep with negative thoughts in your mind. It's of the utmost importance to make yourself feel strong and optimistic at night; to erase all signs, convictions, and feelings of uncertainty and fear; to throw aside every care and worry that would carve its image on your brain and express itself in your face. The worrying mind actually generates calcareous matter in the brain and hardens the cells.

You should fall asleep holding uppermost in your mind those desires and ideals that are dearest to you—those you're the most eager to realize. As your mind continues to work during sleep, these desires and ideals are thus intensified and increased. Purity of thought and loftiness of purpose should dominate your mind when you fall asleep.

When you first awaken in the morning, picture positive qualities as vividly as possible. Say to yourself: "I'm healthy, strong, and buoyant. I will succeed in my goals and be healthy in body and sound in mind because I'm Divine, and Divine Principle cannot be defeated."

Remember this great prayer: "I sleep in peace, I wake in joy, and I live in God now and forevermore."

In a Nutshell

Quite often, answers to the problems that have been on your mind all day are given to you while you're asleep. Remember that you're spiritually recharged during sleep and that adequate sleep is essential to producing joy and vitality in life.

Assume that you now have what you long to possess and that you're now experiencing that which you long to feel. You fall into the deep of sleep and impregnate your subconscious mind.

You're the master of your thoughts, emotions, and responses to life. When you pray, delegate and turn your request over to your subconscious mind with faith and confidence. The deeper mind knows how to solve your problem and presents you with the answer. You will receive an answer, for it is written: "In quietness and confidence shall be your strength."

•• ••

Chapter Ten

Living in the Presence

So many people, when faced with worry and fear, turn to the book of Psalms for comfort and guidance. All 150 psalms inspire us and help us in times of trouble and travail. In previous chapters I showed how Psalms 23 and 91 are especially suited to help us deal with life's problems. In this chapter I want to present another great psalm, number 139, sometimes called "the entire Bible in miniature." As it's a very long psalm, here is an abbreviated version covering its key points:

O Lord, thou hast searched me and known me. . . .
Thou understandeth my thought, afar off.
Thou knowest my path and art acquainted with all my ways.
For there is not a word in my tongue, but, lo, O Lord,
*   thou knowest it altogether. . . .*
Whither shall I go from thy spirit? Or whither shall I flee
*   from thy presence?*
If I ascend up into heaven, thou art there. If I make my bed
*   in hell, behold, thou art there.*
If I take the wings of the morning and dwell in the
*   quttermost parts of the sea,*
Even there shall thy hand lead me and thy right hand
*   shall hold me.*

If I say, surely, the darkness shall cover me; even the night
    shall be light about me. . . .
Yea . . . the darkness and the light are both alike to thee.
For thou hast possessed my reins; thou hast covered me
    in my mother's womb.
I will praise thee; for I am fearfully and wonderfully made:
    Marvelous are thy works and that my soul knoweth right well.
My substance was not hid from thee, when I was made in secret,
    and curiously wrought in the lowest parts of the Earth.
Thine eyes did see my substance, yet being imperfect; and in thy
    book all my members were written, which in continuance
    were fashioned, when as yet there was none of them. . . .
Search me, O God, and know my heart. . . . And see if there be
    any wicked way in me, and lead me in the way everlasting.

It's no wonder that this inspired prayer has been described as the "Crown of all the Psalms." It portrays and reveals our inborn ability to correct or transform all that we consider wrong in our circumstances, through the power of the Creative Presence within, everlastingly responding to the thoughts of our mind and the meditations of our heart.

In some of the most inspired and exalted passages in scripture, Psalm 139 offers the four essential keys to a greater awareness and appreciation of who we are and the realization of our role in life. Briefly stated, these are the four essential truths:

- First, we must accept God as a Loving Presence Who is Omnipresent and universal.

- Second, this Omnipresent God is within us.

- Third, the Presence is Omniscient: God knows all and sees all—and being love, forgives.

- Fourth, we can use these first three truths to heal and restore mind-body conditions and relationships.

Psalm 139 is the Bible in miniature. It poses the deepest, most penetrating question in the Old Testament: "Whither shall I go from thy spirit? Or whither shall I flee from thy presence?" It suggests to us that the Creative Presence is far more than we may have been taught. To think of the Presence is to expand our mind and extend our most basic concepts and opinions of the very nature of God.

When the psalmist states, "If I ascend up into heaven, thou art there: if I make my bed in hell behold, thou art there," is he speaking of literal places somewhere in the skies or in the bowels of earth? Of course not. Modern interpreters of the Bible no longer take the words literally. We know that the words are metaphors for deeper thoughts.

The psalmist is talking about the omnipresence of God; and since this Almighty Presence is omnipresent, It must be in you. It's your very life. This Presence is always waiting for you to call on It. Regardless of the degree of bondage you may be in, this Presence and Power will respond as mercy—soothing, healing, and restoring your soul.

The terms *heaven* and *hell* represent our states of consciousness. Heaven is the mind at peace, a state of rest and relaxation. In heaven we're "resting in God," protected and secure as we claim these qualities of the Omnipresence. *Heaven* is also a reference to the creative act and the power of our mind, beliefs, and ideas. It's the marvel and freedom we possess. In contrast, a "bed in hell" implies a state of immobility, turbulence, and confusion—the inability to move forward or to achieve any kind of progress.

The psalmist reveals his wisdom and understanding of the Creative Principle by implying that it's our choice whether we ascend to heaven or make our bed in hell. We can develop conscious awareness of the Omnipresence and achieve tangible results and peace of mind through our prayers. Or we can focus on limitation and lack. In either event, the loving, intelligent, all-knowing Presence remains the same: forever loving and everlastingly intelligent.

At any moment, in every place, regardless of our present experience, the Divine Spirit will create that which we think

about and feel to be true. Our current lives are testimony to this magnificent and unfailing Principle and Presence. In every circumstance, we can and are urged to "arise, take up our bed, and walk" in the Light of God's love and care.

The purpose of prayer and contemplation is to cleanse the mind and heart and make them obey our conscious direction. We change our habitual thought patterns and processes and make our mind and heart disciples. It's difficult only for a little while, as we persist.

Soon we find our responses changing and following more constructive patterns. We respond (become responsible) more readily to the situation at hand, choosing to "ascend into heaven." We develop more peaceful and congenial attitudes.

Consider for yourself the life-transforming truths offered by the psalmist. *I* is the symbol of the Presence within—the symbol of love, intelligence, and wisdom. When Moses asked God His name, God responded, "I am." Observe what you say following the pronoun *I* because you're announcing your concept of God and of yourself. Don't say—even to yourself—"I'm poor. I'm lonely. I'm not good." If that's how you announce yourself, that's what you will be. Change these negative responses to positive ones. Say instead, "I'm good. I'm healthy. I'm blessed."

The psalmist describes God as an Almighty Presence, not as an anthropomorphic deity floating in the clouds and meting out punishments and rewards according to an unfathomable plan. This belief in a God outside and separate from ourselves is the primary cause of our problems. We separate ourselves from the source of all that can be imagined, the Holy One and Universal Creator of everything—including ourselves. It's this sense of separation that gives birth to the feeling that we're lost souls.

How could we possibly be outside the Holy One? It's a mathematical impossibility. Two infinites would be a contradiction— they would cancel one another out. The fundamental, conceptual premise of Life is *The Lord our God is One Lord.* All else is an elaboration and commentary on this universal, greatest of all truths. Dare and have the heart or courage to believe in and claim a loving, all-knowing God.

It's interesting to note that in at least 27 languages, the words *good* and *God* are synonymous. Let go of the idea of a punishing, reluctant, neglectful Presence, and you will begin an entirely new life and experience.

We experience a transition period when we begin to understand and adopt the principles of the All-knowing Mind of the Infinite. We're neither in heaven nor hell, but in a state of limbo. We seem unable to swim in the great ocean of life or to soar like the eagle to higher realms.

For example, a man who had read my book *The Power of Your Subconscious Mind* mentioned that it made good sense, but that in applying the truths offered, he had lost his sense and feeling of God. He said, "Now, I feel as though I have no God—only a cold, unfeeling principle."

What suggestions can be offered to someone in this state of mind? I believe the kindest thing to tell them is that this lost feeling is a normal transition. I also think it's wise to advise them to remain with their religion; to observe and follow the dogma, rites, and rituals; but continue to pray for wisdom, understanding, and guidance. Tell them to continue to seek, for those who do, with patience and forbearance, find the Loving Presence.

We will soon discover that within Divine Mind are all the characteristics and qualities of love, intelligence, patience, and direction—and these heal the sense of separation from the Source of our life and longing. We do know a loving and caring parent in God. These are the restoring truths of Psalm 139. *O Lord, thou hast searched me, and known me . . . thou understandeth my thought afar off. Thou knowest my path . . . and art acquainted with all my way. . . . Search me, O God, and know my heart . . . And see if there be any wicked way in me and lead me in the way everlasting.*

If ever a word needed to be clarified, it's *wicked.* Far too many people have been told over and again that they are wicked or intrinsically bad. This is a direct result of a misinterpretation and mistranslation of the Bible. The Hebrew-to-English lexicon defines *wicked* as any idea that causes sorrow or unhappiness. It's a term

of mental discomfort. If you find yourself in a state of hell, mental discomfort or wickedness is a signal to redirect your attention and identify with the good—*Arise, take up your bed and walk.*

However, *wicked* has come to signify an unhealthy, unwholesome attitude about ourselves. We think that unless we are perfect, we are sinful or wicked. In fact, it's too much to expect that we must—or even can—be perfect, without sin (which is simply an erroneous use of our faculties). Only God is perfect. It's not given to us to be sinless, but we must and are perfectly able to be sincere—without guile or ulterior motives.

Let go of any idea that you're wicked in the sense of "bad," "evil," or "sinful." If your intent is to better yourself without harming another, you're free and forgiven of wickedness. You are innately, intrinsically good. Accept and acknowledge your royal and Divine inheritance! Dare to believe you are a child of the King of Kings. Walk the Lord's highway. All is yours! To the man or woman who understands God as a loving parent, these words are a source of comfort and support in a time of need.

Please don't be fearful or afraid of a word. Learn and think about what it conveys or means. We should be eager to learn, as children are eager and joyous to discover the world around them.

The open, receptive mind and heart welcome the Higher Understanding that knows, sees, and is concerned for our welfare. The open mind is willing and eager to accept God as all good. How could that possibly be harmful? On the contrary, it's the joy and strength of life. As the mother watches over and protects her child, so the good God watches over each of us. Psalm 139 describes this: *Thou hast covered me in my mother's womb. I will praise thee, for I am fearfully and wonderfully made. Marvelous are thy works; and that my soul knoweth right well.*

Infinite Intelligence created all of your cells, organs, and body from the Divine pattern embodied in the fertilized cell. Infinite Intelligence knows all the processes and functions of your body and knows how to heal and restore any organ. Claim, feel, know, and believe with all your mind, heart, and soul: "The Infinite

Healing Presence moves through every atom of my being, renewing and restoring me to full and radiant health." Picture a river of golden light flowing through and within you—from the crown of your head to the soles of your feet.

If you are in the care of a physician, cooperate fully and remember to pray for his or her guidance and enlightenment to do the right thing in the right way at the right time. Do not begrudge or resent the physician or remedy. Doctors possess a wealth of healing knowledge and have your best interest at heart. Pray this way and you will be directed along the path of ideal healing.

Also use prayer to heal and correct any and all aspects of your life. You will discover health, wealth, and congenial relationships becoming part of your experience.

Guidance is given in the form of inner prompting, urges, and ideas, and we quickly learn to recognize when we are being led along the path of contentment and perfect peace of mind. Meditate and contemplate Psalm 139, this Crown of all Psalms, and you will discover that guidance has already begun. Fear and worry will fade away and be replaced with confidence, optimism, and inspiration, which will seep into your subconscious mind and restore you to a serene and happy life.

In a Nutshell

These are the four essential truths:

- First, we must accept God as a Loving Presence Who is Omnipresent and universal.

- Second, this Omnipresent God is within us.

- Third, the Presence is Omniscient: God knows all and sees all—and being love, forgives.

- Fourth, we can use these first three truths to heal and restore mind-body conditions and relationships.

The Divine Source is Omnipresent and always waiting for you to call upon It. Regardless of the degree of bondage you may be in, this Presence and Power will respond as mercy—soothing, healing, and restoring your soul.

The purpose of prayer, meditation, and contemplation is to cleanse the mind and to make the mind and heart obey our conscious direction. We change our habitual thought patterns and processes and make our mind and heart disciples. It's difficult only for a little while, as we persist.

You are intrinsically good. You are God's child. Accept and acknowledge your Divine inheritance! Dare to believe you are a child of the King of Kings. Walk the Lord's highway. All is yours!

•●• •●•

Chapter Eleven

---·•·---

Three Keys to Peace of Mind

*T*he Bible describes the kingdom of heaven as a "treasure hidden in a field." The parable of the hidden treasure and the pearl says, "The kingdom of heaven is like a merchant looking for fine pearls. When he found one of great value, he went away and sold everything he had and bought it."

The pearl of great value is our awareness and perception that there is only One Power and One Cause in the midst of all phenomena—it's the holy one, the Living Presence of a living God. Historically, pearls have represented valuable ideas that ennoble, inspire, and lift up the minds and hearts of humankind (men and women, boys and girls). The ancients called this pearl of great value *the mind,* and the mystics named it *the Divine.* We call it *Life.* It's God within us, responding to the thoughts of our mind, the meditations of our heart, and our imaginings. The pearl is a metaphor for truth, which sets us free from the detrimental deep-seated feelings and attitudes that hold us back.

A pearl is the product of an irritation within the shell of a mollusk. When a tiny grain of sand or parasite gets inside the shell, the mollusk coats this irritant with many layers of nacre, a luminescent substance that forms a pearl. In the same way, when we become sufficiently irritated or troubled by the way we feel life is treating us, we begin to search for answers and a lasting sense of stability, security, and quietude, while at the same time seeking to

alleviate our aggravations. We will ultimately find our own pearl of great value. Even in the midst of turmoil, therefore, there's a hidden blessing or a benefit to be found—if we have the eyes to see it and ears to hear it.

The thoughtful man or woman is always dissatisfied with lesser quality pearls: passing or temporary happiness and joys. Are we not all seekers? Do we not always yearn for a fairer pearl? Although we might enjoy money, friendship, and art, and should be thankful for them, our search is for that single pearl of greatest value, which the Bible describes as "the kingdom of heaven." What is heaven? What do these words mean to us? Scriptures are written in code, and it's essential to decipher the code to find the very practical truths hidden in scriptures and the holy books of all religions. Modern interpreters say that heaven is a state of consciousness in harmony with the Presence and the thoughts of God. It's the orderly, lawful adjustment of God's kingdom in our own mind, body, and affairs. Heaven is everywhere and is within every one of us. It's a conscious attitude of mind, centered on the ideal state. Obviously the kingdom of God within isn't material; it's spiritual. Heaven is the realm of pure ideas. Earth is the manifestation of these ideas.

To enter heaven, we have to change our negative thoughts, feelings, and attitudes about ourselves, other people, and all things. We have to give up what we now hold in consciousness in exchange for what we want. A new consciousness creates new conditions and circumstances that are more in harmony with our higher ideas. Like the merchant in the parable, when we find the single pearl of great value, we have to sell all of our possessions to obtain it. Our possessions are our preconceived ideas and opinions and any conception of a God Who shows favoritism. Our possessions include ill will, resentment, and anger towards others and ourselves for the mistakes of the past.

This is a lesson in selection, discretion, and values. We have to learn to separate the genuine from the counterfeit; the true from the false; the superior from the inferior; and the valuable from the worthless. Developing a sense of value is one of the most important steps in any person's life. It's not an accident that the person in the parable of the pearl is a merchant, an apparently successful

businessman who possesses pearls to sell. We are all always buying and selling—and judging what is of most value in the marketplace. So we must also choose the thoughts and feelings that will serve us best. The kingdom of heaven is within, and we must learn to be good merchants within—to select our beliefs with all the deliberate care, interest, and involvement of one making an investment in the market. We should choose only those ideas that promote our well-being and prosperity, and reject those that do not.

One of the most important keys to the kingdom of heaven and peace of mind is the spiritual concept of forgiveness. It's through forgiveness that true spiritual healing is accomplished. Forgiveness removes the errors of the mind and creates harmony in every phase of our lives. Errors of the mind, or misunderstanding, are what the Bible refers to as "sin." Sin is simply the failure to realize that the creative, healing power of God is within. If sin were real and enduring, like truth and goodness, it could not be forgiven. However, there's no lasting, binding power in sin.

Once we develop a forgiving attitude, a great light dawns in us, and we see what's meant when we read in the Bible that "the son of man [ourselves] has authority on earth to forgive sins." We forgive ourselves, and are spiritually healed—made holy, wholesome, and complete. This inner change is essential to becoming one with the Healing Presence.

To forgive others makes it possible to be forgiven. Through the Divine law of forgiveness, we cleanse and renew our mind so that we can be forgiven. In forgiving, we are truly and sincerely loving God.

Love is another of the keys to the kingdom and peace of mind. It's the pure essence of being that heals our psychic wounds and makes right anything and everything that may be wrong or in error in our lives. In Divine mind, love is the power that binds the universe together in one magnificent harmony. Love is the principle that sets us on the high road of the ancients to health, happiness, well-being, prosperity, and peace of mind—once we sell all our possessions or false ideas and recognize the living God within. The pearl of great price is our peace of mind in every situation.

Divine love loves for the sake of loving. Just as the sun shines on the just and the unjust alike, love is offered to everyone. When we call to God for help, we are really calling on Divine love. It's the greatest, most intelligent principle that we know. The poet and mystic Lord Alfred Tennyson wrote: "Speak to Him thou for He hears . . . closer is He than breathing, and nearer than hands and feet."

When we become still, we feel the Divine response. A sense of quiet restfulness fills our mind and heart. It has been said that peace is the power at the heart of God and ourselves. It's the pearl glowing with a gorgeous, serene, translucent beauty all its own, permitting the passage of light in and through and all around us, even in the midst of darkness. It's our salvation and the solution to our problems. In times of emergency, Divine love always give us the strength and ability to cope. It supports us, enabling us to manage—usually very well.

On occasion we may require a symbol that helps us to return our thoughts to our Divine center. Why not purchase and mount a pearl? One of my most treasured presents is a small crystal shell in which is embedded a single pearl. This gift from very dear friends serves as an inspiration for me. When nothing else brings calm, to see it shining, softly glowing in the sun, is a reminder of the presence of God. It's a symbol of the kingdom of heaven, God, peace, protection, provision, and happiness—all that we hold to be good and true in life.

Jesus taught to love God with all our heart, mind, and soul. He also advised a rich man, "sell all that thou hast, and distribute unto the poor, and thou shalt have treasure in heaven; and come, follow me." To sell our possessions means to forgive so that we can experience and participate in life more fully. *Follow me* means to follow Jesus's instructions and example. In doing so, we discover the meaning and purpose of our lives and possess enduring peace of mind and lasting happiness.

Happiness usually is equated with recreation and fun. While some recreation is necessary for a balanced life, the truly thoughtful individuals throughout history, including Moses, Buddha, Plato,

Jesus, Mohammed, Emerson, and Einstein, have suggested that happiness is more than fleeting fun. They have said that happiness is instead to be found in creative action and in fearlessly pursuing our own most noble instincts—following the dictates of our heart. This commitment to a higher purpose is another key to peace of mind.

Those who have demonstrated the courage to think independently always seem to be somehow larger than life. For example, while most know Dr. Albert Schweitzer as the selfless physician who devoted his life to treating and healing the natives in the remote jungles of Africa, he was far more than that. In his book *Legacy of Truth*, Dr. J. Kennedy Schultz writes that Dr. Schweitzer has been described as "a renaissance man raised to spiritual dimensions," because of his wide-ranging expertise as a concert organist (and technician) and as an acknowledged authority on Johann Sebastian Bach. Schweitzer received two doctorates in theology and philosophy and was a professor as well as a highly respected biblical scholar. After he read about the need for medical missions, he decided that his real desire was to serve others by becoming a doctor. At the age of 30, he again became a student at the University of Strasbourg, where he was securely positioned for privileged, lifelong professorship, and began his study of medicine.

In his book *Out of My Life and Thought*, he referred to this period as "the most grueling seven years of my experience" as he continued to give sermons every Sunday and organ recitals throughout Europe in order to fund his medical studies.

Only his incredible physical strength and an ironclad dynamic will allowed him to survive and to succeed so brilliantly. The enormous capability and the exceptional education of this practical mystic earned him the respect of the world, which assisted him in supplying all that was needed at his hospital in what is now Gabon in Africa. In 1965, at the age of 90, he passed on, still in full possession of his faculties.

Dr. Schweitzer's philosophy was deceptively simple but all-encompassing. His desire was to impart some truth that would

include all people, whether or not they were religiously inclined. He called this philosophy a "reverence for life." He believed that retaining a sense of the mystery and awe of life is vital. He also believed that everyone needs a purpose in order to realize their God-given and infinite potential, be it humble or very great. It's equally important to develop a dedication to those purposes and become completely involved in them, he argued. Everyone can contribute to life and the welfare of others by using their unique gifts.

When we develop this sense of commitment, we enter into a fuller life and fulfill our purpose in being here. We should, therefore, "sell" all our less inspiring possessions—give up our less noble thoughts—and choose instead to develop a great reverence for life and the peace that passes understanding.

Worry and fear can only dominate your life if you let them. You have the power to eliminate negative thoughts from your life. You have the Presence within you and the strength to change your life. Through prayer and meditation, commitment to your spiritual self, and trust in the Divine, you will overcome your fears. By feeding positive thoughts into your conscious mind, your subconscious mind will respond positively when faced with problems and find solutions that will result in a happier and more peaceful and rewarding life.

In a Nutshell

Are we not all seekers? Do we not always yearn for a fairer pearl? Although we might enjoy money, friendship, and art, and should be thankful for them, our search is for that single pearl of greatest value, which the Bible describes as "the kingdom of heaven."

The kingdom of heaven is everywhere and is within every one of us. It's a conscious attitude of mind, centered on the ideal state. To enter heaven, we have to change our negative thoughts, feelings, and attitudes about ourselves, other people, and all things. We have to select only those ideas that promote our well-being and prosperity, and reject those that do not.

Love is the power that binds us together in one magnificent universe. It's the harmonizing principle that sets us on the high road to health, happiness, well-being, prosperity, and peace of mind.

Remember and apply Dr. Albert Schweitzer's philosophy, which he termed a *reverence for life*. This reverence is a recognition of the very mystery of life—the God-mind that exists in everything in the universe. He also believed and demonstrated that our purpose is realized in serving life and others, not in merely waiting to be served.

•●· ·●·

Biography of Joseph Murphy

Joseph Murphy was born on May 20, 1898, in a small town in the County of Cork, Ireland. His father, Denis Murphy, was a deacon and professor at the National School of Ireland, a Jesuit facility. His mother, Ellen, née Connelly, was a housewife, who later gave birth to another son, John, and a daughter, Catherine.

Joseph was brought up in a strict Catholic household. His father was quite devout and, indeed, was one of the few lay professors who taught Jesuit seminarians. He had a broad knowledge of many subjects and developed in his son the desire to study and learn.

Ireland at that time was suffering from one of its many economic depressions, and many families were starving. Although Denis Murphy was steadily employed, his income was barely enough to sustain the family.

Young Joseph was enrolled in the National School and was a brilliant student. He was encouraged to study for the priesthood and was accepted as a Jesuit seminarian. However, by the time he reached his late teen years, he began to question the Catholic orthodoxy of the Jesuits, and he withdrew from the seminary. Since his goal was to explore new ideas and gain new experiences—a goal he couldn't pursue in Catholic-dominated Ireland—he left his family to go to America.

He arrived at the Ellis Island Immigration Center with only $5 in his pocket. His first project was to find a place to live. He was

fortunate to locate a rooming house where he shared a room with a pharmacist who worked in a local drugstore.

Joseph's knowledge of English was minimal, as Gaelic was spoken both in his home and at school, so like most Irish immigrants, Joseph worked as a day laborer, earning enough to keep himself fed and housed.

He and his roommate became good friends, and when a job opened up at the drugstore where his friend worked, he was hired to be an assistant to the pharmacist. He immediately enrolled in a school to study pharmacy. With his keen mind and desire to learn, it didn't take long before Joseph passed the qualification exams and became a full-fledged pharmacist. He now made enough money to rent his own apartment. After a few years, he purchased the drugstore, and for the next few years ran a successful business.

When the United States entered World War II, Joseph enlisted in the Army and was assigned to work as a pharmacist in the medical unit of the 88th Infantry Division. At that time, he renewed his interest in religion and began to read extensively about various spiritual beliefs. After his discharge from the Army, he chose not to return to his career in pharmacy. He traveled extensively, taking courses in several universities both in the United States and abroad.

From his studies, Joseph became enraptured with the various Asian religions and went to India to learn about them in depth. He studied all of the major faiths and their histories. He extended these studies to the great philosophers from ancient times until the present.

Although he studied with some of the most intelligent and farsighted professors, the one person who most influenced Joseph was Dr. Thomas Troward, who was a judge as well as a philosopher, doctor, and professor. Judge Troward became Joseph's mentor and introduced him to the study of philosophy, theology, and law as well as mysticism and the Masonic order. Joseph became an active member of this order, and over the years rose in the Masonic ranks to the 32nd degree in the Scottish Rite.

Upon his return to the United States, Joseph chose to become a minister and bring his broad knowledge to the public. As his concept of Christianity was not traditional and indeed ran counter to most of the Christian denominations, he founded his own church in Los Angeles. He attracted a small number of congregants, but it did not take long for his message of optimism and hope rather than the "sin-and-damnation" sermons of so many ministers to attract many men and women to his church.

Dr. Joseph Murphy was a proponent of the New Thought movement. This movement was developed in the late 19th and early 20th centuries by many philosophers and deep thinkers who studied this phenomenon and preached, wrote, and practiced a new way of looking at life. By combining a metaphysical, spiritual, and pragmatic approach to the way we think and live, they uncovered the secret of attaining what we truly desire.

The proponents of the New Thought movement preached a new idea of life that is based on practical, spiritual principles that we can all use to enrich our lives and create perfected results. We can do these things only as we have found the law and worked out the understanding of the law, which God seems to have written in riddles in the past.

Of course, Dr. Murphy wasn't the only minister to preach this positive message. Several churches, whose ministers and congregants were influenced by the New Thought movement, were founded and developed in the decades following World War II. The Church of Religious Science, Unity Church, and other places of worship preach philosophies similar to this. Dr. Murphy named his organization The Church of Divine Science. He often shared platforms, conducted joint programs with his like-minded colleagues, and trained other men and women to join his ministry.

Over the years, other churches joined with him in developing an organization called the Federation of Divine Science, which serves as an umbrella for all Divine Science churches. Each of the Divine Science church leaders continues to push for more

education, and Dr. Murphy was one of the leaders who supported the creation of the Divine Science School in St. Louis, Missouri, to train new ministers and provide ongoing education for both ministers and congregants.

The annual meeting of the Divine Science ministers was a must to attend, and Dr. Murphy was a featured speaker at this event. He encouraged the participants to study and continue to learn, particularly about the importance of the subconscious mind.

Over the next few years, Murphy's local Church of Divine Science grew so large that his building was too small to hold them. He rented the Wilshire Ebell Theater, a former movie theater. His services were so well attended that even this venue could not always accommodate all who wished to attend. Classes conducted by Dr. Murphy and his staff supplemented his Sunday services that were attended by 1,300 to 1,500 people. Seminars and lectures were held most days and evenings. The church remained at the Wilshire Ebell Theater in Los Angeles until 1976, when it moved to a new location in Laguna Hills, California.

To reach the vast numbers of people who wanted to hear his message, Dr. Murphy also created a weekly radio talk show, which eventually reached an audience of over a million listeners. Many of his followers suggested that he tape his lectures and radio programs. He was at first reluctant to do so, but agreed to experiment. His radio programs were recorded on extra-large 78-rpm discs, a common practice at that time. He had six cassettes made from one of these discs and placed them on the information table in the lobby of the Wilshire Ebell Theater. They sold out the first hour. This started a new venture. His tapes of his lectures explaining biblical texts, and providing meditations and prayers for his listeners, were not only sold in his church, but in other churches and bookstores and via mail order.

As the church grew, Dr. Murphy added a staff of professional and administrative personnel to assist him in the many programs in which he was involved and in researching and preparing his first books. One of the most effective members of his staff was

his administrative secretary, Dr. Jean Wright. Their working relationship developed into a romance, and they were married—a lifelong partnership that enriched both of their lives.

At this time (the 1950s), there were very few major publishers of spiritually inspired material. The Murphys located some small publishers in the Los Angeles area, and worked with them to produce a series of small books (often 30 to 50 pages printed in pamphlet form) that were sold, mostly in churches, from $1.50 to $3.00 per book. When the orders for these books increased to the point where they required second and third printings, major publishers recognized that there was a market for such books and added them to their catalogs.

Dr. Murphy became well known outside of the Los Angeles area as a result of his books, tapes, and radio broadcasts, and was invited to lecture all over the country. He did not limit his lectures to religious matters, but spoke on the historical values of life, the art of wholesome living, and the teachings of great philosophers— from both Eastern and Western cultures.

As Dr. Murphy never learned to drive, he had to arrange for somebody to drive him to the various places where he was invited to lecture in his very busy schedule. One of Jean's functions as his administrative secretary and later as his wife was to plan his assignments and arrange for trains or flights, airport pickups, hotel accommodations, and all the other details of the trips.

The Murphys traveled frequently to many countries around the world. One of his favorite working vacations was to hold seminars on cruise ships. These trips lasted a week or more and would take him to many countries around the world. In his lectures, he emphasized the importance of understanding the power of the subconscious mind and the life principles based on belief in the one God, the "I AM."

One of Dr. Murphy's most rewarding activities was speaking to the inmates at many prisons. Many ex-convicts wrote him over the years, telling him how his words had truly turned their lives around and inspired them to live spiritual and meaningful lives.

Dr. Murphy's pamphlet-sized books were so popular that he began to expand them into more detailed and longer works. His wife gave us some insight into his manner and method of writing. She reported that he wrote his manuscripts on a tablet and pressed so hard on his pencil or pen that you could read the imprint on the next page. He seemed to be in a trance while writing. He would remain in his office for four to six hours without disturbance until he stopped and said that was enough for the day. Each day was the same. He never went back into the office again until the next morning to finish what he'd started. He took no food or drink while he was working, He was just alone with his thoughts and his huge library of books, to which he referred from time to time. His wife sheltered him from visitors and calls and took care of church business and other activities.

Dr. Murphy was always looking for simple ways to discuss the issues and to elaborate points. He chose some of his lectures to present on cassettes, records, or CDs, as technologies developed in the audio field.

His entire collection of CDs and cassettes contains tools that can be used for most problems that individuals encounter in life. His basic theme is that the solution to problems lies within you. Outside elements cannot change your thinking. That is, your mind is your own. To live a better life, it's your mind, not outside circumstances, that you must change. You create your own destiny. The power of change is in your mind, and by using the power of your subconscious mind, you can make changes for the better.

Dr. Murphy wrote more than 30 books. His most famous work, *The Power of Your Subconscious Mind,* which was first published in 1963, became an immediate bestseller. It was acclaimed as one of the best self-help guides ever written. Millions of copies have been sold and continue to be sold all over the world.

Among some of his other best-selling books were *Telepsychics— The Magic Power of Perfect Living, The Amazing Laws of Cosmic Mind Power, Secrets of the I-Ching, The Miracle of Mind Dynamics, Your Infinite Power to Be Rich,* and *The Cosmic Power Within You.*

Dr. Murphy died in December 1981, and his wife, Dr. Jean Murphy, continued his ministry after his death. In a lecture she gave in 1986, quoting her late husband, she reiterated his philosophy:

> I want to teach men and women of their Divine Origin, and the powers regnant within them. I want to inform that this power is within and that they are their own saviors and capable of achieving their own salvation. This is the message of the Bible and nine-tenths of our confusion today is due to wrongful, literal interpretation of the life-transforming truths offered in it.
>
> I want to reach the majority, the man on the street, the woman overburdened with duty and suppression of her talents and abilities. I want to help others at every stage or level of consciousness to learn of the wonders within.

She said of her husband: "He was a practical mystic, possessed by the intellect of a scholar, the mind of a successful executive, the heart of the poet." His message summed up was: "You are the king, the ruler of your world, for you are one with God."

•●• •●•

HAY HOUSE TITLES
OF RELATED INTEREST

CALM*: *A Proven Four-Step Process Designed Specifically for Women Who Worry,* by Denise Marek

THE POWER OF A SINGLE THOUGHT: *How to Initiate Major Life Changes from the Quiet of Your Mind* (book-with-CD), revised and edited by Gay Hendricks and Debbie DeVoe

THE POWER OF INTENTION: *Learning to Co-create Your World Your Way,* by Dr. Wayne W. Dyer

10 STEPS TO TAKE CHARGE OF YOUR EMOTIONAL LIFE: *Overcoming Anxiety, Distress, and Depression Through Whole-Person Healing,* by Eve A. Wood, M.D.

WHAT TO DO WHEN YOU DON'T KNOW WHAT TO DO: *Common Horse Sense,* by Wyatt Webb

• • •

All of the above are available at your local bookstore, or may be ordered by contacting:

Hay House USA: **www.hayhouse.com**
Hay House Australia: **www.hayhouse.com.au**
Hay House UK: **www.hayhouse.co.uk**
Hay House South Africa: **orders@psdprom.co.za**
Hay House India: **www.hayhouseindia.co.in**

• • •

Notes

Notes

Notes

Res
Av 2008

DATE DUE

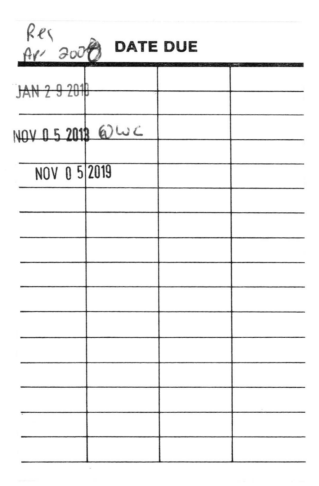

JAN 2 9 2010		
NOV 0 5 2013 ⓦWC		
NOV 0 5 2019		